Cash Management
and the
Demand for Money

New Directions in Management and Economics

. . . a series of authoritative books for more effective decision-making . . .

OTHER SERIES TITLES

M. A. Adelman (ed.), *Alaskan Oil: Costs and Supply*

John S. McGee, *In Defense of Industrial Concentration*

James R. Miller, III, *Professional Decision-Making: A Procedure for Evaluating Complex Alternatives*

E. J. Mishan, *Cost-Benefit Analysis: An Informal Introduction*

Jan Pen, *Income Distribution: Facts, Theories, Policies*

Reginald W. Revans, *Developing Effective Managers: A New Approach to Business Education*

Herman O. Stekler, *Economic Forecasting*

Lester C. Thurow, *The Impact of Taxes on the American Economy*

Richard R. West and Seha M. Tiniç *The Economics of the Stock Market*

Thomas L. Whisler, *The Impact of Computers on Organizations*

J. Peter Williamson, *Investments: New Analytic Techniques*

Cash Management
and the
Demand for Money

DANIEL ORR

PRAEGER PUBLISHERS
New York · Washington · London

PRAEGER PUBLISHERS
111 Fourth Avenue, New York, N.Y. 10003, U.S.A.
5, Cromwell Place, London S.W.7, England

Published in the United States of America in 1971
by Praeger Publishers, Inc.

© 1970 by Daniel Orr

Library of Congress Catalog Card Number: 78–95683

Printed in the United States of America

To
ROBERT CONNELL ORR
valued adviser, lifelong friend

Contents

Preface

In looking back over the completed typescript, I was tempted (sententiously) to discuss this book as a contribution at the "interface between microeconomics and macroeconomics." But that *would* be arrant puffery; actually, the book is concerned with individual decision units throughout, and only in the last chapter, IX, are questions important in aggregative analysis considered. The material developed there is recognizably more primitive and fragmentary than that of the central Chapters III and VI. Which is not to say that I feel apologetic about the efforts of Chapter IX; on the contrary, that chapter is in my view another small vindication of taking a traditional economists' approach, in terms of the behavior of self-serving individual decision units, to important questions (like the determinants of the demand for money) in income and employment theory. Increasingly, the economics profession appears to be turning to the insights to be obtained from dynamic models of individual behavior, in order to predict the time paths and stationary operating characteristics of aggregate variables. The recent literature of investment theory and employment theory has good results to show for taking that approach; and in consumption theory, beginning with the Friedman volume on permanent income, it has long been the standard approach to begin with maximization of a utility stream.

Some, but not all of the recent investment theory literature has taken the Friedman consumption theory approach of positing distributed-lag relations, rather loosely rationalized on grounds of optimizing behavior. The rest of that literature has followed the course of working with maximum conditions obtained from explicit dynamic objective functions, a tradition that was not well developed in economic theory until the operations research boom of post-World War II made available a number of useful analytical tools and conceptual frameworks.

This particular treatment of money demand reported here is very much in the operations research tradition; indeed,, as Chapter VIII shows, there is money to be made where the philosophy of control that is expounded here is ignored. My goal in preparing these chapters was not a financial officer's guide to rational cash monitoring, but some of the results appear to be useful and important to a person so motivated.

Apart from Chapters VIII and IX, which respectively report the results of corporation case studies and extensions to macroeconomics, and Chapter VII, which is a digression on the household demand for cash, the book can be read at two levels:

First, to the reader concerned with application to control problems, the results of Chapters IV–VI contain a number of potentially applicable generalizations of a basic scheme outlined in Chapter III. To that reader, Chapter IX contains little of interest; the first two chapters are useful toward a definition of the control objective, and an understanding of optimization techniques and the cash flow process.

Second, the main motivation and thrust of the work is better prediction and understanding of the demand for cash balances, particularly in the business sector. Chapters IV–VI then serve as tests of the robustness of the basic prediction scheme developed in Chapter III.

By today's prevailing standards, the mathematical methods used here are elementary. A mastery of such standard freshman or pre-freshman books as K. O. May, *Elements of Modern Mathematics* (Addison Wesley, 1959), M. Richardson, *Fundamentals of Mathematics* (Macmillan, 1958) or C. Allendoerfer and C. Oakley, *Principles of Mathematics* (McGraw-Hill, 1960) should suffice to get the reader through all but a few sections.

Many of the results I report here are the product of a long, close and enjoyable collaboration with Merton H. Miller. To him I am profoundly grateful for hundreds of ideas (an extraordinary proportion of which turned out to be good) and hours of advice; he deserves much credit for any substantive merit found in this book, and no blame for its eccentricities. A number of students shared the earlier work reported here—Peter Cuyper, Robert Kramer and Francis Nourie of the Graduate School of Business (Chicago), and Steven Huxley, Dwight Lee and Judy Thomas of UCSD were the chief contributors. Several colleagues at Chicago and elsewhere contributed advice and questions that helped enormously; to collect their names from scattered headnotes would serve academic propriety, but would also make this preface too long. The National Science Foundation provided support for the preparation of this volume. Mrs. Shirley Homewood somehow managed to make a typescript out of those jottings I gave her. My editor, Mrs. Miriam Klipper, was helpful at all stages of production. In particular, she convinced me that an index would little enhance the usefulness of this book; the detailed table of contents and the bibliography-reference index should serve adequately instead. How often does an editor absolve an author (or his "research" assistants) from so much tedium?

I am grateful to Merton Miller and the copyright holders for permission to quote from and paraphrase two Miller-Orr articles: the president and fellows of Harvard College for "A Model of the Demand for Money by Firms" (*Quarterly Journal of Economics* LXXX, August 1966, pp. 413-435), and the American Finance Association for "The Demand for Money by Firms: Extensions of Analytic Results" (*Journal of Finance* XXIII, December 1968, pp. 735-759). Unless explicitly noted to the contrary, the statistical and numerical work in this book was prepared expressly for first presentation here—some of it replicates results presented in earlier Miller-Orr writings.

Finally, I am grateful to Mary Lee Orr for wifely encouragement and forebearance; and to the National Football League and the Columbia Broadcasting System, for a 1969 season of televised football that was of such surpassing dullness that I had no excuse or reason to protract this project.

Cash Management
and the
Demand for Money

I

Objectives and Background

1. MAJOR OBJECTIVES

To look for ways to consolidate and unify ideas and theories seems to be a common impulse. We often hear deplored the divergence between the major branches of economic theory— pricing and allocation opposed to income and employment— and moves to establish common ground are always treated with sympathy and kind regard. Or consider the theory-versus-practice dichotomy, and the occasionally embarrassing, seldom productive pleas for theory that faithfully mirrors practice. In broader scope, there are occasional calls for a better meshing of the social sciences; and indeed, the idea of an all-encompassing unified science with objects of study ranging from subatomic particles to entire societies has been discussed, apparently seriously, by philosophers of science.[1]

Consistency and coherence of thought are doubtless worthy ends, but the impulse to overemphasize their desirability should be resisted. Ideas, theories, and intellectual disciplines can be productive despite fragmentary structure, and we can well wonder whether attempts to reconcile and consolidate existing fragments is usually as productive an allocation of effort as attempts directed at providing new and better fragments.

3

This book does not unify the theories of cash management (understood as good entrepreneurial technique applied to liquid assets), and money demand (understood as a subject of concern and importance for economic stability): do not misunderstand the conjunction in its title. Instead, the topics are pursued parallel to one another. The central focus is a class of short-run models of asset-holders' decision processes, with major emphasis on asset management in business firms. The models are shown, to the extent possible on the basis of a small amount of substantial evidence, to be useful tools for cash management. Some implications of the same models concerning individuals' demands for money are presented, and their status is discussed in light of pertinent available empirical results; but no new empirical evidence on the demand for money is generated by way of testing the model's implications. Finally, the aggregate demand for money is looked at from the perspective of these asset management decision models.

This chapter offers an historical survey of the tradition of short-run optimization in monetary theory, sketches other background material, and previews the issues considered in the remainder of the book. Chapter II examines the important and underdeveloped subject of what variously has been called frictions, transaction costs, transfer costs, or adjustment costs.[2] Different ways of representing adjustment costs are considered, and important features of optimal control response patterns in the presence of such costs are examined. The basic model, which constitutes the point of departure for subsequent analysis in the book, is presented in Chapter III, along with two important and influential predecessor models from the same tradition of short-period optimization. The two chapters that follow are devoted to analytical extensions of the basic model. Chapter IV examines the pattern of optimal response that attends modification of the portrayal of cash flows that feed into the model. Chapter V looks at the effects of changes in the cost structure or objective function confronting the firm. These chapters serve a dual purpose. They constitute evidence on the "robustness" of the basic model, that is, the extent to which its predictions are sensitive to changes in cash flow or cost structure; and they demonstrate the nature of the optimal control response to such important changes when applications are the primary concern.

Chapter VI is short but important. It deals with a three-asset version of the basic model. It too constitutes evidence on the model's robustness; but, more important, it serves as a point of departure from which to consider several issues significant in aggregative theory. Chapter VII is something of a digression; it offers some rather primitive theoretical speculation on household money demand. The central point, that households differ crucially from firms from the standpoint of money demand, is documented at a theoretical level. Chapter VIII in many respects is the most interesting and novel in the book. It compares actual cash management performance in two business firms to hypothetical patterns that would have attended use of the basic model, with surprising results. Chapter IX is an attempt to apply the techniques and results of earlier chapters in the elucidation of some old issues in aggregate theory. The tentative nature of the results developed there must be emphasized. Among the issues touched upon are the workings of monetary and fiscal policy; the consistency of Tobin's version of liquidity preference with the asset management theory discussed earlier in the book; the merits of long run asset preference models developed by Friedman and others; and the indications about the basic model that can be obtained from the existing empirical literature.

2. THE EVOLVING VIEW OF MONEY DEMAND

Notable progress has been made toward clarification of the reasons why money is held,[3] beginning with Keynes' (1930) introduction of asset preference considerations and Hicks' (1935) refreshingly modern discussion of the issues involved in the desirable process of introducing "marginal utility" into the demand for money. Following as it did upon Hicks' discussion, the Keynesian (1936) development of money demand in terms of transactions, precautionary and speculative motives was something of a retrogression away from the line of analysis which this book represents.

As a major consequence of Keynes' discussion, transaction flows and interest rates won acceptance as crucial variables underlying the desire to hold cash. The economics profession initially showed a tendency to attach an excessively pictorial interpretation to Keynes' discussion; in fact, for a time the view of three separate cash balances, one for each motive, seemed to be firmly entrenched.[4] This three-balance interpretation has recently waned, and thanks to the admonitions of Friedman (1956) and others, it is now widely recognized that every unit of cash on hand stands ready to meet a variety of foreseen and unforeseen payment obligations, and yields positive or negative profits in the presence of price level changes. Cash is one of many assets held by an individual household or firm. Each asset yields a stream of value or services, and individuals seek to apportion their total wealth in such a way that the expected utility of the service stream from assets is maximized. The three-part Keynesian "motive" classifies the services yielded by currency and demand deposits, and to a lesser extent by other assets that occasionally are designated as "near money" or "monetary assets." Money and the various distinct monetary assets all are characterized by differing degrees of return, risk, and liquidity. Without attaching the same importance to all of Keynes' motives, Friedman (1956) offers a view of money demand that clearly emphasizes the same basis in maximization of a utility stream.

The widely accepted current view, then, holds that cash may create utility as a *financial* asset and as a *productive* asset. As a financial asset, the value of cash responds to changes in interest rates and in the general level of prices. As a productive asset the role of cash in the income-creation process is active and direct. To the household, money balances provide convenience not unlike the services provided by telephones, automobiles and dishwashers. In the firm, money can be viewed as an input of the production process, which reduces cost when efficiently used to facilitate transactions. Cash, then, derives its value as a financial asset through imperfectly foreseen changes in the price level and return rate on other assets, hence speculatively. Its value as a productive asset stems from the way that it eases the burden of transactions, in the firm or the household.

Neither view of cash—as a financial instrument or a productive input—is adequate by itself. The proper sort of harmony among cash, a portfolio of financial claims, and a holding of physical assets must be found, even if cash is held only because of the productive or convenient services that it yields; and conversely, if the important productive service aspects of cash are not kept in sight in the formulation of portfolio theories, then much of the value of those theories is likely to be lost.

3. RANKING ASSETS ACCORDING TO LIQUIDITY

Why should there be a problem of portfolio balance? Why aren't all financial instruments equally suitable as "temporary abodes of purchasing power"?[5] The answer to the second question, and an important part of the answer to the first, lies in the complex of conventions and institutions that determine the relative liquidity of alternative assets. To respond to those questions with a simple statement about liquidity is but to rephrase the questions in a less explicit form, unless the term is widely and clearly understood. We must be careful to avoid masking vagueness or ignorance behind terms that sound concrete; and since liquidity constitutes an important reason (perhaps *the* reason) why the optimal economic decision process is beset by portfolio considerations, it is worth-while to establish a precise meaning for the term. The definition of liquidity is properly linked to the definition of money.

Analyses of money demand frequently are vague as to the characteristic properties of money, that distinguish it from other assets. In full-scale general equilibrium analyses, for example, there is a residue of controversy as to whether or in what part money is an instrument of debt, or a promise to pay.[6] Fortunately, that question lies outside the modest analytical scope of this book—the concern here is to identify the factors that determine individual decisions to hold particular assets. In pursuit of that concern, it may be necessary to consider two roles played by money, which lead to two alternative views of money; as a medium of exchange, and as a "temporary abode of purchasing power." To emphasize either role to the exclusion of the other leads the analysis astray: the wrong questions are asked, or at least, some potentially important questions are not asked.

It is often stated (and true) that the ability of a good or asset to function as a medium of exchange is determined in part by law and in part by custom, or as we say, it is determined institutionally. We will call any asset that is widely and legally used as an exchange medium, money. That there are different monies such as demand deposits, currency, bank drafts etc., all with slightly different attributes of acceptability, convenience, and safety, need not concern us: we will presume that differences (however measured) among money assets—media of exchange—are smaller and less significant than are the differences between any money asset and any non-money asset. This view is rationalized quite simply: individuals may be willing, under a wide variety of anticipated circumstances, to incur significant expense in order to transfer asset holdings from non-money to money (to obtain purchasing power) or from money to non-money (to obtain interest or other returns). Similarly, we can expect to observe transfers from one class or kind of non-money asset to another, in response to changes in prospect. But it is unusual to find a person, under conditions of normal activity, willing to incur significant expense to transfer from one money asset to another. Such transfers indeed are made frequently and routinely by individuals and businesses: but they are usually made at low cost, with little time spent deciding as to types and amounts, and without the assistance of brokers or other intermediaries. The main gains from such transfers are safety and convenience; and these are subtle gains, in terms of their impact on income and wealth, compared to those realized in an exchange involving money and non-money assets.

All of the conventional media of exchange are (by definition of liquidity) perfectly liquid. Non-money assets can be ranked according to their liquidity, that is, according to the time and expense required to convert them to money. This definition of liquidity might for some purposes be hopelessly and unworkably vague. It will become clear, however, that it is a sufficiently precise definition for our purposes, when the discussion turns to issues for which differences among assets are important. From the definition, short-term debt instruments of the U.S. Government and some corporations are seen to be highly liquid; physical capital that fills some highly specialized role in the production of a single good is highly illiquid. Between the extremes is an array of debt and equity certificates, general-purpose capital equipment and land.

In contrasting money to other assets, the differences between any two money assets were held to be small compared to the differences between any money asset and any non-money asset. Do not infer that the different liquidation costs of various non-money assets are of similar order of magnitude because of the common classification as non-money. In fact, treasury bills are much "nearer" to cash than to machine tools. Assuming that assets are ranked according to liquidity, the dividing line between money and non-monetary assets does not lie at the point of "widest separation" between adjacent asset categories; rather, the dividing line is where common acceptability in exchange no longer characterizes an asset. The conjecture is that all assets can be classed in one category or another, and the "gaps" between money assets will be very small.

Throughout this book the liquidity of an asset will be characterized in terms of *transfer* or *adjustment costs*, costs that attend the acts of obtaining or relinquishing the asset. This representation of liquidity is predicated in part on the belief that information about the expected performance and marketability of assets is itself a marketable commodity, and specialists will organize to provide this information for a fee. That fee then is a part of the cost of adjusting the portfolio. Alternatively, the specialists may deal directly in the asset itself, in which case the transfer cost is in part reflected in a brokerage charge, which varies with the difficulty of "making a market" for the asset. What then becomes of the idea of money as a temporary abode of purchasing power? That phrase has a compelling ring—the frequency with which it is quoted is testimony enough—and it is gratifying that the following analysis does not overlook or dismiss the idea embedded in the phrase. The idea, in fact, is a meaningful one. As we will see when the analysis turns to models that incorporate more than two assets, certain non-money assets such as treasury bills are well suited to serve as temporary abodes of purchasing power. The demand for those assets may be determined in much the same way as the demand for cash.

4. THE IMPORTANCE OF ADJUSTMENT COSTS

The pattern of optimal asset management behavior is quite sensitive to the presence of adjustment (transfer) costs.[7]

The importance of transfer costs can be illustrated with a simple and widely employed model of an individual's optimal asset choice.[8] The analysis assumes that two attributes of assets—return and risk—enter into the asset-holder's utility function; for simplicity, only two assets enter into the decision. In Figure I, point A is the risk-return profile of the first asset, and point B conveys the same information for the second. When every portfolio is properly "balanced," the asset holder chooses the two assets in the combination C^1. All points along the segment $\overline{AB}$ are possible asset mixtures. C^1 is chosen on the basis of a standard type of indifference curve analysis where the arguments of the utility function are risk and return and I^1 is the relevant indifference curve.

Now let the characteristics of the individual's asset preference function change so that the relevant indifference curve is I^2 instead of I^1. The individual's preferred portfolio moves from C^1 to C^2. In adjusting from C^1 to C^2, the asset holder incurs a cost of transfer. It will be a vanishingly small cost in this case, since the information and decision problems are insignificant (there are only two securities). Nonetheless there remains some cost associated with the process of generating and communicating an order to change, and verifying that the order has been fulfilled, even if it is no more than the time and effort spent in telephoning an order.

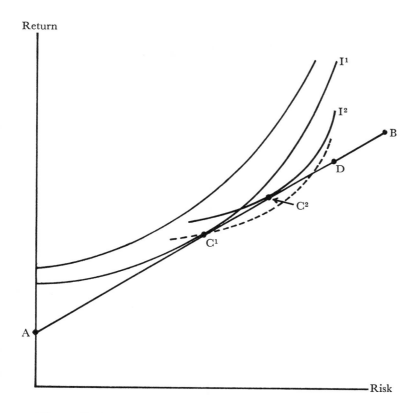

Figure I. M-T Analysis of Portfolio Choice with Shift
in Preference

The foregoing illustration is a simple example of Markowitz-Tobin (M-T) portfolio choice, and it is interesting to use that analysis further, to see how it differs in focus and technique from the analysis of this book. The M-T analysis abstracts from issues of liquidity and liquidity needs; but it can be interpreted as taking the view that both securities, though differing in risk and return, are equally suitable as temporary abodes of purchasing power. Should transaction needs become important at some future date, a mixture of the two securities can be transferred to transactions balances, to maintain the proper portfolio balance. Transfer costs are ignored.

By contrast, suppose that the security A is cash, and there is no separation between transaction and portfolio balances—all transactions are made out of the cash holding represented in Figure I. The presence of adjustment costs will affect the portfolio balance decision: again suppose there is a preference shift represented by the replacement of I^1 by I^2. If a large cash outflow is expected, the move from C^1 to C^2 is not necessarily optimal after that change in the utility function, for the cash drain may create an imbalance that will entail a transfer back to cash. A heavy cash flow after a move to C_2 might move the asset holder to D, say, which is below the new indifference curve through C^1 (indicated by the dashed indifference surface).

A major purpose of this book is to explore the way in which transactions needs and transfer costs affect the management of financial assets. As we will see throughout the remainder of the book, the problem of whether to move from C^1 to C^2 (or to some other portfolio) is one that requires more sophisticated analysis than can be wrung from the M-T model.

5. The Analytic Treatment and Elasticity Implications of Adjustment Costs

Given that adjustment costs are important, and that they can not be handled by conventional static analysis, such as is involved in the Markowitz-Tobin portfolio selection model, it is interesting to ask what analytic approaches can be successfully used. Fortunately, work on other aspects of the problem of optimal asset management can be and has successfully been applied to the control of portfolio assets and cash. The earliest successes in asset management theory are due to Massé (1946), Arrow, Harris and Marschak (1951), and Whitin (1953); all were concerned with the management of physical stock-flow systems, and their work stimulated a large literature that quickly came to be called "inventory theory." Of special importance is the effect that adjustment costs have on the structure of the optimal control response. The literature contains interesting results of major importance which deal with that effect, and these results and other important results from inventory theory will be described in Chapter II.

Striking similarities between transactions balances and stocks of finished goods were perceived early by Baumol (1952), and he developed the parallel to obtain predictions about the demand for cash for transactions purposes. A fortunate emphasis in the early inventory management literature was placed upon costs of adjusting the holdings of physical stocks, and the control responses designed to accommodate those costs found their way into Baumol's discussion of money stocks. Thus, some seventeen years after Hicks (1935) recognized the potential importance of "frictions" in an optimization-oriented approach to the demand for money, an apparatus was provided whereby frictions could be accommodated within the scope of that approach.

For an almost equally long period subsequent to its appearance, Baumol's work was the only explicitly structured and optimization-oriented source of predictions about the demand for money. Empirical tests of its chief hypotheses (concerning transactions and interest elasticities of money demand) typically turned out less than favorable; but instead of searching the vast inventory theory literature for a potentially more suitable paradigm, monetary economists turned to the familiar approach of curve fitting, that is, of structuring an implicit-form demand relation on the basis of empirical observations, without explicit linkage to maximizing behavior.[9]

As we will see in Chapter III, Section 1, the Baumol model (as it now is usually called in the monetary theory literature) predicts constant interest and transactions elasticities of money demand of size $-1/2$ and $+1/2$ respectively. These magnitudes have troubled empirical researchers, who at first kept finding values of approximately 0 (interest) and 1 (transactions) for the elasticities. The predicted constancy of the elasticities has also been bothersome. As we will see, both the constancy and the magnitudes of $\pm 1/2$ are artifacts of the cash flow mechanism and the adjustment cost structure that Baumol inherited from inventory theory. Chapters IV and V develop the nature of this dependence more fully.

The second of the constant elasticity conditions just noted means that the Baumol model implies the existence of pervasive economies of scale in cash management, that is, a decline in cash relative to acitvity in an efficient operation. Whether there are economies of scale in cash management is an important question for the working of monetary policy. When the money supply is expanded, are transactions enabled to expand more, less, or proportionately? Our approach to an answer is to study the money-holding behavior of individuals.

A similar question deals with the response of money demand to changes in interest rates. With a shift in demand (due, perhaps, to a shift in transactions), and no change in supply, will the interest rate respond more, less, or in proportion to the transaction rate increase?

These elasticity issues are consequential. Fortunately, less rigid elasticity predictions can be obtained from models of optimal asset management. This point is of central importance; it was spelled out in some detail in Miller and Orr (1966, 1968), and it will come in for frequent attention in this book.

6. GAUSS AND PARETO ON CASH FLOWS

The structure and effect of transfer cost is but one of the issues important to the effectiveness of asset management modeling. A second major issue is the theoretical implications and empirical congruity of various representations of cash flow. Among the choices to be made at the earliest stage of modeling is whether cash flows should be treated as random, or known with certainty, or a mixture of random and known regular components. The first two choices permit analysis by established methods. The third choice, though patently the most "realistic" and general, encounters an unpleasant fact about stochastic modeling, no matter what the context—a mixture of systematic and random components has never been handled satisfactorily at the same level of analytic generality as each by itself.

The Baumol model used a certainty representation of cash flows, in common with the simple inventory model on which it is based. An early attempt to generalize Baumol's model incorporated a random cash flow mechanism,[10] a commendable move in light of the unpredictability of cash transactions. A random process was also used in Miller and Orr (1966), where it was found, not surprisingly, that properties attributed to the cash flow process affect the demand for money.

Miller and Orr used traditional sources for the cash flow component of their model. Tradition in this subject encompasses hundreds of years; according to Uspensky's (1937) brief historical summary, analysis of stochastic processes can be traced at least as far back as the mid 17th century, to interest in gambling problems on the part of Pascal and Fermat. Not until this century, however, did substantial and useful applications emerge from analyses that used simple stochastic processes.[11]

Overwhelmingly the tradition in stochastic modeling, even in the work done on sequential analysis in this century, is to treat random variables as conforming to certain "rules of good behavior." A random process that in fact hews to those rules is said to be "Gaussian."[12] The simplest example of a Gaussian random process is the Bernoulli process, in which transitions from state to state can be thought of as generated by flips of a coin.[13] In a Bernoulli process, the state-to-state transitions are defined by the forward difference equation

$$(2) \qquad B_{t+1}(x) = pB_t(x-1) + qB_t(x+1) \qquad p+q = 1.$$

$B_t(x)$ denotes the probability that the random variable (e.g. a cash balance) takes the value x during the time period $[t, t+1)$.[14] The values p and q indicate the probabilities of an increase and a decrease, respectively, in the value of the random variable. The process is defined for integer values of the random variable, and one-unit changes can occur at regularly spaced unit-interval points in time, e.g. once a day.

A second analytical favorite from the Gaussian family of processes is the Poisson process, in which transitions are defined by the differential equation

$$(3) \qquad P_t'(x) = -(\lambda+\mu)P_t(x) + \lambda P_t(x+1) + \mu P_t(x-1).$$

This process differs from the Bernoulli process in a crucial way: integer changes in the cash balance can take place at *any* point in time. Notationally, λ and μ are probability constants; in a cash flow context, μ is the "arrival rate" of cash into the balance, and λ is the "departure rate" of cash from the balance. $P_t(x)$ is the probability of a cash balance of x at time t, and $P'_t(x)$ is the first time derivative of $P_t(x)$.

Like all random processes that are attracted to the Gaussian, the Bernoulli and Poisson processes embody a stability and regularity that are manifested in a number of ways.[15] Let b_t and p_t be samples of the value of x taken at time t from (2) and (3) respectively. Sequences of such observations will have two important properties: first, in both cases, the sample mean values of changes (first differences) over time

$$\overline{\Delta b}_t = \sum_{j=1}^{t} (b_j - b_{j-1})/t, \quad \overline{\Delta p}_t = \sum_{j=1}^{t} (p_j - p_{j-1})/t$$

will rapidly converge to fixed values $E(\Delta b)$ and $E(\Delta p)$ as t increases. Second, the same sort of rapid convergence in time will hold for the sample variances

$$S_{\Delta b}^2 = \sum_{j=1}^{t} (\Delta b_j - \overline{\Delta b}_t)^2/t, \quad S_{\Delta p}^2 = \sum_{j=1}^{t} (\Delta p_j - \overline{\Delta p}_t)^2/t$$

to the fixed values $\sigma_{\Delta b}^2$ and $\sigma_{\Delta p}^2$. It is the going terminology, in referring to these convergence properties of mean and variance, to say that Gaussian processes are characterized by *finite* mean and variance; and in fact, when exact analytical expressions for means and variances of such processes are obtained by integration, the results are finite.

When will an actual time series (as opposed to a series generated by a theoretical Bernoulli or Poisson process) display the convergence in sample behavior that is a requisite of Gaussian behavior? The mathematician Paul Lévy has established a simple necessary and sufficient condition for Gaussian behavior: the largest observation (in absolute value) that the process generates must be *asymptotically negligible* compared to the sum of the observations as the number of observations increases.[16] Precisely, let $x_1, x_2, \ldots$ denote a sequence of independent and identically distributed random variables. Then, if and only if there exists an $\mathcal{N}$ corresponding to any arbitrarily small ϵ such that

$$|x_k|/\sum_{t=1}^{n}|x_i| < \epsilon \text{ for all } n > \mathcal{N}, \quad |x_k| = \max \, (|x_1|, \ldots, |x_n|)$$

will the x sequence have the Gaussian properties of stability.

The Gaussian process is a special member of a family, called the family of stable processes. The characterizing property of stable processes is revealed if we form the n'th partial sum of the mutually independent and identically distributed random variables $x_1, x_2, \ldots$: $S_n = \sum_{j=1}^{n} x_j$. Then stable processes have the simple property that

$$S_n \underset{d}{=} \gamma_n x + \delta_n,$$

which we read "the sum of n changes has the same distribution as a single change, up to a linear transformation involving the *location parameters* γ_n and δ_n." The *exact* meaning of the phrase "has the same distribution" will be developed in the next few pages; for the time being, we will assume that the meaning is sufficiently clear. This invariance of the form of the distribution of changes under addition extends to processes that do not have Gaussian properties. For years, the accepted descriptive terminology for these other processes was "stable non-Gaussian processes." Mandelbrot has, for historical reasons, used the terms "stable Pareto-Lévy processes" and "stable Paretian processes." The defining property of stable processes, their invariance of form under addition, is the source of considerable convenience in analytic work.

Before exploring the stable processes and their properties it is useful to establish this

Definition. Let x be a random variable with the probability density function $f(x)$. The characteristic function ϕ of f, defined for real ξ, is

$$\phi(\xi) = \int_{-\infty}^{\infty} e^{-i\xi x} f(x)\,dx.$$

Characteristic functions (like generating functions and Laplace transforms) are analytic transforms; for the analysis of certain properties of $f(x)$ it is most convenient to work in the domain of the transform $\phi(\xi)$ rather than directly with the probability function $f(x)$ itself. Notably, the sum of two random variables x_1 and x_2 with distributions f_1 and f_2 has a distribution (called the *convolution* of f_1 and f_2, denoted f_1*f_2) with the characteristic function $\phi_1\phi_2$. The convolution thus has a characteristic function that is the product of the individual characteristic functions of f_1 and f_2.

The importance of characteristic functions in discussing stable Paretian processes, however, transcends these facts of convenience. For with the exception of two important special cases (associated with the normal and Cauchy distributions) the probability functions of stable processes are unknown, and only the *logarithms of their characteristic functions* can be written out in explicit form!

To see how these facts are all related, we write down that single analytic expression:

$$\log \phi\ (\xi) = i\delta\xi - \gamma|\xi|^{\alpha}[1 + i\beta(\xi/|\xi|)\ \tan\ (\alpha\Pi/2)],$$

which contains four real parameters α, β, γ, and δ. These parameters determine the character of the distribution of x, and hence the character of the stochastic process determined by changes in x.

Following Fama's lucid discussion (1963) we note that δ is a *location* parameter; if α is greater than 1, $E(x) = \delta$. β is an *index of skewness*, $-1 \le \beta \le 1$; a value $\beta = 0$ implies symmetry in the distribution of $x.\gamma$ is a scale parameter. Finally, α is called the "characteristic exponent": it determines the total probability mass in the tails, or the *kurtosis* of the distribution. With $\alpha = 2$, the Gaussian or normal member of the family of stable distributions is generated; and the mean and variance are respectively δ and γ. With $\alpha = 1$ and $\beta = 0$ the Cauchy case is realized.

With these definitions and forms established, the notion of the stability of stochastic processes can be made more precise. The n-fold convolution of the random variable x with probability density function $f(x)$, has the characteristic function whose logarithm is

$$n \log \phi(\xi) = i(n\delta)\xi - n\gamma|\xi|^{\alpha}[1 + i\beta(\xi/|\xi|) \tan (\alpha\Pi/2)].$$

Stability, then, means precisely invariance of the parameters α and β, and proportional expansion of γ and δ, under successive additions.

For stable distributions with $\alpha < 2$, Lévy has shown that an asymptotic form of *the law of Pareto* is always observed: that is, there exists a constant P such that (for symmetric distributions with mean $\delta = 0$)

$$X \overset{\lim}{=} \infty \ Pr(|x| > X) = 2(x/P)^{-\alpha},$$

whence the name "Paretian." Pareto's law was believed (by Pareto) to be of importance in describing the distribution of personal income in any society. Compared to random variables that are attracted to the Gaussian, random variables that are attracted to others among the stable laws with characteristic exponent < 2 will have a much larger concentration of observations in the extreme tails of the distribution. Later we will see how the issue of Gaussian versus Paretian behavior emerges from cash flow data (Chapter IV).

7. HOUSEHOLD VERSUS CORPORATE MONEY DEMAND

At a suitably general level, the motives for holding cash and the services rendered by cash balances will be the same for modest households and major corporations. Nonetheless, it is a mistake to suppose that the same techniques of cash management are appropriate for both classes of decision maker; in fact the analysis of following chapters suggests that the two cases are significantly different. It might well follow, then, that the money demand function of the household sector differs widely from the demand for money by firms. Harking back to the motives for money-holding, and the early inventory management models of the demand for money, much of the discussion suggests that only households were being considered. The introduction of "precautionary" motives (and occasionally, the discussion of precautionary *balances*) is perhaps the most conspicuous feature that points to a preoccupation with households at the expense of firms in the earlier discussion of motives. Another development that indicates an excessive preoccupation with households is the heavy reliance on simple inventory control models, like the Baumol model, as guides to the prediction of money demand. In view of the overwhelming importance of the cash holdings of corporations and other businesses and business-like agents such as individually owned firms, partnerships, and agencies, the widespread attempts to comprehend money demand in terms of forces that are thought to affect the typical household are a little bit puzzling. Corporations alone hold nearly half of the economy's cash balances, and at any point in time the U.S. Treasury may hold deposits equivalent to 2 per cent or so of the money supply (though their balances are not normally counted as a part of the money supply). State, county, and municipal governments plus large private businesses swell the non-household total, and further depress the importance of households in the total picture.

Important differences between corporate and household cash flows are (obviously), in the *magnitude* of the total flow in any period of time; and perhaps also in the *pattern* of the flow over time. Economizing portfolio adjustments are practical and sensible only when cash flows attain some minimal magnitude. Moreover, wage and salary receipts, an extremely important component of the household cash inflow, show a much higher degree of regularity than can be expected in the cash inflow of a corporation. If these considerations of magnitude and regularity are not exploited in the modeling process, the models may not yield accurate and useful predictions of money demand. In the following chapters, especially Chapter VII which deals further with problems of household money demand, the importance of some of these differences is explored. Meantime, the next section previews two more issues that must be resolved in constructing asset management models.

8. CONTROL AND PREDICTION

The utility of asset management analysis depends on how well it works, an issue that will be considered from two points of view. First, does it yield more substantial and useful predictions of money holding than are otherwise obtainable? Does it tell us anything new about crucial relationships in the economy, such as money supply, interest rate, and physical investment tieups? This is the prediction aspect of the analysis, and is paramount to academic economists and government policy makers. A second aspect, occasionally thought (mistakenly) to be intimately related to the first, is: does the asset management analysis offer a means to the improved control of corporate cash balances?

Suppose in fact that the asset management approach provides a control device superior to any previously available. It doesn't follow that the predictive quality of the analysis will be high. In the first place, data will be consistent with the older control procedures, until the superior technique becomes widespread. Secondly, an asset management model may misrepresent or distort certain features of the real world. The distortion may not weaken the model as a control instrument (compared to available alternatives), but the value of the model for prediction may be weakened. For example, a model predicated on Gaussian cash flows may produce some improvement in cash management procedures, but Paretian properties of the actual cash flows may underlie large errors of prediction. Finally, devices that are good for control of individual decisions may tell us nothing useful about aggregate data; and conversely, a device that tells us a lot about the behavior of aggregates may be worthless for control purposes, possible examples in the latter category being certain classes of linear estimates.

At this time, only the rather skimpy discussions of Chapters VIII and IX can be offered concerning the usefulness of asset management models for control and prediction purposes.

NOTES

1. Oppenheim and Putnam (1958). But also see the amusing discussion of the ideas and career of Auguste Comte, the "father of unified science," in Hayek (1955).
2. "Friction" is an outmoded catchall phrase to rationalize imperfect achievement or restoration of equilibrium in static models. "Transaction cost" is the

most widespread and popular of the terms in current use. It will be avoided in this book, since the term "transaction" is reserved to describe ordinary cash payments and receipts; these should not be confused with portfolio adjustments. "Transfer cost" was to my knowledge first used by Hicks (1935) to describe such obstacles as brokerage and paper-work costs to "perfect" portfolio adjustment; the term was adopted by Miller and Orr (1966). Adjustment cost is the term popularly used in the capital theory literature, and is perhaps the most descriptive of the terms. Hereafter we will use the terms adjustment cost and transfer cost interchangeably.

3. Reasons for concern over the demand side of "the money market" will not be touched upon here. See Patinkin (1965), Johnson (1962), Friedman (1956), Bailey (1962), or almost any other book on monetary theory for a discussion of the importance of money demand to the analysis of aggregated general equilibrium systems.

4. This view is evident in some of the comparatively recent asset management and empirical money demand literature. In some cases it is possible to interpret analyses that deal with, for example, transactions balances as saying that crucial variables affect money demand *through* the transactions motive; other motives are ignored for purposes of compactness in discussion. In other cases it is inescapable that the analysis relies on the additivity of the balances associated with different motives to explain outcomes or discrepancies.

5. The quoted phrase is attributed to Milton Friedman by Johnson (1962).

6. This controversy is discussed at length in the recent book of Pesek and Saving (1967).

7. The *structure* of transfer costs—that is, the particular functional forms chosen to represent them—has crucial effects on the asset management process; hence, it should not be inferred that the mere presence of these costs is the whole issue. The importance of transfer cost structure is examined in Chapter II, Section 2.

8. The model we use here was introduced, I believe, by Tobin (1958). See also Markowitz (1959).

9. Some of the empirical work proceeds without any reference to optimization objectives. Other work, based mainly on Friedman's (1956) organizing theme, professes a goal of uncovering maximizing behavior; the approach to optimization taken in that literature differs from, and may even be inconsistent with, the approach taken here. See Chapter IX, Section 7.

10. See Patinkin (1965), chapter 5 and appendixes. This model is discussed in Chapter III, Section 3.

11. See Feller (1951), and a discussion by B. Mandelbrot (1963a) of the contributions of Bachelier and others to the theory of price movements. Possibly the climactic work in the application of simple stochastic processes is sequential analysis; see A. Wald (1944), which lays the theoretical groundwork for sequential analysis.

12. Or more strictly, the term is that such random variables are "attracted to the Gaussian" (see Gnedenko and Kolmogorov (1954) or Feller (1966)).

13. A bit of terminology may be useful here. A stochastic process is simply the behavior of a random variable that takes different values over time. If changes in the value of the variable take place at regularly spaced time intervals (or if the value of the variable is observed at regularly spaced intervals) the process is defined over a *discrete time* domain. Each change point (or observation) is

a *stage* of the process. The values that the process can assume are the *states* of the process. The *transition rule* of the process attaches probabilities of change from one state to another. If the process is *Markovian*, the transition rule does not depend on the history of the process; only upon the current value. If the process is *stationary*, the mean value of successive observations over time will converge to a fixed value.

14. In demarcating time intervals, the convention of using a square bracket if the interval contains its end point, and a regular parenthesis if it does not, will be observed. Thus, $[t, t+1)$ denotes the time interval beginning at t, and running up to but not including $t+1$.

15. This discussion of Gaussian (and the later discussion of Paretian) stable processes draws heavily on Mandelbrot (1963a), as well as Feller (1966), Mandelbrot (1963b) and Fama (1963).

16. See Feller (1966), chapter vi, especially the "historical notes" on pp. 176 and 169. I first learned of Lévy's role in establishing the critical importance of asymptotic negligibility from B. Mandelbrot.

II

Control Decisions for Randomly
Disturbed Systems

1. Alternative Treatments of Time in Stochastic Economic Models

A dominant tradition in economic theory is to rely on deterministic or full certainty assumptions in the construction of models. Apart from asset management (and, of course, econometric theory), there is no part of economic theory in which the analytical tradition is mainly stochastic. The few scattered stochastic models that have been developed to consider traditional questions yield results which indicate the significant implications of ignoring uncertainty so widely. As a case in point, recent work suggests that the efficiency and welfare properties of competitive market allocation no longer can be shown to exist when uncertainty is recognized analytically unless the opportunity is provided in the market system to insure against all risks.[1]

There are reasons, of course, to rely on deterministic models. The process that is modeled may not be affected seriously by random forces.[2] Furthermore, predictions are harder to obtain from stochastic models. The classical mathematical techniques of maximization, so useful in dealing with deterministic models, are not immediately applicable to stochastic models—a random function has no gradient. To cope with this second rationalization for ignoring uncertainty, a variety of alternative objectives have been proposed for stochastic cases, to replace the simple maximization-of-returns hypothesis. The simplest and in many other respects the most satisfactory objective when returns are stochastic is the maximization of *expected* return.[3]

A second important structural consideration is whether a model is dynamic or static. There has been concern in the main line of economic analysis over that dichotomy for some time. The calculus of variations was applied early to significant problems by Charles Roos (1925) and G. C. Evans (1930), and Samuelson's influential work (1946) goes deeply into dynamic phenomena. Formally, time can be incorporated into a model as a continuous flow; decision rules or control actions then are characterized as functions of time, and are optimized by methods of the calculus of variations. It is essential to this approach that control actions be continuously modifiable over time. Alternatively, time can be viewed as a sequence of discrete, perhaps equally spaced points. The discrete treatment is particularly useful in modeling processes that are monitored only occasionally, once per day or once per quarter, say. Control actions are taken only at specific intervals of time, and an action taken at time t affects all outcomes until time $t+1$. In that framework, an optimal sequence of actions can be selected by methods of the ordinary calculus.[4]

In dealing with stochastic models in discrete time, a third category can be added to the static and dynamic alternatives. "Steady state" analysis of a stochastic model is motivated in very much the same way as is the traditional static analysis of a deterministic model. That is to say, it is concerned with "average" or "normal" performance of the controlled system over time.[5] The remainder of this Section describes the three analytic modes in greater detail.

Dynamic Models. As a preliminary, three real-valued vectors are defined. $\mathbf{c}_t^k$ is the vector of values chosen by the decision-maker at time k to be the value of *control instruments* as of time t. $\mathbf{x}_t$ is a vector of *exogenous variables*. The elements x_{jt} are random variables. At time k, the probability density function $f^k(\mathbf{x}_t)$ is attached to $\mathbf{x}_t$. $f^k(\mathbf{x}_t)$ is, in short, a probability estimate formed at time k regarding the outcomes in period t. As time passes and new information is gathered, this estimate can change. Values of $\mathbf{x}_t$ are realized (revealed) during $[t, t+1)$; that is, at time $t+1$, the values of $\mathbf{x}_t$ will be known with certainty. Finally, $\mathbf{S}_t$ is the *state* of the activity at time t. The state vector contains all numerical information available at time t, and relevant to the choice of future controls $\mathbf{c}_t^t$, $\mathbf{c}_{t+1}^t$, . . . , $\mathbf{c}_{t+n}^t$, ... Consecutive state vectors $\mathbf{S}_1$, $\mathbf{S}_2$, . . . are related by the *state transition mapping*

$$(1) \qquad \mathbf{S}_{t+1} = \mathbf{S}(\mathbf{S}_t, \mathbf{c}_t^t, \mathbf{x}_t).$$

The decision maker is assumed to maximize expected returns. The maximum value of the return that can be realized in the first period (in the interval $[0, 1)$) is denoted

$$R_1^0 = \max_{\mathbf{c}_0^0} E[R(\mathbf{S}_0, \mathbf{c}_0^0, \mathbf{x}_0)] = \max_{\mathbf{c}_0^0} \int_{\mathbf{x}_0} R(\mathbf{S}_0, \mathbf{c}_0^0, \mathbf{x}_0) f^0(\mathbf{x}_0) d\mathbf{x}_0.$$

The term R_1^0 is a special one-period member of the returns set R_t^k, read "the return that is expected to accrue during $[t-1, t)$ as of time k". In general,

$$R_t^k = \max_{\mathbf{c}_t^k} [R(\mathbf{S}_k, \mathbf{c}_t^k, \mathbf{x}_t)]$$

is the return that is expected at time k to accrue during $[t-1, t)$. The R_t^k are random variables, as their values will depend on the random variables $\mathbf{x}_k$, $\mathbf{x}_{k+1}$, . . . , $\mathbf{x}_t$.

If the decision maker's planning horizon is N periods, the dynamic decision problem is to find

$$(2) \qquad \Pi_N(\mathbf{S}_0) = \max_{\mathbf{c}_0^0} \sum_{t=1}^{N} R_t^0 = \max_{\mathbf{c}_0^0} \sum_{t=1}^{N} \int_{\mathbf{x}_t} R(\mathbf{S}_0, \mathbf{c}_t^0, \mathbf{x}_t) f^0(\mathbf{x}_t) d\mathbf{x}_t.$$

Note that the maximization is specified to involve the control decision of the first period, $\mathbf{c}_0^0$. In order to find the optimal value of $\mathbf{c}_0^0$, it is generally necessary to assign tentative values to subsequent controls, $\mathbf{c}_1^0$, $\mathbf{c}_2^0$, . . . , $\mathbf{c}_n^0$ over the *entire* planning horizon. At time $t=1$ information not available at $t=0$ is at hand; that is, the value of $\mathbf{x}_0$ has been revealed, and is incorporated into $\mathbf{S}_1$ through the state transition mapping (1). $\mathbf{S}_1$ of course affects the choice $\mathbf{c}_1^1$. Because of the gain in information that results when the value of $\mathbf{x}_1$ is revealed, the "time zero" values c_1^0, $c_2^0, \ldots, c_N^0$ will probably differ from the values chosen a period later $c_1^1, c_2^1, \ldots, c_N^1$. In both periods the decision process involves the choice of $N+1$ controls: the first one binding in the current period, the remaining N tentative. The choice problem at time 1 is thus extended to encompass periods $1, \ldots, N+1$; the objective is

$$\frac{\max}{c_1^1} \sum_{t=1}^{N+1} R_t^1.$$

Note that so long as N is finite and the individual R_t^k are bounded, the objective will be bounded at every decision time k. The objective that governs the choice of the horizon length N is to capture all measurable future impacts of the current choice. That is, N is a horizon of adequate length if and only if optimal values for current controls, chosen from horizons of different lengths N and $N+z$, satisfy the condition

$$(3) \qquad |\, \mathbf{C}_0^0(N) - \mathbf{C}_0^0(N+z)\,| < \epsilon, \; z = 1, 2, \ldots$$

where ϵ is a vector of arbitrarily small constants, and $\mathbf{C}_0^0(j)$ denotes the optimal control decision to be taken at time 0, obtained from a j-period horizon model.[6]

Occasionally it is possible to characterize a general solution independent of time, or a *stationary control policy*, that applies in every period. A stationary policy is a mapping of a state vector into an optimal current decision vector, of the form

$$c_t^t = \mathbf{C}(\mathbf{S}_t) \qquad t = 0, 1, \ldots.$$

A condition for the existence of such a solution is that the probability function of the random vector $\mathbf{x}$ must be *stationary*; that is, $f_t^k(\mathbf{x}_t) = F(\mathbf{x}_t)$ for all k and t. Certainly, if $\mathbf{x}$ is perceived in two different periods to be governed by a *different* probability law, the best control response will differ between those periods, even if the initial state vectors are the same in the two periods.[7] The assumption of stationarity also applies to the decision objectives and costs confronting the firm—these, too, are held to be unchanging over time.

Under the assumption of stationary $\mathbf{x}$, the control policy usually is found (if it can be found) by consideration of the problem in this form:

$$(4) \qquad \Pi_{\infty} = \mathbf{c}_0^0 \,\epsilon\, \mathbf{C}(\mathbf{S}) \overset{\infty}{\underset{t=1}{\overset{\max}{\sum}}} \alpha^{\,t-1} R^{\,t},$$

where α is a discount factor $0 < \alpha < 1$. Inclusion of the discount factor reflects a general economic fact, which was conveniently ignored in the preceding N-period horizon formulation: present returns are prized more highly than future returns. The inclusion of α also reflects the mathematical fact that in its absence, the value of (4) is unbounded, and hence a maximum can not be found. In addition to the contrast between an infinite and an N-period horizon, (4) is distinguished from (2) by the fact that (2) seeks an optimum for the specific initial state $\mathbf{S}_0$, while (4) seeks to define the appropriate $\mathbf{c}_0^0$ contingent on *any* $\mathbf{S}_0$ that can arise. This change is indicated in (4) by the removal of $\mathbf{S}_0$ as an argument of the objective Π; and by making the first period decision $\mathbf{c}_0$ conform to the general decision rule $\mathbf{C}(\mathbf{S})$. When a general solution for (4) can be located analytically, it is usually found by exploiting the structure

$$(5) \qquad \Pi_{\infty} = \overset{\max}{\mathbf{c}_0^0(\mathbf{S}_0)} \Big[R_1^0 + \overset{\infty}{\underset{t=2}{\sum}} \alpha^{t-1} R_t^0 \Big] = \overset{\max}{\mathbf{c}_0^0(\mathbf{S}_0)} [R_1^0 + \alpha \Pi_{\infty}].$$

The procedure is to find a payoff function $\Pi\infty$ that satisfies the "fixed point" condition of the mapping (5), that is, the transformation of Π_{∞} into itself. Generalized analytical solutions of this type typically are not easy to find, and have been located only for a few specific versions of the expected returns function R.

In summary, a dynamic analysis can conveniently assume an infinite horizon, if stationarity is also assumed. The fixed point property of (5) can sometimes then lead to a decision rule that will apply in all periods. Alternatively, the analysis can proceed over a finite (N period) horizon, whether stationarity is assumed or not. In a finite horizon analysis without stationarity, it usually is necessary to confine the search to the specific numerical vector $\mathbf{c}_0^0$ that is the best response to the observed vector $\mathbf{S}_0$.

For further discussion of these decision structures, the reader is referred to Karlin (1955).

Static Analysis.[8] The difference between static and dynamic analysis lies entirely in the horizon period that is specified; in a static analysis, the objective involves only one period:

$$\overset{\max}{\underset{\mathbf{x}_0}{\mathbf{c}_0^0}}\ R_1^0 = \int R(\mathbf{c}_0^0,\ \mathbf{S}_0,\ \mathbf{x}_0) f^0(\mathbf{x}_0)\, d\mathbf{x}_0.$$

A static analysis is acceptable and appropriate so long as (a) essential conditions affecting objectives, costs, and the exogenous vector **x** are unchanged over long periods of time (long, meaning length of the order of an adequate horizon period or greater); or (b) current decisions have no effect on future returns. In cases where essential changes *do* occur or current decisions *do* affect future returns, the solutions obtained from static analysis generally will be non-optimal, and in fact they may be disastrous. Examples of problems for which a static analysis is appropriate are not numerous. One very simple inventory decision model, called the "newsboy" or "Christmas tree" model,[9] exploits the fact of obsolescence to truncate the decision process at one period (today's newspaper has virtually no market tomorrow; Christmas trees are a dreg as of late December 25). A second topic for which static analysis is the preferred mode, is commercial bank deposit creation by member banks of the Federal Reserve System. The Fed's biweekly reserve call is structured in such a way that credit decisions by a commercial bank have very little meaningful persistence into the future—current decisions primarily affect the current period.[10] Static analysis also has been applied to perfectly competitive markets by Nelson (1961) and Tisdell (1968).

Because static models are much easier to handle analytically than their dynamic counterparts, a reduction—approximation technique has been suggested, whereby dynamic problems are "converted" to one-period (static) problems. The trick is to represent the effects of current decisions on future costs, and to incorporate that representation as a part of the current period objective function.[11]

Steady State Analysis. This third analytic mode combines features of both static and dynamic analysis. Like the latter, it seeks to optimize the expected performance of a system over

time. Like the former, it does not deal explicitly with an un-
folding sequence of events over time. The steady state objective
function is

$$\max_{\mathbf{c}_0^0(\mathbf{S})} \left[\lim_{\mathcal{N} = \infty} \sum_{t=0}^{N} R_t^0 / \mathcal{N} \right].$$

Steady state analysis usually begins by imposing a restriction on
the form or structure of the decision policies to be considered.
Rather than an optimal policy from the unconstrained set of
conceivable policies, the decision process searches for optimal
values of specific numbers associated with a specific form of
decision rule. Examples will be found below in Section 2 and
Chapter III of how this restriction of the policy set operates.

Steady state analysis differs from an unrestricted infinite-
horizon dynamic analysis in only one other important respect:
there is no discounting of future returns under steady state
analysis. The absence of discounting has been considered in
some detail by Hadley (1964), who finds that true dynamic
analysis by providing for compounding of returns or costs, takes
into account the "interest on the interest" effects neglected by
steady state analysis. It is also important to keep in mind that
steady state analysis embodies the same assumptions of stationarity mentioned earlier in the discussion of infinite-horizon
dynamic analysis. Thus, steady state analysis will probably be
found unsuitable for circumstances in which important changes
at specific times can be anticipated.

Throughout this book, the steady state approach will be
relied on almost exclusively for analysis of the effects of uncertainty on asset management decisions. The extent of reliance on
steady state analysis is a measure of the lack of substantial
results on fully dynamic problems. It is believed, nonetheless,
that results and ideas from the steady state analysis are valuable.

2. RESPONSE DISCONTINUITY AND ADJUSTMENT COSTS
IN OPTIMAL CONTROL

In some important classes of application, the best control
action that can be taken over a wide range of states is "continue

to do just what you're doing now". Only when the initial values lie outside a specified region in state space does the control response depart from an established routine. Various phrases have been used to describe such jumpy control responses: "trigger rules", "bang-bang policies", "random walk policies", and "control limit policies" are four of the suggestions. All these designations reflect the importance of a violation of some boundary in state space before a significant change in the control decision takes place. Terminology is certainly of small importance, but the absence of any universally used designation suggests dissatisfaction with the existing choices. In the following, the term "relaxation response policies" will be used; the term is after "relaxation cycles", irregular movements caused by gross changes in regime.[12]

The appropriateness of a relaxation control response for a particular circumstance is determined and indicated by the objective function. Typically, costs attach to such control adjustments as production rate changes or cash balance replenishment. At least two conditions, associated with the cost of adjustment, will optimally lead to the use of relaxation response policies. First, let the control cost incurred at time t depend on changes in the control vector[13] $\Delta \mathbf{c}_t = \mathbf{c}_t - \mathbf{c}_{t-1}$ as well as on the level of the control vector $\mathbf{c}_t$; and let the cost be of the form

$$\gamma(\mathbf{c}) = \begin{cases} \gamma_1 + \gamma_2 |\Delta \mathbf{c}| + \gamma_3 \mathbf{c} & |\Delta \mathbf{c}| > 0 \\ \gamma_3 \mathbf{c} & \Delta \mathbf{c} = 0 \end{cases}$$

where γ_1, γ_2, and γ_3 are constants. That is, let the cost contain a "lumpy" component γ_1, invariant over nonzero values of the change $\Delta \mathbf{c}$, but equal to 0 when the change itself is equal to zero.

Second, and more surprising, a relaxation response is indicated when the cost of control is of the form

$$\gamma(\mathbf{c}) = \begin{cases} \gamma_2 |\Delta \mathbf{c}| + \gamma_3 \mathbf{c} & |\Delta \mathbf{c}| > 0 \\ \gamma_3 \mathbf{c} & \Delta \mathbf{c} = 0 \end{cases}.$$

This second case shows that the "lumpy" component of response cost is not requisite of relaxation control. In this second case, the control cost term has a "kink" at $\Delta \mathbf{c} = 0$; that is, the left-hand and right-hand derivatives of the function $\gamma(c)$ are different at $c = 0$. The control value responds to that kink in a manner directly analogous to the response of output to shifts in cost in the Sweezy theory of oligopoly demand.

(s, S) *Policies and "Lumpy" Adjustment Cost (Scarf)*. The effects of lumpy and kinky costs of response on the control regime can be illustrated in two examples from the literature of asset management. The first case involves a *lumpy* cost of placing orders to replenish inventory. Suppose that an order can be placed at the end of a period, and it will be filled before the beginning of the next period. To further simplify notation, denote the stock on hand *after* an order is delivered by y; and denote the stock level before an order by x. The order, then, amounts to $y - x$. Let *sales* be a discrete-valued random variable, denoted z, with the probability mass function ϕ_z. The expected one-period costs of operation have three components:

$$(6) \begin{cases} \text{Ordering cost:} & \gamma(y - x) = \begin{cases} 0 & y - x = 0 \\ \gamma_1 + \gamma_2 \cdot (y - x) & y - x > 0 \end{cases} \\[2ex] \text{Shortage cost:} & \sigma(y) = \sum_{z=y+1}^{\infty} \sigma \cdot (z - y)\phi_z \\[2ex] \text{Holding cost:} & \eta(y) = \sum_{z=0}^{y} \eta \cdot (y - z)\phi_z. \end{cases}$$

Let $C_N(x)$ denote the minimum expected present value of costs over an $\mathcal{N}$-period horizon. Then we can write the firm's objective as: find

$$C_N(x) = \underset{y \geq x}{\min} \{\gamma(y - x) + \sigma(y) + \eta(y) + \alpha \sum_{z=0}^{\infty} C_{N-1}(y - z)\phi_z\}.$$

Scarf (1960) has proved the following[14]

Theorem: When $\sigma(y) + \eta(y)$ is convex, and $\gamma(y - x)$ is of the form (6), there always exist numbers S and s, $S > s$, such that

$$\text{if } x \geq s, \text{ let } y = x, \text{ and}$$
$$\text{if } x < s, \text{ let } y = S$$

are the optimal rules for selecting y.

A time series of inventory levels, then, will appear as is shown in Figure II when ordering conforms to the optimal policy. It is to be emphasized that in this model, sales demand is a random variable, and ordering decisions can be made only at regularly spaced points in time (every Friday noon, say). The rationale for the (s, S) policy, as it is called,[15] is straightforward: the "lumpy" cost of ordering, and higher holding costs following an order, are sustained only to avoid even larger expected costs of shortage. Demand uncertainty makes it too costly to hold enough stock so that the probability of shortage is identically equal to zero. Even if sales, a random variable, has an upper bound, it will always pay to accept occasional shortages, because the holding cost of a marginal unit of stock will eventually exceed the benefit, in the form of lower shortage probability, than the unit of stock affords.

The (s, S) policy can be applied directly to the study of cash management, to cases in which cash flows have a large and persistent negative drift; and indeed, the important and widely cited contributions of Baumol (1952), Tobin (1956) and others can be viewed as simplified applications to the problem of. money balance maintenance.

[U, D] *Policies and "Kinky" Adjustment Cost* (*Eppen-Fama*). The

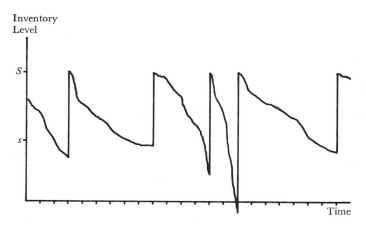

Figure II. Hypothetical Performance of (s, S) Control Policy over Time

second case that calls for a relaxation control response is one in which the control cost is *kinky*. The setting differs from that of the (s, S) policy in that the sales variable z can be negative, as well as positive. While negative sales is a questionable concept, a slight reinterpretation avoids difficulty; let the random variable z be regarded as a deviation of actual sales from the mean sales rate $\bar{z}$. Then actual sales $= z + \bar{z}$, and z is the change in inventory when output is set equal to the mean sales rate. Output can be increased above the normal level or reduced below the normal level. The output rate is designated p. Then with a starting inventory level of x, the realized inventory level at the end of the first period will be

$$x + p - (z + \bar{z}) = y - z,$$

where $y = x + p - \bar{z}$ is the expected inventory level at the end of the first period. Eppen and Fama (1969a) and Beckmann (1961) have described the optimal policy[16] under the condition that the expected holding and shortage costs are of the same forms analyzed by Scarf, that is,

$$\eta(y) = \overset{y}{\underset{z=-\infty}{\Sigma}} \eta \cdot (y - z)\phi_z$$

$$\sigma(y) = \overset{\infty}{\underset{z=y+1}{\Sigma}} \sigma \cdot (z - y)\phi_z$$

and the cost of adjusting the production rate is of the kinky form

(7) $$\gamma(p - \bar{z}) = \gamma \cdot |p - \bar{z}| = \gamma |y - x|.$$

The objective of the producer is to find

$$C_N(x) = \overset{min}{y} \left\{ \gamma |y - x| + \eta(y) + \sigma(y) + \alpha \overset{\infty}{\underset{z=-\infty}{\Sigma}} C_{N-1}(y - z)\phi_z \right\},$$

where α is the time preference (discount) factor.

The structure of the optimal policy is indicated by the

Theorem: If $\eta(y) + \sigma(y)$ is convex, and $\gamma(p - \bar{z})$ is of the form (7), there exist numbers U and D such that the optimal policy is

(a) if $x > D$, let $p < \bar{z}$, $\bar{z} - p = x - D$
(b) if $D \geq x \geq U$, let $p = \bar{z}$
(c) if $U > x$, let $p > \bar{z}$, $p - \bar{z} = U - x$.

That is, when the initial inventory x lies outside the range $[U, D]$, minimal corrective steps are taken to move the expected inventory level at the beginning of the next period back within the range. When inventory x is within the range, the production rate is left at its normal value $\bar{z}$. A stock level, then, would optimally behave over time as is shown in Figure III, given the assumptions analyzed in this case.

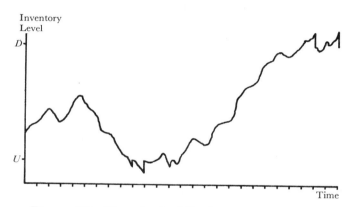

Figure III. Hypothetical Performance of $[U, D]$
Control Policy over Time

Just as the optimality of the (s, S) policy hangs on the condition that randomly generated flows go in one direction only, so the optimality of the $[U, D]$ policy is dependent on the condition that randomly generated flows move the stock symmetrically in both directions, upward and downward. Thus, both the specific form of the adjustment cost and the structure of the random exogenous flows are important in determining the optimal policy form in each case.

The Unconventional Character of Relaxation Control. Other circumstances can be envisioned such that a relaxation response

may well be optimal. Suppose, for example, the *holding* cost is
of the form

$$\eta(.) = \begin{matrix} 0 & x < K \\ \eta.x & x \geq K \end{matrix}$$

that is, inventories can be maintained costlessly over a significant range of levels. However such a case has never to my
knowledge been considered sufficiently important to warrant
analysis. Relaxation response control rules derive their practical
importance from the configuration of control costs, not holding
costs, it would seem.

Relaxation control responses are not the standard stuff of
economic analysis. In the business cycle literature, the principle
of acceleration is a time-honored explanatory device that embodies the very antithesis of relaxation control. In naïve accelerator models, a rigid relationship between attainable output
and existing capital is posited, which ignores slack due to capital
flexibility or idle capacity. Even in more sophisticated versions
which provide for input substitution, such as the recently
fashionable flexible accelerator, there is a linear rather than a
relaxation relation between the control variable (investment) and
the forcing variable (desired output). Similarly, linear relationships are ubiquitous in the literature on inventory cycles.

In the literature on money demand, regular functional relationships between desired cash and the crucial determining
variables, interest and the transactions volume, are widely met.
Belief in functional regularity shapes and conditions both predictions about response to monetary policy and the design of
empirical tests that attempt to gauge the response of money
demand to changes in important variables. It will be of interest
to see whether standard monetary policy predictions and empirical test procedures hold up if relaxation control regimes are
optimal. These issues must wait until Chapter IX.

3. STATIONARY OCCUPANCY PROBABILITIES FOR FINITE RANDOM PROCESSES

A dynamic analytic approach was taken in the two papers,

by Scarf (1960) and Eppen and Fama (1969a), in which optimality theorems were given for different relaxation response policies (Section 2 above). In both cases, the optimality of a particular policy class was established over a finite horizon of unrestricted length. The analysis was restricted by the condition that the random sales variable z be stationary and independent over the $\mathcal{N}$ periods, that is, $\phi_t(z) = \phi_z$ for all $t = 1, \ldots, \mathcal{N}$. Establishing necessary and sufficient conditions for the optimality of a policy class is difficult, and thus far the dynamic analytical approach has been the only successful route to that goal.

Finding the optimal numerical values in a specific case for policy parameters[17] is yet another difficult problem, but one that has been approached with success through several analytic modes. Usually numerical approximation methods are used to obtain specific solutions in dynamic approaches to optimization within a restricted policy class. Eppen and Fama (1968) offer a good example of a successful numerical approach to the problem of finding best values of U and D under different specific cost and demand circumstances.

Steady state analysis is useful as an alternative approach for obtaining specific solutions. It is a superior mode to dynamic numerical analysis for some purposes, such as describing the average behavior of randomly shocked systems when a particular policy form is used over a long period of time. Also, it is usually straightforward to find optimal policy parameters from steady state analysis. The objective function can usually be expressed in terms of the policy parameters, and optimized with respect to the policy parameters by routine techniques of differential calculus. The ways in which optimal policy parameter values depend on the structures of cost and demand can be seen in the first-order conditions; occasionally, these relationships are quite simple.

The behavior over time of important stock and flow variables, like production rates and inventory levels, can be related to the values assigned to policy parameters, once the parameters have been characterized. Then we can study the specific effects of cost structures and demand conditions on the behavior of the stocks and flows. The main virtue of the steady state approach is its analytic simplicity. That simplicity is obtained at the cost of restricted attention to a narrow class of policy forms which can be specified in terms of a small number of policy parameters.

A crucial step in steady-state analysis, then, is to characterize the relations between important stocks and flows on the one hand, and the random exogenous process and the policy controls on the other. In many cases, linking up can be achieved through the *steady state distributions* of the flow rates and stock levels. Such distributions, when they can be found, describe the behavior of stocks and flows *during a "typical" period in the indefinite future.* Suppose, for example, that we are told that the steady state distribution of inventory levels is $\Theta(X)$. The function Θ assigns a probability to the event that the inventory level x is no greater than the value X. But a time must be specified for which the statement is true; it is not true today, for example, if $\Theta(X) > 0$, and the inventory level is known to be more than X today; and it is unlikely to be true tomorrow if inventory is far above the level X today. Clearly, the known initial condition—today's inventory—affects our judgment about the relative likelihood of different inventory positions tomorrow. Accordingly, steady state distributions are defined as limits of sequences: let $\Theta_1(X)$ be the distribution describing the inventory position tomorrow, $\Theta_2(x)$ the following day, and so on. Then if

$$\Theta_X = \lim_{t = \infty} \Theta_t(X)$$

can be shown to exist, as it can under many practical circumstances, the steady state distribution is defined, and inventory levels are subject to a probability law that is stationary over time. Recall that stationary demand and cost conditions were held to be requisite for a stationary operating policy; stationary operating policies are further requisite to the existence of steady state distributions, so far as practical discussion is concerned.[18]

Such distributions, if they exist, adequately represent the dependence of production rates and inventory levels on the policy parameters. That is, if the steady state distributions are known, no additional information other than the objective function is needed to optimize the values of the policy controls. It will now be seen that under simple circumstances, that the parameters of the $[U, D]$ policy can be optimized, once the steady state distribution of inventory is known explicitly in terms of the policy controls.

Recall that the costs realized by the firm in one period are given by the expression

$$\gamma \cdot |p - \bar{z}| + \{\eta \cdot (y - z) | y \geq z + \sigma \cdot |(z - y)| z > y\}.$$

The cost coefficients γ, η and σ, and the stock-flow variables y and z, are defined above (page 32). Let the probabilities that govern the flow of sales demand be of the symmetric Bernoulli form[19]

$$\phi(\bar{z} - 1) = \phi(z + 1) = 1/2.$$

Thus, in any day, sales can take the values $\bar{z} \pm 1$; and the distribution is symmetric around the mean and median value $\bar{z}$. Control decisions are made once per day.

So long as the inventory level is in the interval $[U, D]$, the production rate is fixed at $\bar{z}$, and the transition rule governing movements in inventory is described by the forward equation

$$\theta_{t+1}(x) = \theta_t(x - 1)/2 + \theta_t(x + 1)/2, \ D \geq x \geq U,$$

where θ is the density function of the distribution Θ. When x lies below U or above D, an adjustment is made in the production rate; if $x = D + 1$, output in the next period is reduced by one unit to $\bar{z} - 1$; or if $x = U - 1$, output in the next period is increased by one unit to $\bar{z} + 1$. These production rules lead to two important boundary conditions, on the argument that upward adjustment from $U - 1$ to U or downward adjustment from $D - 1$ to D follows instantaneously:

$$\theta_{t+1}(U - 1) = \theta_{t+1}(U)$$

and

$$\theta_{t+1}(D + 1) = \theta_{t+1}(D).$$

The steady state condition is that, for any arbitrarily small ϵ, there must exist some value t such that

$$\left| \theta_{t+k}(x) - \theta_t(x) \right| < \epsilon$$

for all x and k. The condition can be fulfilled only for t sufficiently large so that the value of x at time 0 is no longer influential. The implication of the steady state condition is seen readily: if $D - U > 2$, and $x = D$ at time 0, the probability that $x = U$ at time 1 is zero. However, after the process has been in operation for a large number of periods, the probability of finding $x = U$ is no longer zero; and eventually, the probability of finding $x = U$ in successive periods does not change perceptibly *from the vantage point of time* 0.

The desired steady state occupancy probabilities can be found in a number of ways. If specific numerical values of U and D are known, it is a simple matter to solve the system

(8) $$B . \theta_x = \theta_x$$

(9) $$\mathbf{1} . \theta_x = \mathbf{1},$$

where θ_x is the vector of steady state probabilities, $\mathbf{1}$ is the unit vector of the same dimension as θ_x, and B is the matrix of Bernoulli transition probabilities described in the transition relations. The matrix B is of the form

$$B = \begin{bmatrix} 1/2 & 0 & 1/2 & 0 & \cdots & 0 \\ 1/2 & 0 & 1/2 & 0 & \cdots & 0 \\ 0 & 1/2 & 0 & 1/2 & \cdots & 0 \\ \vdots & & & & & \\ \vdots & & & & & \\ \vdots & \cdots & 1/2 & 0 & 1/2 & 0 \\ 0 & \cdots & 0 & 1/2 & 0 & 1/2 \\ 0 & \cdots & 0 & 1/2 & 0 & 1/2 \end{bmatrix}$$

and is of rank $D - U + 2$. To satisfy (8) it is necessary and sufficient that θ_x have equal elements—thus, the occupancy probability density function is uniform over the integer points in $[U-1, D+1]$. To satisfy (9), the value of each component must be $1/(D-U+2)$.

An alternative solution technique is to solve the second order difference equation

(10) $$\theta_x = \theta_{x+1}/2 + \theta_{x-1}/2$$

subject to the boundary conditions

(11) $$\Sigma\theta_x = 1$$
$$\theta_{U-1} = \theta_U$$
$$\theta_{D+1} = \theta_D.$$

The equation (10) has the characteristic equation

(12) $$\xi^2 - 2\xi + 1 = 0.$$

The solution to (10) is of the form

(13) $$\theta_x = A\xi_1^{*x} + B\xi_2^{*x},$$

where ξ_1^* and ξ_2^* are the roots of the characteristic equation (12), and A and B are arbitrary constants that are valued to conform to the boundary conditions (11). Since ξ_1^* and ξ_2^* both are equal to 1, the solution (13) is of the form

$$\theta_x = A + Bx.$$

Apparently, the number of boundary conditions is excessive, since there are only two constants to be determined. But note that one of the last two conditions of (11) is redundant, since

$$A + BD + B = A + BD$$
$$A + BU - B = A + BU;$$

both imply only that $B = 0$. The solution then is $\theta_x = A$; it is uniform over the range $[U-1, D+1]$, and the probability mass assigned to each integer point in the range is determined by fulfillment of the first boundary condition. The steady state occupancy probability, characterized in terms of the policy controls U and D, is

$$\theta_x = 1/(D-U+2).$$

The problem of characterizing the steady state behavior of randomly shocked processes is more difficult when higher-order transition relations are encountered. Suppose, for example, that rather than (10), the transition relation were

$$\theta_{t+1}(x) = \theta_t(x-2)/16 + \theta_t(x-1)/4 + 3\theta_t(x)/8$$
$$+ \theta_t(x+1)/4 + \theta_t(x+2)/16,$$

a fifth-order system. The solution method used for the earlier second-order example is harder to apply in this case; however, such higher order and more complicated variants will arise later on (Chapter IV). As in the simple Bernoulli case, such higher order problems are simpler in the absence of drift; that is, when the expected change between periods is zero. All cases involving drift are decidedly more difficult and troublesome to analyze, regardless of the order of the transition relation. This, too, is an issue that will receive consideration in Chapter IV.

Once the steady state density function θ_x is located in terms of U and D, it is a simple matter to find optimal values of those control limits, since operating costs can be related quite simply to θ_x. Expected costs of holding relate to the expected value of x, conditional on $x > 0$; and shortage costs relate to the mean value of the negative tail (if any) of $\int\theta_x$. The expected cost of changing the output rate is inferred from the probability of a change, and the fact that output changes are all of unit size. Output changes occur with probability $\theta_D + \theta_U$, or $2/(U - D + 2)$. The expected cost of operation in a typical future period, then, is[20]

$$2\gamma/(D - U + 2) + \eta D/2 - \sigma U/2, \ D \geq 0, \ U \leq 0.$$

Each expression can be minimized in terms of U and D, and the arrangement of U and D about 0 is the one that yields the lowest value overall.

In the next chapter, these analytical approaches will be applied to the problems of cash management.

Notes

1. See, for example, Radner (1968).
2. It is contended by Haavelmo (1959), for example, that stochastic effects are of secondary importance in capital theory, even when considering the investment decision of the individual firm.

3. A variety of objections have been raised concerning the selection of a simple expected returns maximization hypothesis. The most prominent one, perhaps, is that risk and return frequently are found to be positively associated with one another; and as return increases, so does the dispersion of prospective outcomes. That dispersion is held to be a bad thing. In the usual applications of dynamic asset management models, to the control of finished goods inventory or cash balances, ignoring risk can be justified on the ground that even the riskiest alternative is unlikely to lead to a ruinous outcome. For a lengthy and accessible discussion of the strategic and psychological issues underlying choice of objective for decision making under uncertainty, see Luce and Raiffa (1957), chapter 13; or, see Marschak (1951).
4. The decision-theoretic setting of asset management problems is well treated in an essay by Arrow, Karlin and Scarf (1958).
5. See Karlin (1958b); also Arrow, Harris and Marschak (1951).
6. The existence of "adequately long" horizons is an issue considered in Dvoretzky, Keifer and Wolfowitz (1952). A thorough and illuminating background discussion of the importance of horizons in decision problems is to be found in Charnes, Drèze and Miller (1966). The definition of adequate horizon length is, of course, related to the definition of a limit for the optimal initial control: that limit exists if and only if for arbitrarily small ϵ there exists an N such that (3) holds.
7. Stated formally, if $S_j = S_t$ and $f^j(x_j) \neq f^t(x_t)$, then $c_j^j \neq c_t^t$.
8. Care should be taken to avoid confusion: recall that we are concerned with stochastic models, which differ in important ways from the conventional static models of economic theory.
9. See, for example, Manne (1961), pp. 117-121.
10. On commercial bank reserves and credit policy, a number of papers are available, beginning with Edgeworth (1888). For a more recent view see Poole (1968), and Thore (1968). Both Poole and Thore provide extensive references.
11. This reduction-approximation technique was first proposed, I believe, by Arrow (1957). The same idea is developed by H. D. Mills (1962), and it is discussed further and applied with some success by E. S. Mills (1962), especially chapter 7.
12. To the best of my knowledge, Georgescu-Roegen (1951) was first to analyze relaxation phenomena in economic dynamics. The best-known study involving the application of relaxation methods in economics, probably, is Hicks (1950). The importance of relaxation responses in decision and control processes has been evident since the work of Arrow, Harris and Marschak (1951) and Massé (1946). Two studies, by Beckmann (1961) and Orr (1962), apply a relaxation approach in the theory of production.
13. Notation: When the superscript used in Section 2 is suppressed, it is implied that the control value in both planned and executed in the period of the subscript. When the subscript is also suppressed, the discussion applies to every time period.
14. Scarf's analysis and proof embodies a continuous-valued random sales variable, a more challenging case to handle analytically.
15. The terminology has caught on from Dvoretzky, Keifer and Wolfowitz (1953).
16. Beckmann does not consider the questions or issues of optimality, but simply derives operating rules under the indicated cost circumstances. Eppen and Fama provide an optimality proof under assumed conditions that are in some

respects less and in other respects more restrictive than those indicated in my discussion. The Eppen-Fama proof can be extended to the case described in the text, if it is specified additionally that the random variable z has a finite domain, that is, there exists a K such that $|z_t| < K$ for all t. Their proof is less restrictive than the text indicates, in that it doesn't require that the "normal" production rate be equated to mean sales. I have attempted to emphasize the gross effects of the cost structure and the probability function ϕ on response; I have taken care to avoid unsupportable statements in the process of description, but the descriptions are certainly not everywhere faithful in detail to the originals from whence they derive. It should be noted that Eppen and Fama motivate their analysis in the context of cash balance control. In that context, x can be interpreted as a cash balance, z as a cash flow (net daily payment or receipt), and p as a purchase (or sale) of securities.

17. For the s, S policy, the action level s and the return level S are complete characterizations of the operating rules. They are the "policy parameters."

18. It may be possible to devise "ergodic theorems" (convergence proofs) for cases in which the policy is non-stationary. Whether examples exist, or interesting ones can be constructed, I do not know.

19. For a full description and analysis of the Bernoulli process, and a cryptic exposition of the difference equation techniques used here, see Feller (1951) or later editions. Fuller treatment of difference equations is available in Goldberg (1958) or Baumol (1951).

20. The alternatives follow from a result of Eppen and Fama (1969a): $D \geq 0$ and $U \leq 0$ in all instances.

III

The Basic Model and Important Precursors

1. The Baumol Model

Baumol's work on the demand for money (1952) and most of the subsequent literature that followed from it, is adapted in a simple way from the (s, S) inventory policy (Chapter II, Section 2). The objective of Baumol's analysis is to find an optimal pattern of asset transfer to replenish a cash balance that is steadily drawn down over time. The model incorporates (i) a known constant cash flow rate of \$m per day; (ii) the requirement that all demands for payment from the cash balance be filled immediately, (iii) a lumpy cost of transfer from assets into cash, denoted γ, and (iv) an opportunity cost of holding cash, denoted v, equal to the interest foregone on the single earning asset available in the economy, "bonds".

The decision rule used in Baumol's analysis calls for the sale of \$M worth of bonds every M/m days. Receipts from sale of bonds are obtained immediately. The objective, then, is to minimize daily operating costs with respect to M. The costs are

$$c = \gamma m/M + vM/2,$$

where γ and v are cost coefficients, m/M is the probability of a transfer into cash on a randomly chosen future day, and $M/2$

is the average value of the cash balance over time. Differentiation reveals that the optimal transfer size $M*$ is given by

(1) $M* = (2\gamma m/v)^{1/2},$

the familiar square root law that dates back to the "economy in manufacture" literature of the 1920's.[1] The operating rule that led to (1) will generate a cash balance that takes the sawtooth pattern of Figure IV over time. The regularity of that

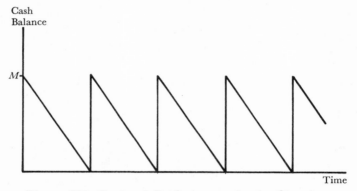

Figure IV. Optimal Performance in the Simplest
"Baumol" Case

pattern implies that the mean cash balance is half the optimal transfer size; $\overline{M} = M*/2$. Subsequent research by Tobin (1956) established that the policy form analyzed by Baumol is optimal for the assumed circumstances.

In contrast to the burgeoning theoretical and applied literature on the control of physical output, which generalized in a variety of interesting directions, the small number of works on the control of cash stayed very close to Baumol's formulation. For a long time, the Baumol model was *the* optimal asset management approach to the demand for money.

The approach has been met with some dissatisfaction, arising in good part out of the healthful spirit of empiricism that is said to distinguish contemporary economics. The most important weakness of the model as a predictor of money demand is its implied demand elasticities for money, with respect to the interest rate and the transactions rate. The model's predicted elasticities are too rigid and of the wrong size; they are $1/2$ with respect to m, the transactions variable, and $-1/2$ with respect to ν, the interest rate. Early empirical tests, especially those by Friedman (1959) uncovered larger elasticities for both transactions and interest: in the neighborhood of 1.8 and 0, respectively.[2] On this evidence, the asset management approach was found wanting. The numerous possible variations on the Baumol model, embodying different cash flow and operating cost assumptions, were left unconsidered until recently. As will be seen throughout this book, a proper choice of departure from the Baumol model can generate elasticity predictions that differ significantly from his.

2. Cash Flow Processes

The theory of random processes over discrete domains has for the most part dealt with variables that can increase or decrease over time, as we might expect, given the historical concern with gains and losses from gambling. By contrast, applications of the theory in economics and management usually have dealt in processes that move in only one direction, the most obvious and important example for present purposes being the Baumol model of money demand (Section 1). We have but to look at the behavior of a business firm's cash balance over time to realize that it sustains random increases as well as decreases; and an analysis that provides the possibility of random movement in both directions has a better chance of predicting well than a model in which the random movements of the balance are in a single direction. A two-month sequence of the daily payments and receipts of a business firm (net of portfolio actions taken to correct the cash position) is displayed in Figure V.

As it turns out, a more "realistic" accommodation of cash flows can significantly affect predictions of the demand for money. In this chapter, we begin the process of analyzing money demand under a variety of conditions, but one condition

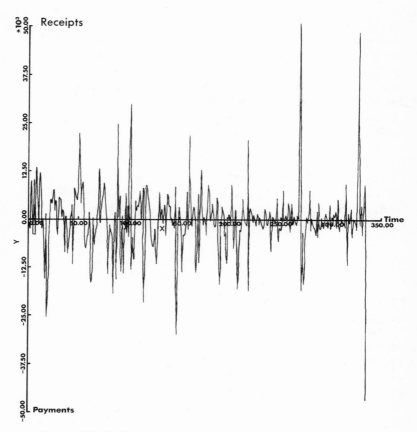

Figure V. Daily Net Cash Flow Volumes, Corporation

remains fixed throughout the analysis: cash balances are permitted to move randomly in the upward as well as the downward direction. Not only is the two-way flow a more realistic
(descriptive) picture; the restriction to flows in one direction
constricts the scope of analysis and biases predictions. As we
will begin to see in this chapter, it is almost impossible to pre-
judge the degree and extent to which money demand predictions will be sensitive to the structure of the predictive model;
the statement that predictions are biased by one-way cash

flows must be supported by evidence. That evidence is provided in this chapter.

Section 3 describes Patinkin's (1956) model of money demand, which was the first to build randomness into both the payment and receipt flows. I believe the treatment given here is the first in which Patinkin's model is formulated explicitly as an optimization process. The model relies on a combinatorial analysis provided by A. Dvoretzky.

3. THE PATINKIN-DVORETZKY MODEL

This model, which was constructed to analyze transactions and precautionary demand, embodies a number of novel and unique features.[3] Patinkin follows Hicksian monetary analysis[4] in assuming that cash flows occur, and costs can be incurred, throughout the time intervals $[t, t + 1)$, $[t + 1, t + 2)$, . . . , but cash management decisions can be made only at the times t, $t + 1$, ... (This construction has subsequently virtually disappeared from monetary analysis.) During each time interval, $2N$ transactions of equal size m occur; N are payments and N are receipts. Thus, at each point in time when a cash management decision is made, the cash flow has netted out to zero. However, the payments and receipts can occur in a random order, and as a consequence shortages can occur during the intervals between management decisions unless adequate protective steps are taken at the beginning of the period. The cash manager wants to minimize the sum of two costs: the cost of holding cash to prevent shortages, and the cost of running out of cash between control decisions.

Patinkin's treatment of the model is verbal-descriptive. The model is seen to rationalize the holding of cash by a utility-maximizing decision-maker.

Formally, the control problem confronting the decision-maker is to choose an initial cash balance mM at time t, given that (1) during the *budget period* $[t, t + 1)$, N receipt and N payment transactions of m dollars each will occur, in a random order;[5] (2) a cost of holding cash is incurred, that is directly proportional to the size of the initial balance mM; and (3) a shortage cost is incurred if payment transactions accumulate in excess of receipt transactions at any time during the budget period in an amount *greater than Mm*.[6] The shortage cost is a simple penalty that can be incurred no more than once during an interval between control decisions; multiple shortages during a budget period do not affect cost.

An optimal plan needs to consider only the current period, since the netting out of payments and receipts means that there is no persistence of random effects or costs between periods.

To analyze the model formally, it is necessary to calculate shortage probabilities for each possible initial state mM. Clearly, if $M \geq N$, the shortage probability is zero, since the most unfavorable of the possible sequences of transactions is N payments followed by N receipts. Conversely, if $M = 0$, only the most favorable sequences, in which total payments never exceed total receipts, will result in no shortage. The probability that one of the favorable sequences occurs is given as $1/(N+1)$.[7] The best value for M is likely to lie somewhere between the extremes of 0 and N.

Patinkin enlisted Aryeh Dvoretzky to calculate a distribution of shortage probabilities $F(2N, M)$: the probability that at any stage of a randomly ordered sequence of N receipt days and N payment days, the payment days will outnumber the receipt days by M or more (more than $M-1$).

Dvoretzky proved that

$$F(2N, M) \approx e^{-M^2/N},$$

where the approximation sign signifies that the two sides of the expression approach the same limit as N increases. The exact expression is

(1) $F(2N, M) = N!^2/(N-M)!(N+M)!$

The courageous or persistent reader can verify that for $2N = 30$, the fit achieved by Dvoretzky's approximation is not bad: a few sample points are offered in Table I to support this judgment. The choice of 30 as a value for $2N$ reflects the view that a month is as natural a "budget period" as can be conceived *a priori*.

TABLE I

M	Dvoretzky Approximation (A)	Actual Value (B)	Ratio (A/B)
1	.96722	.96744	.999
2	.87517	.87702	.998
3	.74082	.74413	.996
4	.58665	.59093	.993
6	.30119	.30485	.988
8	.11844	.11968	.989
10	.03567	.03546	1.007
12	.00823	.00782	1.052

Using Dvoretzky's approximation, we can set up the decision problem quite simply. The decision-maker seeks a value of M to minimize the expected cost of cash management[8]

$$(2) \qquad E(c) = vm(M - 1) + \rho\, e^{-M^2/N},$$

where v is the cost per period of holding a dollar of cash, m is the size of all payment and receipt transactions, and ρ is a penalty incurred should payment obligations exceed cash on hand during the time between cash management decisions.

The first-order condition for a minimum on $E(c)$ is

$$0 = vm - \frac{2\rho M}{N}\, e^{-M^2/N}$$

or

$$(3) \qquad Me^{-M^2/N} = vmN/2\rho.$$

The left side of (3) behaves like the function xe^{-x}: it takes a zero value at $M = 0$, rises to a value of $(N/2e)^{1/2}$, when $M = (N/2)^{1/2}$ and then falls as M approaches its natural upper limit of N. Thus, if

$$(4) \qquad vmN/2\rho > (N/2e)^{1/2},$$

the first order condition cannot be satisfied by any of the feasible values of M. In that circumstance, the indicated optimum is $M = 0$. In the following, we assume that

(5) $vmN/2\rho \leq (N/2e)^{1/2}$,

in which case, the first order conditions hold at the single point $M = (N/2)^{1/2}$ when (5) holds as an equality, or at two values of M, when $(N/2e)^{1/2} > vmN/2\rho$. In the second case, there will be a question as to which root yields a lower value of the objective function (2). In fact, the smaller root always indicates a maximum on (2), and the larger, a minimum, as seen in Figure VI. Thus, in general, the objective function (2) takes

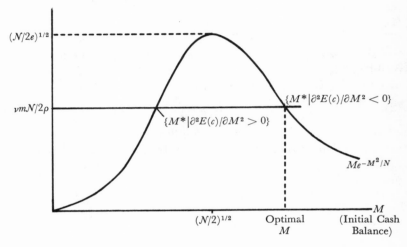

Figure VI. Solution Structure for Patinkin-Dvoretzky Model

its minimum at a value $M \geq (N/2)^{1/2}$. Suppose Patinkin's "budget period" of $2N$ days is one month in length; then $M \geq (7.5)^{1/2}$, i.e. $M \approx 3$ or more, depending on the specific values of v, m and ρ.

From the expression

$$Me^{-M^2/N} = vmN/2\rho$$

and from the fact that the optimal $M^* \geq (N/2)^{1/2}$, we can deduce that

(a) as v or m increase, M^* decreases
(b) as ρ increases, M^* increases

(c) as $\mathcal{N}$ increases, M^* always increases if $\dfrac{M^{*3}}{\mathcal{N}^2} e^{-M^2/\mathcal{N}} > vm/2\rho$, and decreases otherwise. If $(1/8e\mathcal{N})^{1/2} > vm/2\rho$, M^* *always* increases when $\mathcal{N}$ increases.

The statements (a) and (b) follow trivially from the slope of the left side of (3) in the range $\mathcal{N} > M > \left(\dfrac{\mathcal{N}}{2}\right)^{1/2}$. The statement (c) requires explanation.

Let the condition (3) be written

$$V(M^*, \mathcal{N}) = K\mathcal{N}.$$

Then, the differential of the equation (3) is

$$\frac{\partial V}{\partial \mathcal{N}}\, d\mathcal{N} + \frac{\partial V}{\partial M}\, dM^* = Kd\mathcal{N}.$$

We see that

$$\frac{\partial V}{\partial \mathcal{N}} = \frac{M^{*3}}{\mathcal{N}^2} e^{-M*2/N} \qquad \frac{\partial V}{\partial M^*} = \left(1 - \frac{2M^{*2}}{\mathcal{N}}\right) e^{-M*2/N}.$$

It follows from $M^* \geq (\mathcal{N}/2)^{1/2}$ that $\partial V/\partial M^* \leq 0$. The differential, then, can be written

$$\left(1 - \frac{2M^{*2}}{\mathcal{N}}\right) e^{-M*2/N}\, dM^* = \left[\frac{vm}{2\rho} - \frac{M^{*3}}{\mathcal{N}^2} e^{-M*2/N}\right] d\mathcal{N},$$

and if dM^* and $d\mathcal{N}$ are to move in the same direction, their coefficients must have the same sign, i.e. $\partial V/\partial \mathcal{N} < 0$ is necessary. The value of $\dfrac{M^{*3}}{\mathcal{N}^2} e^{-M*2/N}$ increases monotonically over the interval $(\mathcal{N}/2)^{1/2} < M^* < \mathcal{N}$. Thus, the coefficient of $d\mathcal{N}$ takes its greatest value if $M^* = (\mathcal{N}/2)^{1/2}$; its value there is $\dfrac{vm}{2\rho} - (1/8e\mathcal{N})^{1/2}$. If its value is negative there, it is negative everywhere, and dM^* and $d\mathcal{N}$ take the same sign everywhere.

From the conditions (a–c) a couple of useful facts emerge. First, there are two distinct measures of the transaction rate, m and $\mathcal{N}$. These have opposite effects on the optimal cash balance: M^* varys inversely with m and directly with $\mathcal{N}$.

Recall that N is a measure of the "budget period" over which the firm's cash flow by assumption must net out to zero; while m is a measure of the actual daily inflow or outflow *during* the budget period. If a budget period exists at all, it is almost surely less variable in duration than the cash flow is variable in volume. It would seem then that the logical choice of a transaction measure is m. There is, of course, the objection that m is highly variable within a budget period, but in other contexts, such as the theory of sequential sampling, this has not proved to be too serious an objection. Instead of looking at N as a number of days, Patinkin treated it as a number of transactions. The suggested modification of introducing m as the daily volume has added appeal from the fact that institutional considerations pertaining to cash shortages make the day-ending cash balance more important than its behavior *within* a day. By protecting against M days' drain, the cash holder is expressing concern over something more meaningful than M successive payment transactions.

If m is accepted as the relevant transactions measure, we note from (3) that the transactions rate m and the interest rate v affect the optimal initial cash balance in precisely the same way. As we will see, this intuition-violating and putatively counterfactual prediction is as much an artifact of the "budget period" hypothesis as it is of our use of m instead of N as the cash flow measure. The importance of having cash flows zero out every $2N$ days can be seen from the analysis of an otherwise similar model that omits the budget period construction. The model's predictions of demand elasticities will be looked at in Section 6.

4. THE BASIC MODEL: STRUCTURE[9]

In large business firms, the cash balance fluctuates irregularly (and to some extent unpredictably) over time in both directions—building up when operating receipts exceed expenditures and falling off when the reverse is true. If the build-up is at all prolonged, a point is eventually reached at which the financial officer in charge decides that cash holdings are excessive, whereupon he transfers a sizable quantity of funds to the control of the portfolio staff for temporary investment, or to loan retirement. In the other direction, in the face of prolonged cash drain, a level will be reached where the portfolio managers will be instructed to liquidate securities or where the firm will borrow to restore the cash balance to what it regards as an adequate working level.

This section presents a model that incorporates both the "up and down" cash balance movement characteristic of business operations, and the critical, lumpy transfer cost feature of the Baumol model, while relaxing some of the restrictive specifications of the Patinkin-Dvoretzky model. In particular, the specification of a budget period, over which receipts are equal to payments, is eliminated; and the firm can engage in cash balance management actions at any point in time. We will see that the basic model to be developed here can be generalized and modified in various ways.

Of the model's main structural features, some will be recognized as technical simplifications to permit compact and transparent solutions in analytical form. Others, however, are of a substantive nature and raise important empirical and economic issues. Full consideration of the more important issues is best postponed until the model and its major empirical implications have been set forth.

The model incorporates these conditions:

1. The cash manager operates in a two asset environment, as in the Baumol and Patinkin analyses: one asset is the firm's cash balance, and the other is a separately managed portfolio of liquid assets (such as Treasury bills, certificates of deposit, commercial paper or other money market instruments) whose marginal and average yield is v per dollar per day.

2. Transfers between the two asset accounts may take place at any time at a given marginal cost of γ per transfer, independent of the size of the transfer, the direction of the transfer or of the time since the previous transfer.

3. Such transfers may be regarded as taking place instantaneously; the lead-time involved in portfolio transfers is short enough to be ignored. This condition eliminates the need for

an explicit buffer stock whose function in stochastic inventory problems is to protect against runouts during the lead-time. While an assumption of zero lead time may seem quite strong, it is actually not unrealistic; at least, not for large firms with specialized staffs that monitor the cash balance and the portfolio closely. Dealings in most of the major money market instruments can be initiated by large firms by placing a telephone call, with delivery for the start of the next business day (and in some special cases even during the same day).[10]

4. Consistent with prevalent banking custom, the existence of a compensating balance requirement is assumed. It is further assumed that those requirements imply that the firm's cash balance is never allowed to fall below zero. Zero, of course, is a crucial point even in the absence of compensating balances, since overdrafts are never allowed for business firms. Even firms with open lines of credit must go through the formality (and expense) of arranging a transfer to the cash balance before checks will be cleared through an overdrawn account. In practice, compensating balance requirements may imply that cash normally never falls below some level that is substantially greater than zero.[11] The precise agreement that is negotiated between the firm and its banks will depend basically on the cost of the banking services—mainly check processing and loan accommodation—that the firm actually uses. Since compensating balances are a price charged by the bank in lieu of service charges, they will be regarded as completely exogenous to the problem of cash balance management.

5. An important point of contrast to the earlier Baumol and Patinkin models is the treatment of cash flows. It is assumed that cash flows are completely stochastic, and behave as if generated by a stationary Gaussian random walk. Given this framework, it is convenient and yet sufficiently general for our purposes to suppose that the sequence of individual cash receipts and payments resembles a sequence of independent Bernoulli trials. In particular, let $1/t$ be some small fraction of a working day such as $1/8$, i.e. an "hour." Then suppose that during any such hour the cash balance will increase by $+m$ dollars with probability $p = 1/2$, and that it will decrease by $-m$ dollars with

probability $q = 1 - p = 1/2$. Hence, over an interval of, say, n days, the distribution of changes in the cash balance will be binomial with mean $\mu_n = ntm(p - q) = 0$ and variance $\sigma_n^2 = 4ntpqm^2 = ntm^2$. This binomial distribution in turn will, of course, approach normality as n and t increase. Most of the subsequent discussion in the text will focus on the special symmetric or zero-drift case in which $p = q = 1/2$, although derivations for the more complicated non-symmetric cases are of interest, and will be carefully looked into in Chapter IV.[12]

6. Finally, structural conditions are imposed on the firm's objective function. It is assumed that the firm seeks to minimize the steady state cost of managing the cash balance under some "policy of simple form." In the present context, the simplest and most natural such policy is the two-parameter control-limit policy illustrated in Figure II. That is, the cash balance is allowed to wander freely until it reaches either the lower bound, zero, or an upper bound, h, at which times a portfolio transfer will be undertaken to restore the balance to a level of z. Hence, the policy implies that when the upper bound is hit there will be a lump sum transfer *from* cash of $(h - z)$ dollars; and when the lower limit is triggered, a transfer *to* cash of z dollars (Figure VII).

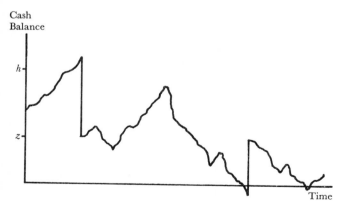

Figure VII. Hypothetical Performance of (h, z) Control Policy

Given this policy structure, and our other assumptions, the steady state expected cost per day of managing the firm's cash balance can be expressed formally as:

(6) $E(c) = \gamma P(T) + \nu E(M),$

where $P(T)$ is the probability of a portfolio transfer (either from or to cash) during any randomly chosen day in the distant future; γ is the cost per transfer; $E(M)$ is the average daily cash balance; and ν is the earning rate per dollar held in the security portfolio. The firm's objective is to minimize $E(c)$ with respect to the upper bound on cash holding, h, and the return point, z.

5. OPTIMAL VALUES OF THE BASIC POLICY CONTROL LIMITS

The most crucial job in finding optimal values for h and z is to characterize the steady state occupancy probability distribution of cash balances; for once that distribution has been found, it is a small thing to calculate $P(T)$ and $E(M)$ for substitution into (6).

Recall from condition 5 that the cash balance moves t times per day, m dollars at a time. Using a relaxation response policy of the assumed structure, let the domain of the cash balance be $0, m, 2m, \ldots, hm$; when the points 0 or hm are reached, let a transfer to or from the earning portfolio return the balance to the point zm. When changes are generated by a symmetric Bernoulli process, the transition rules (forward equations) are[13]

$$P_{t+1}(xm) = 1/2 \{P_t[(x-1)m] + P_t[(x+1)m]\} \quad 0 < x < z, \; z < x < h$$
$$P_{t+1}(zm) = 1/2 \{P_t[(z-1)m] + P_t[(z+1)m] + P_t(m)$$
$$+ P_t[(h-1)m]\}$$

$$P_{t+1}(m) = 1/2 \, P_t(2m)$$
$$P_{t+1}[(h-1)m] = 1/2 \, P_t[(h-2)m],$$

where $P_k(j)$ denotes the probability that the cash balance is precisely $\$j$ at time k.

This system of equations is less cumbersome to work with if we make a simple notation change. Instead of carrying the size of an individual cash transaction through the analysis, let the cash domain be normalized on m; that is, let $\$m$ be the standard cash unit instead of $1. With this notation change, we invoke the steady state condition (pass to the limit $t = \infty$) to obtain the difference equations

(7)
$$P_x = 1/2 \, [P_{x-1} + P_{x+1}] \quad 0 \le x \le h, \, x \ne z$$
$$P_z = 1/2 \, [P_{z-1} + P_{z+1} + P_1 + P_{h-1}]$$

with two boundary conditions

$$P_0 = P_h = 0$$

and the probability density condition

$$\sum_{x=0}^{h} P_x = 1.$$

To obtain a solution to this system is neither routine nor difficult. First, note that the characteristic equation of (7) is

$$0 = \xi^2 - 2\xi + 1$$

with the double root $\xi^* = 1$. The solution form for (7), then, is

$$P_x = A\xi^* + Bx\xi^* = A + Bx,$$

where A and B are two arbitrary constants. Two troublesome facts emerge; the same solution regime cannot hold at 0 and h, since

$$A + B \cdot 0 = 0$$

implies $A = 0$, and

$$Bh = 0$$

implies $B = 0$. A way around this problem is offered by the stipulation that the solution is

(8)
$$\begin{cases} A + Bx & 0 \le x \le z \\ C + Dx & z \le x \le h; \end{cases}$$

that is, two different probability regimes prevail over two intervals of the cost domain. The break-point at z is suggested by the linearity of the solution in x, by the zero probability masses at the terminal values 0 and h, and by the fact that P_z

is greater than $(1/2) P_{z-1} + (1/2)P_{z+1}$. With the solution form (8) there are four arbitrary constants, A, B, C and D; and there are four independent boundary conditions, $P_0 = 0$ which implies $A = 0$; $P_h = 0$ which implies $C = -Dh$; a "splicing" condition at the point z, which implies $D = Bz/(z-h)$; and the density condition $\sum\limits_{x=0}^{h} P_x = 1$, which can be rewritten

$$1 = B\sum_{x=0}^{z} x + D\sum_{x=z+1}^{h} (x-h) = B\frac{z(z+1)}{2} + \frac{Bz}{(z-h)}\left[\frac{h(h+1)}{2} - \frac{z(z+1)}{2}\right] + Bzh$$

(since there are $h - z$ terms of the form $-Dh$ present) to yield

$$B = 2/zh.$$

Thus, the stationary occupancy probability density is given by

(9a) $P_x = 2x/zh$ $0 \le x \le z$,

and

(9b) $P_x = 2(h-x)/h(h-z)$ $z \le x \le h$.

The stationary occupancy probability function, then, is triangular in form, with range bounded by 0 and h, and mode at z. The mean value $\sum\limits_{x=0}^{h} xP_x$ is

(10) $E(M) = (h+z)/3.$

This expression can be calculated directly (a rather tedious process that is made possible by the information $\sum\limits_{x=1}^{h} x^2 = h(h+1)$ $(h+2)/6$; or the mean value can be ascertained from any number of ancient "statistics" texts that discuss the triangular density function).

   The steady state probability of a transfer to or from the portfolio during some randomly chosen future day is denoted $P(T)$ and is found from the expression

$$P(T) = (t/2) P_1 + (t/2) P_{h-1};$$

from the values (9) we see that

(11) $$P(T) = t/z(h - z).$$

The rationale, of course, is that t transactions per day take place; and should a transaction occur when the cash balance is in the state 1 (or state $h - 1$), the probability is $1/2$ that a transfer to cash (to the portfolio) will occur.

Finally, the optimization process is more transparent if we substitute $\mathcal{Z} = h - z$ in the terms (10) and (11). The firm's objective then can be rewritten: find

(12) $$\mathop{\min}_{\mathcal{Z}, z} E(c) = \frac{\gamma t}{z\mathcal{Z}} + \frac{vm(\mathcal{Z} + 2z)}{3},$$

which is obtained by substituting (10) and (11) into (6), and noting that v is the portfolio earning rate per dollar, so vm is the earning rate per standard transaction unit. The necessary conditions for a minimum are

$$\frac{\partial E(c)}{\partial z} = -\frac{\gamma t}{z^2 \mathcal{Z}} + \frac{2 vm}{3} = 0$$

$$\frac{\partial E(c)}{\partial \mathcal{Z}} = -\frac{\gamma t}{\mathcal{Z}^2 z} + \frac{vm}{3} = 0,$$

which together yield the optimal values[14]

(13) $$z^* = \left(\frac{3\gamma t}{4 vm}\right)^{1/3}$$

and

$$\mathcal{Z}^* = 2z^*,$$

or in terms of the original policy variables

(14) $$h^* = 3z^*.$$

The structure of the optimal solution can be further illuminated if we return to a dollar denomination (instead of the transaction unit denomination of $\$m$ that underlay our derivation of the steady state distribution) in measuring the cash balance. In (13) the optimal bounds are given in units of

m. To obtain the optimal bounds in single dollar units, simply multiply the expression (13) by m to obtain

$$(15) \qquad z^* = \left(\frac{3\gamma m^2 t}{4\nu}\right)^{1/3};$$

and similarly to obtain h^* in dollar units. Note that $m^2 t$ is the daily variance of changes in the cash balance. We can write (15), then, as

$$(16) \qquad z^* = \left(\frac{3\gamma \sigma^2}{4\nu}\right)^{1/3},$$

a form which elucidates the relationship between the control (or prediction) model, and the variability of observable daily changes that are to be controlled or predicted.

This solution has a number of interesting and in some respects quite surprising properties. Notice first that despite the symmetry of the Bernoulli process and of the cost of returning the system to z the solution turns out to be asymmetrical. The optimal return point lies substantially *below* the mid-point of the range over which the cash balance is permitted to wander. The optimal rule structure implies that sales of portfolio assets will take place with greater average frequency and in smaller "lots" than purchases.[15] Some insight into the economics of the solution structure can be gained from Figure VIII in which the transfer cost and the holding cost are plotted separately as functions of z when h takes its optimal value. The transfer cost is a symmetric U-shaped function with minimum at the mid-point, $z = 1/2h^*$. The idle balance cost, by contrast, is a linear increasing function of z throughout; its value at $z = h^*$ is twice the value at $z = 0$. Hence, it obviously is uneconomical to set z greater than $h^*/2$ since both costs are increasing in the range $(h^*/2, h^*)$. Some cost reduction can be achieved by reducing z below $h^*/2$, since the transfer cost function is relatively flat in the region of its minimum.

But more surprising, the optimal z^* always lies at $1/3\, h^*$, regardless of the relative magnitudes of the cost coefficients γ and ν. Changes in the ratio γ/ν serve only to shrink or dilate the system as a whole; there is no change in the internal balance

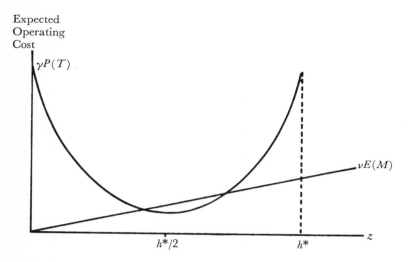

Figure VIII. Components of Expected Operating Cost,
(h, z) Policy

between z and h. The explanation lies in the structure of the cost function (12). Note that z and $\mathcal{Z}$ enter symmetrically into the transfer cost component, but that z enters with twice as much weight as $\mathcal{Z}$ in the holding cost component. Hence, whenever $\mathcal{Z} < 2z$ a reduction in z by some small amount Δ, combined with an increase in $\mathcal{Z}$ of double that size, will leave the holding cost unchanged, but lower the transfer cost; and, conversely, when $\mathcal{Z} > 2z$ a Δ increase in z combined with a 2Δ decrease in $\mathcal{Z}$ will permit some net cost savings to be effected.

An important issue, that we will look at with care in Chapter V, is the effect of changes in the cost function on the optimal solution structure.

6. Implications for the Demand for Money

For economists, the major interest in the solution lies in its implications for the demand for money by firms. That demand can be identified with the average cash balance associated with an (h, z) policy; it is $\dfrac{h^* + z^*}{3}$. Substituting the optimal values of h^* and z^* from (16) and (14), we obtain

$$(17) \qquad\qquad \overline{M} = \frac{4}{3}\left(\frac{3\gamma\ \sigma^2}{4\nu}\right)^{1/3}$$

as an expression of the firm's average cash balance (or demand for money) in terms of the important determining variables— cash flow data and operating costs. As in the case of Baumol's model (Section 1), the demand for money is an increasing function of γ, the cost of transferring funds to and from the earning portfolio; and a decreasing function of ν, the interest rate or opportunity cost incurred on funds held in the cash balance. The novelty of (17) is the explicit inclusion of the cash flow variance in the money demand equation. The variance is a measure of what is often referred to in the monetary literature as the "lack of synchronization" between cash receipts and payments. The Patinkin model of course attacks precisely the same phenomenon, but in asserting that payments and receipts are equal in volume over his budget period, Patinkin imposes a "global" synchronization. The "local" lack of synchronization that remains in his model is handled within the cash balance, with no recourse to purchases or sales of securities. Hence his emphasis on shortage costs instead of transfer costs.

The presence of the variance of cash flows as a "synchronization variable" in the money demand function raises the question of how (17) is to be interpreted when transactions elasticities are under discussion. In the Baumol model, the transaction rate is clear and unambiguous, and the predicted transaction demand elasticity is of the "correct" sign. In the Patinkin model, the measure of transaction rates is ambiguous; and if the most natural-seeming measure is chosen, the sign of the transaction elasticity is negative, rather than positive as prior reasoning and empirical testing leads us to expect.

In empirical studies of money demand, total sales is usually taken as the measure of the transactions variable. It is clear that there will be some relation between total sales on the one hand, and the transactions variable that the basic model reveals to be important, namely the transactions variance, on the other. Total sales is an approximation of the positive changes in the cash balance, summed over a time interval. But the relation is a loose one, and only wide limits can be established for the elasticity of the demand for cash with respect to sales that is implied by the basic model. The ambiguities stem from the fact that the sales rate may change in any of several different ways, each with a different impact on the firm's need for cash. As one simple possibility, the model can accommodate a doubling of sales by doubling each separate receipt and expenditure invoice, and increasing the step size from m to $2m$. The model then would predict, on the basis of (17), that the optimal balance should rise by a factor of $2^{2/3}$. As another possibility, a doubling of sales may come about because transactions occur twice as often; that is, t is doubled in value, with no change in the average invoice. The "law of large numbers" is strongly operative in this event, since there will be additional opportunities for offsetting changes, and the desired balance increases by a factor of only $2^{1/3}$. Thus, the model offers a range of possible sales elasticities, from $1/3$ to $2/3$, and that range becomes even larger when we allow for the possibility of increases in transaction magnitude accompanied by decreases in transaction frequency, or vice versa. The contrast with respect to money demand elasticity predictions between this model, and the two important predecessors provided by Baumol and Patinkin, should be quite clear. The Baumol model, which has served as the hypothetical basis for a substantial amount of empirical research, unambiguously predicts interest and transaction elasticities of equal magnitude but opposite sign: respectively minus and plus $1/2$. The rigidity and small value of the transaction elasticity prediction has been a particular source of difficulty, in much but not all of the empirical research done on the question of whether there are "economies of scale" in cash holding.

Patinkin's model is also suspect on the basis of the elasticity predictions that it yields. Based on the first order maximum relation (3) we obtain

(18) $$m = 2\rho M e^{-M^2/N}/\nu N,$$

which expresses our transaction variable as a function of our decision variable, instead of vice versa. We have that the transactions elasticity

$$\eta_m = \left[\frac{dm}{dM} \cdot \frac{M}{m} \right]^{-1} = \mathcal{N}/(\mathcal{N} - 2M^2).$$

The inversion of $\frac{dm}{dM}$ is permissible because $M^* \geq (\mathcal{N}/2)^{1/2}$, and dm/dM is monotonic and (18) is continuous for all M in the interval $(0, \mathcal{N})$. Note that v and m can be interchanged in (18) so that $\eta_v = \eta_m$.

So far as the signs and magnitudes of these elasticities are concerned, recall that $M^* \geq (\mathcal{N}/2)^{1/2}$. Hence the denominator is negative in all cases. When

$$(\mathcal{N}/2)^{1/2} \leq M^* < \mathcal{N}^{1/2} \quad , \quad \eta < -1 \; (|\eta| > 1)$$
$$\mathcal{N}^{1/2} \leq M^* < \mathcal{N} \qquad \qquad -1 < \eta < 0.$$

Thus, the question of inelastic or elastic money demand hangs on the location of M^* vis-à-vis $\mathcal{N}^{1/2}$. There remains the troublesome issue that the transaction and interest elasticities are of the same sign.

The basic model, then, appears to offer advantages over both predecessor models in terms of elasticity predictions. In succeeding chapters we continue to develop and rationalize the basic model. The main objective of this effort is to establish that the model is "robust," that is, that its important money demand predictions do not fail when the model is modified in the direction of greater realism. In the next chapter, the effects of changes in the basic Bernoulli cash flow process are examined. Before turning to modification and extension, however, we should ask how well the decision rules of the basic model can be expected to do, in comparison to conceivable alternative decision rules.

7. The Issue of Optimality

The results presented in the preceding section on the demand for money by firms depend in a critical way on the (h, z) policy form that firms are assumed to employ. Hence, the results are no better than the policy itself—if the policy is easy to surpass for control purposes, it probably will be ineffective in predictive applications. The neatest way to resolve this issue is exemplified in the work of Scarf (1960) and Eppen and Fama (1969a), described in Chapter II, Section 2. They list the conditions that imply the optimality of other policies of simple form. Unfortunately, no such general proof exists for the (h, z) policy.

Evidence beyond mere conjecture does exist to support the idea that (h, z) policies cannot be improved upon under the following assumed cost conditions:

1. Cash shortages are not permitted (that is, they are infinitely costly).
2. Holding costs (the opportunity cost on the cash balance) are linear in the amount of cash held.
3. Adjustment costs are "purely lumpy."

The first evidence that can be mustered in support of the (h, z) policy is the numerical results of Eppen and Fama (1968). They generated numerical solutions to a variety of optimal cash balance problems. Every time they considered a case which embodied the three assumed cost conditions, their discrete dynamic programming routine indicated that a solution of the (h, z) policy type was optimal—and further, the indicated numerical optima for h and z always took the ratio of 3:1.

Second, an optimality proof can be sketched quite simply, based on the additional condition

4. Cash flows conform to a symmetric Bernoulli process.

Following Scarf (1960), we define $C_N(x)$ as the minimum cost over an N-period horizon achievable with an initial cash balance of \$$x$. We have

$$C_N(x) = \overset{\text{min}}{z} \{ \gamma(z - x) + L(x) + \frac{\alpha}{2}[C_{N-1}(z+1) + C_{N-1}(z-1)],$$

where $\gamma(z - x)$ is the transfer cost, given by

$$\gamma(z - x) = \begin{cases} 0 \text{ if } z = x \\ \gamma \text{ if } z \neq x \end{cases}$$

$L(x)$ is defined for integer-valued x; it is the one-period cost of operation, given by

(19)
$$L(x) = \infty \qquad x = -1$$
$$L(x) = vx \qquad x \geq 0,$$

$L(x)$ is convex over the range $[-1, \infty]$.

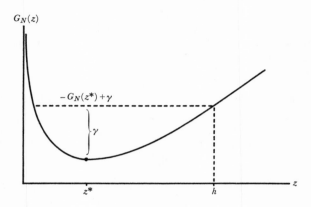

Figure IX. Optimality of (h, z^*) when $G_N(z)$ is convex

Observe the function $G_N(z)$:

(20) $\qquad G_N(z) = L(z) + \frac{\alpha}{2}[C_{N-1}(z+1) + C_{N-1}(z-1)].$

Proposition: if $G_N(z)$ is shaped as in Figure IX (nonincreasing up to z^*, and nondecreasing thereafter) the optimal response will be of the form

If $x = 0$ or $x \geq h$ transfer to z^*
if $0 < x < h$,   do nothing

where h satisfies the conditions

$$G_N(h) \geq G_N(z^*) + \gamma$$
$$G_N(h-1) < G_N(z^*) + \gamma.$$

Proof: The proof follows from Figure IX; it is seen that $G_N(0) > G_N(z^*) + \gamma = C_N(0)$ and $G_N(h) \geq G_N(z^*) + \gamma = C_N(h)$. What is true for $G_N(0)$ and $G_N(h)$ is also true for $G_N(\zeta)$, $\zeta < 0$, $\zeta > h$.

Proposition: $G_N(z)$, defined in (20), is shaped as in Fig. IX, over the integer range $z \in (0, \infty)$, if $L(x)$ is given in (19).

Proof: $G_N(z)$ declines *at least* up to $z = 0$ (by (19)). Let z^* denote the value at which $G_N(z)$ begins to increase. Then for $z > z^*$, we have

$$\Delta G_N(z) = G_N(z) - G_N(z-1)$$

is nowhere negative. This fact hangs on the appropriateness of the (h, z) policy if $G_N(z)$ is shaped as in Fig. IX:

$$\begin{aligned} C_{N-1}(x) &= G_{N-1}(x) & 0 < x < h \\ C_{N-1}(x) &= G_{N-1}(z^*) + \gamma & \text{otherwise.} \end{aligned}$$

It follows that $\Delta G_N(z) \geq \nu$ for all $z > z^*$.

Together, the two propositions identify sufficient conditions for the optimality of the (h, z) policy.

For proof of (h, z) optimality under less restrictive conditions, see Chitre (1969).

NOTES

1. For references, see K. J. Arrow (1958).
2. A fuller (but far from comprehensive) discussion of elasticity findings is offered in Chapter IX, Section 2.
3. Patinkin (1956), chapter 5 and appendices.
4. Hicks (1935).
5. The canonical probability model for Patinkin's case is an urn containing N black and N white balls. The balls are drawn from the urn *without* replacement, and the sequence of black and white balls corresponds to a receipt and payment sequence.
6. Take care to note that mM is the number of dollars held in the initial cash balance, while M is the number of consecutive payment transactions that can be covered by that initial balance; furthermore mM is the unconditional expected level of the cash balance throughout the entire period. Also see note 8 below.
7. See the expression (1) in the following text. It is derived in Patinkin (1956), Special Appendix to chapter v by Aryeh Dvoretzky, pp. 450-456.
8. The objective (2) is apparently what Patinkin has in mind; Dvoretzky's work provides information necessary for the analysis of such an objective. It contains a weakness, however; it overlooks the possibility that the cash balances can take a negative value more than once during the decision period. The probability of repeated shortages is an exceedingly difficult matter to analyze. In any event, if ψ is the cost of remedying a single shortage event, the objective (2) will be biased, by failing to recognize that the cash balance can go negative repeatedly during $2N$ trials. The maximum number of times the cash balance can go negative is $N - M$, if we assume that each time the balance goes negative, a costly remedial action is taken to restore it to a zero level.
9. The model developed and analyzed here and in Section 5 and 6 was first

presented in Miller and Orr (1966). The analysis here differs in small ways from that presentation.

10. As it has been described thus far, the model sounds like a mechanism for controlling transactions balances, as indeed it is. But what of the other motives? The absence of a lead time pretty well removes the need to hold cash against "unforeseen contingencies" so long as there is a holding of liquid earning assets; the precautionary motive is of small moment if condition 3 is observed. So far as the speculative motive is concerned, nothing prevents the firm from speculating on changes in interest rates—if it wishes. As a practical matter under present-day conditions, with securities of very short maturity always available, most of the firm's speculative activity would be expected to take the form of changes in the maturity structure of the portfolio, and hence is not considered by the analysis in its present form. The optimal cash holding, however, might be affected indirectly, to the extent that the prospect of speculative gains were reflected in the value of ν.

11. In practice, compensating balances usually call for the maintenance of some average balance. Typically, the term over which the averaging is done is not specified, and the whole arrangement is pretty loosely structured. The matter of compensating balances is considered in more detail in Chapter V, Section 1 below.

12. These increments or decrements represent only "operating" cash transactions and are to be regarded as exclusive of cash flows stemming from the portfolio, either transfers or run-offs of securities held. The proceeds of matured securities are assumed to be immediately reinvested.

The Bernoulli process is by no means restrictive in this context. The properties of the Bernoulli process that are crucial for our present purposes are not the implied regular timing or constant size of change; the critical features are serial independence (which precludes discernible or regular cyclic movements); stationarity (which precludes a persistent trend); and the absence of frequent "huge" changes—the process must be Gaussian. Any of a number of other familiar generating processes with these features might equally well have been used, all leading to the same solution for the problem.

That the results are not dependent on the assumption of a Bernoulli process can be verified by reference to Savage (1965) on the "surveillance problem," a special case of which is very similar to and has the same solution as this cash balance problem. In that paper, and in later work with Gordon Antelman, Savage uses Poisson and Weiner processes as the generating mechanism. Our reason for relying on the Bernoulli process here is its great simplicity, which permits the solution to be developed with only the most elementary methods. This also makes it much easier to bring economic intuition to bear in interpreting the results.

13. See Chapter II, Section 3 above.

14. Second order maximum conditions also hold for these values.

15. The greater size of security purchases just cancels out the greater frequency of sales so that no drift is communicated to the volume of earning assets held in the earning portfolio. This property follows directly from the probabilities of passage in a symmetric Bernoulli process: Prob (first passage at 0 when process originates at $z) = \dfrac{h-z}{h}$ and Prob (first passage at h when process originates at $z) = 1 - \dfrac{h-z}{h} = \dfrac{z}{h}$. See Feller (1951), chapter xiv.

IV

Sensitivity Analysis and Analytic Extensions of the Basic Model: Cash Flows

1. INTRODUCTION

The central role of maximization models in the prediction of microeconomic relationships is as old as economic theory. In the formulation of these models, a compromise between analytical viability and descriptive realism is usually called for, and the need for that compromise has been a source of recurrent controversy as to whether predictions obtained from maximization models have any value. There are two sources of support for belief in the potential of a particular theory: empirical tests which fail to refute both its predictions and antecedent conditions or "assumptions"; and further theoretical work which shows that predictions of the model do not change much even when the model's antecedent conditions are substantially modified.

In this chapter and Chapter V, evidence of the second type is developed regarding the basic model of Chapter III. The main purpose of this chapter is to see whether control decisions and money demand predictions are modified in important ways when the Bernoulli cash flow process that was used in the basic model is changed substantially.

A number of interesting and reassuring facts emerge from

this sensitivity analysis of cash flows, but an extremely deep and possibly important question is ignored or glossed over. The question is whether cash balances in particular, and dynamic economic processes in general, can be validly represented as simple first order Markov processes. A second question, that is considered in this chapter, asks whether the Bernoulli process of the basic model is a logical choice to describe cash flows, when attention is restricted to first-order Markov processes.

The first question is not avoided because of any difficulty in testing data for serial independence. Such a test would be a reasonable and easy first step in examining the Markovian hypothesis. Rather, the question is avoided because the existing literature on the prediction and control of stochastic systems doesn't offer much in the way of help should cash flows reflect significant higher order dependencies. On this issue, we may be acting like the man who dropped a coin in an alley, and looked for it in the street under a lamppost, because the light was better there; or we may be acting like economists often do when they consider the empirical properties of their theories.

The second question, about the representative quality of the Bernoulli cash flow, asks about the effect of real-world deviation from the assumed pattern of regularly timed and identically sized transactions. In reality, the timing of cash balance changes is irregular, and the average magnitudes and frequencies of individual receipts and payments probably differ markedly. *A priori*, there is no way to judge the significance of these irregularities of timing and size. It is unlikely that cash balances will be controlled, or cash flow data will be obtained, at time intervals shorter than a day. Conceivably over a day much of the irregularity in individual transactions will cancel out.

The issue that must be resolved concerning the basic model as a control scheme is whether the Bernoulli process yields good predictions of the steady-state distribution of the cash balance. Based on the success of Wald's theory of sequential analysis (Wald, 1944, 1946, 1947), we can state in advance that the Bernoulli predictions will be good (in the sense that only small improvements can be obtained and only by the use of mechanisms so complicated as to be virtually intractable), so long as these conditions are satisfied: (i) the distribution of daily changes in the cash balance must conform to a simple Gaussian hypothesis, with standard deviation that is not large compared to the optimal range (O, h^*) in the control policy; (ii) any *drift* in the cash balance must be detected and incorporated into the analysis, and (iii) the sequence of daily changes must not show significant patterns of serial correlation.

The second and third conditions are analyzed in Sections 2 and 3 below. The basic model can be used successfully, even if the two conditions do not hold strictly, so long as systematic movements in the cash flow persist over a time interval that is long compared to the mean elapsed time between transfers to adjust the cash balance. The basic model can be altered quite easily to take account of drift.

If the first condition is met, the Wald theory rationalizes a Bernoulli approach in the analysis of cash management and money demand. The first condition has two important parts: the cash balance must conform to a simple Gaussian hypothesis; and the standard deviation of cash balance changes must be "small" compared to the width of the optimal control range. If the Gaussian hypothesis is acceptable, but the cash flow is excessively variable, then Bernoulli predictions of the steady state cash balance will be found inaccurate. It is difficult to state rigid conditions that will assure that the ratio h^*/σ will be "sufficiently large," but it is desirable that there be a large number of cash account transactions between portfolio-cash transfers. The ratio of h^*/σ depends on economic considerations, as is seen in the expression $h^* = (81\gamma\sigma^2/4\nu)^{1/3}$. γ and ν are respectively coefficients of adjustment response cost and the opportunity cost of holding cash. Numerical examples that are developed throughout this chapter suggest that even when the ratio h^*/σ is quite small, the accuracy of predictions remains good. This numerical evidence is summarized in Section 7.

There are benefits in assuming that cash balance changes are distributed in accord with one of the stable laws, if the assumption can be sustained. It is easiest to work with a process that doesn't change in basic form over time, and only the stable laws have that invariance property. If daily changes can be viewed as drawings from a Gaussian population, then the sample variance offers a good measure of the diffusion rate of the cash balance—the speed at which it approaches the control limits. For a Gaussian population, Bernoulli approximations can confidently be used. However, if the daily cash balance changes are distributed in accord with another of the "stable Pareto-Lévy" laws, then predictions of the diffusion rate based upon the sample variance will be systematically too low. An optimization or prediction routine based upon Gaussian premises then will underestimate first passage times and the frequency of transfers.

Fortunately, non-Gaussian behavior can be approached by elementary methods. In Section 4, processes that can be viewed as the result of mixing or pooling transactions from two distinct regimes are analyzed. Section 5 explores the significance of these results on pooling for the issue of stable non-Gaussian cash flows. The first order of business, discharged in Sections 2 and 3, is to examine the effects of non-stationarity.

The analytical parts of this chapter are exceedingly tedious, and the reader will probably want to avoid details of calculation unless he has a specific application in mind.

2. NON-STATIONARITY IN THE CASH FLOW PROCESS[2]

The basic model of Chapter III was developed under the assumption that cash flows have zero drift; that is, that the probability of a payment equals the probability of a receipt on the occasion of each transaction. The symmetry assumption implies that the expected change in the cash balance over time is zero. Care must be taken to avoid the construal that cash balances don't change much over time in the stationary case. Actually, the cash balance will reach any arbitrarily high or low level if it is allowed to proceed in an uncontrolled fashion long enough. This is implied by fundamental results on Bernoulli trials, summarized in the

Theorem:

Let the excess of "successes" over "failures" after $2N$ Bernoulli trials be denoted S_{2N}. Then, if $p = q = 1/2$,

$$Pr\{|S_{2N}| \geq M|S_0 = 0\} = 2^{-2N} \sum_{j=M}^{N} \frac{(2N)!}{(N+j)!\ (N-j)!}$$

Proof:

The result follows from the binomial formula for exactly $N + M$ successes (or failures) in $2N$ symmetric trials:

$$\binom{2N}{N+M} = 2^{-2N}(2N)!/(N+M)!\ (N-M)!\ .$$

It follows as a corollary that for any finite M,

$$\lim_{2N=\infty} Pr\{|S_{2N}| \geq M|S_0 = 0\} = 1.$$

The issue, then, that is involved in a stationarity assumption is *not* that cash balances can't move about freely to extremely high or low values; rather, it is that they can not drift systematically toward ever-increasing accumulation or deficit of cash.

In any model that embodies a drift or trend, it is necessary to assume that over a long period of time, some process or activity outside the model periodically transfers excess funds out of the portfolio (if the drift is positive), or feeds additional funds into the portfolio (if the drift is negative). We should note, however, that the theorem just stated implies that the same transfer provisions will on occasion be necessary even if cash flows are subject to no drift.

Without stationarity, the analytical expressions for the components of expected cost in the (h, z) policy turn out to be extremely cumbersome. In general, the transition probabilities for a nonstationary Bernoulli process which drifts between 0 and h, and returns to z upon encountering either barrier, are

$$f_{t+1}(x) = pf_t(x-1) + qf_t(x+1) \qquad 0 < x < h,\ x \neq z$$
$$f_{t+1}(z) = p[f_t(z-1) + f_t(h-1)] + q[f_t(z+1) + f_t(1)]$$
$$f_{t+1}(0) = 0$$
$$f_{t+1}(h) = 0$$
$$p + q = 1.$$

Stationary occupancy probabilities are obtained by solving the system of equations

(1) $\qquad f(x) = pf(x-1) + qf(x+1) \qquad 0 < x < h,\ x \neq z$

(2) $f(z) = p[f(z-1) + f(h-1)] + q[f(z+1) + f(1)]$

(3) $f(0) = f(h) = 0,\ \sum_{x=0}^{h} f(x) = 1.$

For notational convenience, let $p/q = r$. Then the general solution for (1) is

(4) $\begin{cases} f(x) = A + Br^x & 0 \le x \le z \\ f(x) = C + Dr^x & z \le x \le h, \end{cases}$

which contains four arbitrary constants, to be assigned values to satisfy the conditions (2) and (3). Since $f(0) = 0$, it follows that

(5) $0 = A + B$ $\qquad\qquad B = -A.$

Similarly,

(6) $D = -Cr^{-h}.$

From (4)

(7) $A(1 - r^z)/(1 - r^{z-h}) = C.$

Finally, the density condition on the occupancy probabilities,

$$1 = \sum_{x=0}^{h} f(x)$$

yields the result

(8) $C = (1 - r^z)/[z(1 - r^{z-h}) + (h - z)(1 - r^z)] = (1 - r^z)/\Delta.$

The values (5)–(8) may be combined to obtain a specific expression for the stationary occupancy probabilities of x, in terms of p and q. From the density, it is possible (but tedious) to calculate the mean cash balance in the steady-state:

$$E(x) = \sum_{x=0}^{h} xf(x) = \sum_{x=0}^{z} xA(1 - r^x) + \sum_{x=z+1}^{h} xC(1 - r^{x-h}).$$

Substitution and manipulation gives

$$E(x) = \frac{1}{\Delta}\left[\sum_{x=0}^{h} x(1 + r^{z-h+x}) - r\sum_{x=0}^{z} xr^{x-1} - r^{z-h}\sum_{x=0}^{z} x - r^z \sum_{x=z+1}^{h} x \right.$$
$$\left. - r^{1-h} \sum_{x=z+1}^{h} xr^{x-1} \right],$$

where Δ is defined in (8). From the identity

$$\sum_{x=1}^{K} x r^{x-1} \equiv \frac{d}{dr} \sum_{x=0}^{K} r^x = [1 - (K+1)r^K + Kr^{K+1}]/(1 - r^2)$$

and after some substitution, we obtain

$$E(x) = \frac{1}{2\Delta} [h(h+1) - r^{z-h} z(z+1) - r^z h(h+1) + r^z z(z+1)]$$

$$+ \frac{r}{\Delta(1-r)} [z(r^z - r^{z-h}) + h(1 - r^z)].$$

By adding and subtracting z a couple of times from the numerators, we finally find that

$$(9) \qquad E(x) = \tfrac{1}{2}[(q-p)^{-1} + h + z - hz(1 - r^{z-h})/\Delta]$$

an expression which lacks some of the straightforward character of its counterpart value in the zero drift case.

As in that stationary case, the probability of a transfer can be computed with reference to the occupancy probabilities for states 1 and $h-1$. The expression is

$$P(T) = p f_{h-1} + q f_1 :$$

a transfer occurs if the cash balance is in the state $h-1$ and a receipt comes in (with probability p); similarly for a payment when the balance is in state 1. By this argument we obtain

$$P(T) = [q(1 - r^{z-h})(1-r) + p(1 - r^z)(1 - r^{-1})]/\Delta,$$

which reduces to

$$(10) \qquad P(T) = (q-p)^{-1}[z - h(1 - r^{-z})/(1 - r^{-h})],$$

where as before $r = p/q$. In both expressions (9) and (10), the term $(q-p)$ is the *drift rate*, or mean change in the cash balance per transaction. The objective function

$$E(c) = \gamma P(T) + \nu E(x)$$

becomes extremely cumbersome upon substitution of (9) and (10). However, the important qualitative properties of the optimal solution and the demand for money in the presence of drift can be seen with the help of constructed numerical examples. Table II presents three sets of numerical results, for cases in which the critical cost ratio γ/mv takes the values 5, 50, and 500. In all three cases, the calculation assumes exactly one payment or receipt transaction of size m per day. To illustrate the significance of the calculations and the numerical values selected for the cost ratios, consider the second case. Suppose that v, the interest rate, is 7.2% per year, or $.0002 foregone per day on each *dollar* held in the cash balance. If the daily transaction unit m is $\pm$ $5,000, then, mv, the daily interest foregone per transaction unit held, is $1. If the transfer cost γ is $50, the crucial γ/mv is 50. The same value can be obtained with lower interest rates and higher daily transaction sizes, or vice versa; or the coefficient γ can be varied without changing the ratio. Other things equal, a ratio of 500 implies very small daily cash flows, and a ratio of 5 implies daily cash flows on the order of $50,000 a day net (assuming that a $50 transfer fee and a 7.2% interest rate are reasonable order-of-magnitude estimates).

For extreme positive drift (the value $p = .9$), the stochastic element in the cash flow becomes relatively unimportant, and the control rules resemble those of a Baumol model, in which *all* cash transactions are receipts.[3] In the Baumol version with $p = 1$, the cash balance is allowed to build up to the amount $h/m = (2\gamma/mv)^{1/2}$. A security purchase then returns the balance to zero, whereupon the process of accumulation of h units begins once again. As p falls, and hence as the upward drift becomes less pronounced and then changes to downward drift, the optimal return point z^* increases steadily in value. The behavior of the upper bound, h^*, however, is somewhat surprising. For the case $\gamma/mv = 5$, the upper bound behaves in the same way as the return point—it increases steadily with reductions in p. However, when γ/mv takes the larger values 50 and 500, the return point behaves strangely: h^*/m first declines; it reaches a minimum while still in the zone of net upward drift, then begins an increasingly rapid increase once the zone of negative drift ($p < .5$) is entered.

The column headed $E(x)/m$ in the table shows the behavior of the mean cash balance as a function of drift. Its behavior also

TABLE II

Responses to, and Effects of, Drift in Cash Flow

p	μ/m	σ^2/m^2	Case 1: $\gamma/mv = .5$			Case 2: $\gamma/mv = 50$			Case 3: $\gamma/mv = 500$		
			z/m	h/m	$E(x)/m$	z/m	h/m	$E(x)/m$	z/m	h/m	$E(x)/m$
1.0	1	0	–	3.16	1.58 (Baumol)	–	10.00	5.00 (Baumol)	–	31.62	15.81 (Baumol)
.9	.8	.36	.78	4.10	1.93	1.17	10.58	5.31	1.62	30.36	15.39
.8	.6	.64	.97	4.19	1.99	1.52	10.02	5.06	2.18	27.41	14.02
.7	.4	.84	1.14	4.30	2.03	1.91	9.51	4.77	2.89	24.11	12.41
.6	.2	.96	1.33	4.45	2.06	2.46	9.39	4.56	4.10	20.90	10.63
.55	.1	.990	1.44	4.55	2.07	2.85	9.60	4.51	5.23	20.29	9.96
.53	.06	.996	1.48	4.59	2.07	3.03	9.75	4.49	5.89	20.54	9.79
.51	.02	.999	1.53	4.64	2.07	3.24	9.93	4.47	6.72	21.17	9.67
.5	.0	1	1.55	4.66	2.07	3.35	10.04	4.47	7.21	21.63	9.61
.49	−.02	.999	1.58	4.69	2.07	3.46	10.16	4.45	7.76	22.21	9.56
.47	−.06	.996	1.63	4.74	2.07	3.71	10.42	4.43	9.02	23.68	9.44
.45	−.1	.990	1.68	4.79	2.07	3.96	10.73	4.41	10.46	25.52	9.35
.4	−.2	.96	1.82	4.94	2.07	4.73	11.66	4.36	14.16	30.96	9.56
.3	−.4	.84	2.13	5.29	2.05	6.33	13.93	4.40			
.2	−.6	.64	2.48	5.70	2.03	7.75	16.26	4.71			
.1	−.8	.36	2.83	6.15	2.04	8.94	20.00	5.09			

is crucially sensitive to the value of γ/mv: for the small value, the normalized mean increases steadily as the value of drift decreases. For the two large values, the mean balance first decreases, and then begins to increase again in the region of negative drift.

It is difficult to find any reason or order in the behavior of the control units h and z for extreme values of drift. The limits do not converge monotonically toward the optimal values suggested by the Baumol model as p approaches zero or unity. Furthermore, the sensitivity of optima to the value of the ratio γ/mv is puzzling. The ratiocination of Miller and Orr (1966) on this issue notwithstanding, extreme values of drift seem to induce rather strange behavior.

3. THE IMPORTANCE AND IMPLICATIONS OF DRIFT

It is possible to find some comfort in the numerical cases of Table I, however. Data on daily corporate cash flows suggest that drift simply is not an important consideration, at least not over periods as long as a month.[4] For values of p which imply low drift, in the range $.6 > p > .4$ say, the demand for money is remarkably stable—in no case does the maximum value of $E(x)$ over this range exceed the minimum value by more than 12%; and the error of estimate over the range when $p = .5$ is assumed is never much more than 10%. It would be interesting to know just how costly it is to operate as though drift were absent, when it in fact is present. Table III indicates the magnitude of the costs involved in erroneously using a zero-drift model when drifts of various values are actually present.

A second issue also should be considered. Conceding that the mis-estimation of *extreme* drift is costly, how likely is it that drift will prove to be a problem in actual operating circumstances? Various answers to this question can come out of any *a priori* discussion. It may be the view that drift *is* significant, at least on a seasonal basis: that is to say, at least in some months, the net accumulation of one type of transaction—either payments or receipts—will swamp the diffusion effect noted in the zero-drift case. Even if there is extremely pronounced seasonal drift

TABLE III

The Costs of Error in Drift Estimation

p	Case 1 $-\gamma/m\ \nu=500$			Case 2 $-\gamma/m\ \nu=50$			Case 3 $-\gamma/m\ \nu=5$		
	$p=.5$ cost (A)	Min. cost (B)	$(A)/(B)$	(A)	(B)	$(A)/(B)$	(A)	(B)	$(A)/(B)$
.90	41.53	29.74	1.40	12.06	9.96	1.21	3.87	3.48	1.11
.80	34.39	26.58	1.29	10.44	9.18	1.14	3.60	3.40	1.06
.70	27.10	22.86	1.19	8.88	8.27	1.07	3.37	3.28	1.03
.60	19.78	18.42	1.07	7.52	7.34	1.02	3.20	3.18	1.01
.55	16.50	16.07	1.03	7.00	6.95	1.01	3.14	3.14	1.00
.54	15.94	15.64	1.02	6.92	6.89	1.00	3.13	3.13	1.00
.53	15.43	15.25	1.01	6.85	6.83	1.00	3.13	3.12	1.00
.52	15.00	14.91	1.01	6.79	6.78	1.00	3.12	3.12	1.00
.51	14.65	14.63	1.00	6.73	6.73	1.00	3.11	3.11	1.00
.49	14.32	14.29	1.00	6.67	6.66	1.00	3.10	3.10	1.00
.48	14.37	14.26	1.01	6.65	6.64	1.00	3.10	3.10	1.00
.47	14.58	14.31	1.02	6.65	6.63	1.00	3.10	3.10	1.00
.46	14.96	14.46	1.03	6.67	6.63	1.00	3.10	3.09	1.00
.45	15.50	14.69	1.06	6.70	6.63	1.01	3.10	3.09	1.00
.40	20.03	16.64	1.20	7.10	6.78	1.05	3.12	3.09	1.01
.10	—	—	—	14.24	9.57	1.49	3.98	3.45	1.15

pattern, it does not undermine the general approach of the basic model, so long as the drift rate remains stable over a period that is long compared to the interval between portfolio management adjustment transfers. Thus, if adjustment transfers are made at three day intervals on the average, while the period of pronounced drift is a month or more, there is no large problem: the appropriate drift model is used during the time period when drift is present, and it is modified in response to (or anticipation of) changes in the drift rate.[5] If, on the other hand, cash flows are characterized by extreme drift over short periods, then the steady state mode of analysis may be inappropriate: transient effects may dominate the longer-term movements that are well-handled in the steady-state approach.

In discussing drift, it is interesting and important that the daily cash transactions of two remarkably different corporations appear to be driftless. Table IV shows that over a fifteen-month period, there was no significant drift in the cash account of the Union Tank Car Corporation; nor was there significant drift within subperiods of three months' duration or greater. The data may suggest the presence of a seasonal component in cash flows (although the series is too short to be reliable on this point): but there is no clear evidence of drift. Similar evidence, not presented here, is to be found in an eighteen-month daily cash ledger series generously made available by another and much larger corporation, the name of which I am not authorized to disclose.

4. Importance of the Symmetry Assumption

The Bernoulli process used in the basic model embodies a second characteristic that may be important: it is symmetric around the mean change. A variety of driftless processes may depart from symmetry, and they may be important in describing cash flows. In this section, a number of driftless asymmetric processes will be examined, and the implications of approximating them by a Bernoulli process will be considered.

The first case involves an asymmetric flow that is important in the analysis of "three asset" versions of the basic model,

TABLE IV

Drifts in Daily Cash Balance Data, Union Tank Car Corporation

Month Number	Receipts–Payments during Month	Cumulative Receipts–Payments as of Month's End	Cumulative Mean Daily Flow, Month's End	Receipts–Payments during Quarter
1	$ – 2,997	$ – 2,997	– 136	$
2	27,972	24,975	568	
3	8,817	33,792	512	33,792
4	12,216	21,576	245	
5	40,975	62,551	569	
6	– 19,097	43,454	329	9,662
7	– 39,449	4,005	26	
8	17,026	21,031	119	
9	– 9,841	11,190	57	– 32,264
10	– 21,646	– 10,456	– 48	
11	– 1,180	– 11,636	– 48	
12	10,952	– 684	– 3	– 11,874
13	– 490	– 1,174	– 4	
14	3,632	2,458	– 8	
15	27,827	30,285	90	30,969

Daily standard deviation $\sim 8,800$.

which are developed in Chapter VI below. Suppose the cash balance level is initially z, and once per period a cash receipt or payment occurs. With probability 1/3 let the transaction be a receipt of two units, and with probability 2/3 let the balance move down one unit as a result of a payment (as in a pure Bernoulli application, the transaction size unit and time unit are presumably selected to best fit a set of observations). The expected "first passage time" (the expected nu.nber of elapsed periods until 0 or h are reached) from an original position at z is denoted D_z and is given by the relation

$$(11) \qquad D_z = \tfrac{1}{3}D_{z+2} + \tfrac{2}{3}D_{z-1} + 1 \qquad (1 \le z \le h - 1),$$

a non-homogeneous third order difference equation. The three boundary conditions are $D_0 = 0$, $D_h = 0$, and $D_{h+1} = 0$.[6] The mean first passage time is important in the analysis, since its reciprocal is the steady state probability of cash-portfolio transfers.[7]

In this simple asymmetric case, an exact solution for the mean first passage time may be obtained. The characteristic equation of the difference equation (11) is $\xi^3 - 3\xi + 2 = 0$, which has roots $\xi = 1$, $\xi = 1$, $\xi = -2$. The solution of (11) is thus of the form

$$D_z = A + Bz + C(-2)^z + \theta,$$

where A, B and C are arbitrary constants whose values are determined by boundary conditions, and θ is a particular solution of the system. We see that $-z^2/2$ satisfies (11), and assign that value to θ. The first boundary condition gives $D_0 = A + C = 0$, or $C = -A$. From $D_h = 0$ we obtain

$$B = \frac{A}{h}[(-2)^h - 1] + \frac{h}{2}$$

and substituting these values of B and C into $D_{h+1} = 0$ gives

$$A = h(h+1)/2[(3h+1)(-2)^h - 1].$$

Thus, the exact solution is

$$D_z = \frac{h(h+1)}{2[(3h+1)(-2)^h - 1]} + \frac{zh}{2} + \frac{z(h-1)[(-2)^h - 1]}{2[(3h+1)(-2)^h - 1]}$$

$$+ \frac{h(h+1)(-2)^z}{2[1 - (3h+1)(-2)^h]} - z^2/2.$$

Now suppose the values $h = 9$ and $z = 3$ are used in conjunction with the asymmetric process which led to the duration expression (11). The expected duration until passage at 0 or 9 is $D_z = 9 + 75/1556$ or 9.04. The best simple Bernoulli approximation uses σ, the standard deviation of cash balance transactions, as a unit of change in the cash balance.[8] With the process $P_x = \frac{1}{3}P_{x-2} + \frac{2}{3}P_{x+1}$, the transaction variance is 2, and $\sigma = \sqrt{2}$.

Table V compares numerical passage time and mean cash

TABLE V

Cash Balance Behavior with an (h, z) Policy and
$$P_x = \tfrac{1}{3}P_{x-2} + \tfrac{2}{3}P_{x+1}$$

h	z	Mean Balance	Bernoulli Mean Balance	Passage Probability*	Bernoulli Best Passage Probability Estimate
6	2	2.4536	2.6667	.2388	.2500
6	3	2.8462	3.	.2291	.2222
36	3	12.7821	13.	.0282	.0200
36	6	13.7823	14.	.0127	.0111
36	9	14.7825	15.	.0090	.0082
36	12	15.7829	16.	.0073	.0068
36	15	16.7833	17.	.0063	.0064
36	18	17.7839	18.	.0058	.0062

* The likelihood of reaching 0 or h during a randomly selected time period far enough in the future so that the probability estimate is unaffected by initial conditions, i.e. the steady-state passage probability.

balance results for this asymmetric generating process, to the same results obtained via the best Bernoulli approximation. The Table suggests that the relevant properties of the process, namely the passage probabilities and mean cash balances, are remarkably well predicted by the Bernoulli model.

As an aid in the analysis of more complicated non-symmetric processes, Feller suggests a technique for obtaining bounded approximate solutions for the mean passage times.[9] The technique was not necessary in the preceding simple case, but it is useful in the analysis of more complicated problems, including some that can be generated by pooled Bernoulli processes.

Every discrete cash-flow process can be represented by a difference equation. If there is no drift in the cash flow, the characteristic equation of the difference equation has a double root at 1; and thus $A + B_z + \theta$ (where θ again denotes a particular solution and A and B are arbitrary constants) is a formal solution to the difference equation, albeit one that does not satisfy the full set of boundary conditions. For the case of equation (11), if A and B are valued so that the approximate solution $A + Bz - z^2/2$ takes the value 0 at 0 and h, then it happens that the approximate solution is negative at $h + 1$, and

$D_{h+1} \leq 0$ holds instead of $D_{h+1} = 0$. That is, the boundary conditions $D_0 \leq 0$, $D_h \leq 0$, $D_{h+1} \leq 0$ are satisfied when

$$A = 0$$
$$A + Bh - h^2/2 = 0$$

or $B = h/2$. With A and B so valued, the expected first passage time is approximated by $z(h - z)/2$, or with $h = 9$, $z = 3$, 9 periods. To establish a lower bound on the exact expected passage time D_z, we use the result that any linear combination of solutions of a difference equation is also a solution; and so the difference $A + Bz + \theta - D_z = z(h - z)/2 - D_z$ is also a formal solution to the difference equation (11) with *non-positive* boundary values. Since we know that $D_z = 1 + \sum_x D_x P_{x-z}$ (where P_{x-z} is the probability of transition from x to z) and $D_x < 0$ instead of $D_x = 0$ for $x < 0$ and $x > h$ when the approximation $D_x = x(h - x)/2$ is used, it follows that $z(h - z)/2 - D_z \leq 0$, or $D_z \geq z(h - z)/2$.

We can also specify A and B so that the solution expression $A + Bz - z^2/2$ is zero for $z = 0$ and $z = h + 1$. The approximation solution thus obtained has $A = 0$, $B = (h + 1)/2$, and takes the value 10.5 for $h = 9$, $z = 3$. Here we have the expression $z(h + 1 - z)/2 - D_z$ satisfying the difference equation (11) with *non-negative* boundary values, and so the relation $D_z \leq z(h + 1 - z)/2$ follows. Thus, when $h = 9$, $z = 3$, it follows that $9 \leq D_z \leq 10.5$.

This method for deriving upper and lower bounds on the true duration expression can readily be extended to more complicated cases. To show how the process extends, consider the steady-state transition probabilities

$$(12) \qquad P_x = \tfrac{1}{5}P_{x+4} + \tfrac{1}{5}P_{x+1} + \tfrac{1}{5}P_{x-1} + \tfrac{2}{5}P_{x-2},$$

which imply the duration relation

$$D_z = \tfrac{1}{5}D_{z-4} + \tfrac{1}{5}D_{z-1} + \tfrac{1}{5}D_{z+1} + \tfrac{2}{5}D_{z+2} + 1.$$

An explicit solution involves the roots of a sixth degree polynomial. The process is driftless and so there will be two unit roots and an approximation solution of the form $A + Bz + \theta$. The particular solution is $\theta = -\tfrac{5}{26}z^2 = -z^2/\sigma^2$ where σ^2 is the variance of the cash balance transition relation (12). An underestimate is obtained by setting A and B so that the approximation expression is zero for $z = 0$ and $z = h$. The overestimate is obtained by setting A and B so that the expression is zero for $z = -3$ and $z = h + 1$. The bounds are

$$\frac{5}{26}z(h-z) \le D_z \le \frac{5[(h+1)^2 - 9]}{26(4+h)}(3+z) + \frac{45}{26} - \frac{5}{26}z^2.$$

Although the cash balance jumps around more freely here than in the previous example of Table V, sensitivity to the breadth of the range $(0, h)$ is not markedly more acute. When $h = 9\sigma \sim 21$ and $z = 3\sigma \sim 7$ we have $\frac{1715}{13} \le D_z \le \frac{2275}{13}$, and with $h = 60$, $z = 20$, $\frac{4000}{26} \le D_z \sim \frac{4717}{26}$. In each case, the lower bound on D_z is the Bernoulli estimate of D_z used in sequential analysis.

That the approximation technique is useful when cash balance changes are pooled simple processes is evident from the preceding example. The regime (12) could result from component processes having the transition relations

$$P_x = \tfrac{1}{2}P_{x+4} + \tfrac{1}{2}P_{x-1}$$
$$P_x = \tfrac{1}{3}P_{x+1} + \tfrac{2}{3}P_{x-2},$$

if the probability that an observation conforms to the first process is $2/5$, and to the second process $3/5$.

To obtain the stationary occupancy probabilities and the mean cash balances that result when the illustrative pooled process is controlled by an (h, z) policy, it is necessary to solve the system (12) with the boundary conditions

$$P_\xi = 0 (\xi \le 0)$$
$$P_\eta = 0 (\eta \ge h)$$

$$P_z = \tfrac{1}{5}(P_{z+4} + P_4 + P_3 + P_{z+1} + P_{z-1}) + \tfrac{2}{5}(P_1 + P_{z-2} + P_{h-2}) + \tfrac{3}{5}P_{h-1}$$

$$\sum_x P_x = 1.$$

Since the stationary density function obtained from this system will certainly not be triangular (as in the case of a symmetric Bernoulli process and an (h, z) policy) the mean cash balance will not be $(h + z)/3$. However, the error introduced into the mean balance estimate by using a single-step symmetric Bernoulli process to represent the more complicated process (12) is remarkably small and virtually independent of the values of h and z, as seen from the numerical examples of Table VI.

TABLE VI

Mean Cash Balance
When the Generating Process (12) Is Controlled by the Basic Model

h	z	Bernoulli Mean Balance Estimate	Actual Mean Balance
9	3	4.	4.3161
12	3	5.	5.3198
12	4	5.3333	5.7460
36	6	14.	14.3362
36	9	15.	15.3661
36	12	16.	16.3797
36	15	17.	17.3827
72	6	26.	26.3407
72	12	28.	28.3813
72	18	30.	30.3883
72	24	32.	32.3932
72	30	34.	34.3963
72	36	36.	36.3985
105	10	38.3333	38.7058
105	20	41.6667	42.0577
105	30	45.	45.3968
105	35	46.6667	47.0651

These results on pooled processes are particularly important, since such pooling may be an important explanation of non-Gaussian behavior in cash flow. In the next section, the issue of "Paretian" behavior in the cash flow series is related to the results developed in this section on asymmetry and the pooling of heterogeneous generating processes.

5. ASYMMETRY, POOLING, AND "PARETIAN" BEHAVIOR

Table VII reports a matter of concern, the excessive concentration of daily net cash transactions in the tails of a sample distribution of daily net transaction sizes. That is, there are many days when very large net receipts or very large net payments are observed, and the dispersion of transaction sizes from the mean value suggests that a Gaussian hypothesis may lead to serious error. Similarly, if the cumulative second moment of the data sample is chronologically exhibited, it may fail to converge toward any fixed value, and this too may be taken as evidence of "Paretian" rather than "Gaussian" behavior. Under a Pareto-Lévy hypothesis, the analytic mode employed in the basic model may be inappropriate. Results do exist concerning first passage times and passage probabilities for stable non-Gaussian processes,[10] and these conceivably could be utilized as a basis for a revision of our earlier analysis.

Table VII

Dispersion of Daily Cash Balance Changes,
Union Tank Car Corporation

Interval	No. of Observations	Gaussian Prediction
$x < \mu - 3\sigma$	2	.45
$\mu - 3\sigma \leq x < \mu - 2\sigma$	9	7.15
$\mu - 2\sigma \leq x < \mu - \sigma$	21	45.41
$\mu - \sigma \leq x < \mu$	130	104.98
$\mu \leq x < \mu + \sigma$	147	104.98
$\mu + \sigma \leq x < \mu + 2\sigma$	16	45.41
$\mu + 2\sigma \leq x < \mu + 3\sigma$	5	7.15
$\mu + 3\sigma \leq x$	4	.45

Likelihood of observed mass $> |3\sigma| = \binom{334}{6}(.00135)^6 \, (.99865)^{328} = .0002$

However, a more direct approach can be based on the view that the observed cash transactions result from the mixing or pooling of two distinct Bernoulli regimes. If this hypothesis is appealing it affords a simple way to determine the optimal control procedures for a specific application. The pooling hypothesis also makes it possible to assess the error encountered with a simple Bernoulli approximation, if the true process displays "stable Paretian" properties.

To see how pooling leads to Paretian symptoms, consider two zero-mean Gaussian populations, X: $\mathcal{N}(0, 1)$ and Y: $\mathcal{N}(0, 4)$, and let a sample be drawn from the two populations with probability .9 and .1 respectively. If z represents an element of the sample, we then have

$$P(z \in X) = .9, \quad P(z \in Y) = .1,$$

and as the size of the sample increases, we can represent the sample variance by

$$S_z^2 \cong .9\sigma_x^2 + .1\sigma_y^2,$$

or for large samples, $S_z^2 \sim 1.3$ and $3S_z \sim 3.42$. In the population Y, an observation greater in absolute value than 3.42 lies outside the range $\pm 1.71\sigma_y$, and occurs with probability .08726. Suppose now that the sample is composed of 300 observations; we expect thirty will be drawn from the population Y, and of these, we expect that 2.7 will lie outside the range ± 3.42. Were the observations drawn from a homogeneous Gaussian population with variance 1.3, the expected number of observations outside the ± 3.42 range would be .4 in a sample of size 300.

Therefore, if there is reason to suspect that the transactions of certain distinct days are generated in a radically different way from most days (as would be the case, say, if dividend dates or payroll days are important) then the effect of pooling provides good reason to expect a higher-than-normal frequency of outliers beyond 3σ. If the cash flow can best be represented by drawing from *many* different populations, the pooling approach may be less efficient than direct use of a stable non-Gaussian hypothesis.

What effect do pooling and similar departures from the binomial have on the steady-state probability distribution of cash balance levels? The results of Section 4 on asymmetric generating processes suggest that even a high degree of irregularity in the true generating process leads only to small errors in Bernoulli predictions of mean cash balances and mean passage times. Thus, there is some ground for hope that Paretian behavior generally will not prove excessively troublesome in the analysis of cash flows. This, of course, remains only a hope until supporting experience is accumulated. Fragments of experience, in which the basic model was used for prediction and control purposes, is reported below in Chapter VIII.

6. IMPLICATIONS OF IRREGULARLY TIMED TRANSACTIONS

Two implications of the Bernoulli process, the regularity of cash transactions in time, and the size uniformity of all transactions, are aesthetically displeasing and frequently challenged. The Bernoulli process appears particularly weak *a priori* when the structure of individual transactions is considered; and if the basic model is to be used as a control instrument, the patent unrealism of the Bernoulli process may be a genuine drawback. For irregular transaction sizes or the bunching of transactions during very short time intervals may lead to significant "spillovers," to the effect that transfers, which supposedly occur when the cash balance just reaches zero or the upper bound h, actually occur when the balance is substantially below zero or above h. More important, those size irregularities can ruin the accuracy of passage time and transfer probability estimates. A failure of these estimates can lead to distortion of expected cost and non-optimal decisions. Whether the irregularity of transaction flows is an important consideration to the design of control rules must be judged in light of experience. The results of Chapter VIII suggest that it need not be important. If experience shows it to be important, new questions concerning control must be answered.

When the model is used in prediction, net daily cash flows can be expected to be the most refined type of data available. Because individual transactions can't be observed, the implied regular spacing of transactions in time loses much of its objectionability. The issue then is whether observed daily changes vary widely in size, and that, once again, is the Gaussian vs. Paretian issue that was considered in Section 5.

For the reasons mentioned, the regularity of transactions is unlikely to be a pressing issue in prediction applications; and the more highly aggregated are the data that are used, the less pressing the objection is likely to be. The lack of dependence of predictions on the Bernoulli hypothesis can be further verified by using a process with irregularly timed transactions to generate cash flows in the basic model. A useful representative of the class of processes that move at irregular intervals in the Poisson process, alluded to in passing earlier (Chapter I, Section 5), and treated in detail by Feller (1951), chapter XVI.

Suppose a cash balance is subject to instantaneous change due to payment or receipt transactions. All changes are of the same size,[11] and they occur randomly in time. The cash flow is characterized by two properties: it is homogeneous in time, and future changes are independent of the timing and pattern of past changes. These two properties mean that the probability of any change or set of changes in the cash balance is the same in any time interval of length Δt, regardless of where in time the interval occurs; and is independent of the history of events leading up to the interval.

The cash flow is described mathematically in terms of probabilities $P_n(\Delta t)$ and $Q_n(\Delta t)$ which respectively denote the probability of exactly n receipts and exactly n payments during an interval of length Δt. Then $P_0(\Delta t)$ is the probability of zero receipts, $1 - P_0(\Delta t)$ is the probability of one or more receipts, and similarly for $Q_0(\Delta t)$ and $1 - Q_0(\Delta t)$. Assume that

$$\lim_{\Delta t = 0} \frac{1 - P_0(\Delta t)}{\Delta t} = \lambda, \quad \lim_{\Delta t = 0} \frac{1 - Q_0(\Delta t)}{\Delta t} = \mu,$$

where λ and μ are positive constants. For a small interval Δt, then, the probability of one or more receipts is $\lambda \Delta t + o(\Delta t)$, and the probability of one or more payments is $\mu \Delta t + o(\Delta t)$. The term $o(\Delta t)$ denotes "small trash," a quantity of smaller order of magnitude than Δt, which vanishes as Δt goes to the limit. Two postulates for the Poisson process are suggested by the assumed limits: (1) For all t and small Δt, the probability of one receipt during $(t, t + \Delta t)$ is $\lambda \Delta t$, and the probability of one payment during $(t, t + \Delta t)$ is $\mu \Delta t$. These results are independent of the number of receipts and payments prior to t. (2) The probability of more than one change in any direction during $(t, t + \Delta t)$ is $o(\Delta t)$. The attribution of probabilities in the two postulates is arbitrary; the assignment of $\mu \Delta t$ as the probability of one payment and $o(\Delta t)$ as the probability of more than one payment leads to useful and familiar results, but it is not an implication of analysis.

From the postulates for the Poisson process, these forward equations are derived:

$$(13) \qquad f_{t+\Delta t}(x) = f_t(x)(1 - \lambda\Delta t - \mu\Delta t) + f_t(x-1)\lambda\Delta t \\ + f_t(x+1)\mu\Delta t + o(\Delta t),$$

where $f_t(x)$ denotes the probability of occupying the integer-valued state x at time t. Roughly, the forward equation (13) states that the cash balance can be in the state x at time $t + \Delta t$ by (a) staying there since time t; (b) moving there by a receipt or (c) by a payment during the Δt interval; or (d) moving there during the Δt interval as a result of more than one receipt and/or payment.

Transposing $f_t(x)$, dividing by Δt, and going to the limit as $\Delta t \to 0$, we obtain the differential equation

$$\frac{\partial f_t(x)}{\partial t} = -(\lambda + \mu) f_t(x) + \lambda f_t(x-1) + \mu f_t(x+1).$$

The steady-state condition is $\partial f_t(x)/\partial t = 0$. Invoking that condition we get the system of equations.

$$(14) \qquad (\lambda + \mu) f_x = \lambda f_{x-1} + \mu f_{x+1},$$

and when an (h, z) policy is used, several boundary conditions are implied:

$$(15) \qquad f_0 = 0, f_h = 0,$$

$$(16) \qquad (\lambda + \mu)f_z = \lambda(f_{z-1} + f_{h-1}) + \mu(f_{z+1} + f_1),$$

and

$$(17) \qquad \sum_x f_x = 1.$$

If we divide both sides of (14) and (16) by $\lambda + \mu$, then we replicate the asymmetric Bernoulli cash flow system treated in Section 2, where $p = \lambda/(\lambda + \mu)$ and $q = \mu/(\lambda + \mu)$. The two systems are equivalent from the standpoint of our money demand problem, for the mean cash balance and the mean passage time will be the same in the two cases. There will be non-trivial differences between the two processes: the diffusion rate may be quite different over short periods of time and hence the second and higher moments of the distribution of passage time may differ. Such a difference in higher moments stems from the fact that over any fairly long time interval, such as a day, the number of cash transactions is fixed in a Bernoulli process, while the number of transactions is a random variable in a Poisson process. In the context of relaxation response policies, the farther apart the control limits are, the smaller will be the difference between the passage time distributions of the Poisson and Bernoulli processes.

7. When Is the Control Range "Large Enough" Compared to the Process Variability?

Throughout this chapter, we have emphasized the desirability that the control range $(o, h*)$ be "large" compared to the standard deviation of the daily cash flow, which in the Bernoulli case is

$$\sigma = [E(x^2) - (Ex)^2]^{1/2} = 2m(pqt)^{1/2}.$$

The magnitude of distortion that results from various small values of $h*/\sigma$ is not easy to assess analytically. However, numerical evidence that is scattered throughout this chapter suggests that fairly wide departures from the Bernoulli process can occur in cash flows, with surprisingly little loss of accuracy in the Bernoulli predictions. Table V is relevant to the question. It shows that only small departures from predicted mean balances and passage probabilities will occur in response to a radical shift in the cash flow regime, so long as $h*/\sigma$ is moderately large (the Table's smallest value, 6, shows small errors of estimate).

Table VI conveys further information. It presents actual mean cash balances and Bernoulli estimates when the cash flow generating process is of the complicated form (12). Recall that bounds were established on the passage probabilities for this process in Section 4. Again, values of $h*/\sigma$ in the range of 6-10 seem to preclude extremely large cost penalties.

Notes

1. Most of the substance of this chapter and Chapter V first appeared in Miller and Orr (1968).
2. This Section is a revised version of Miller and Orr (1966), Section II-5 and Appendix. The interpretation of analytic and numerical evidence here differs substantially from the interpretation of the earlier paper.
3. Analysis of the Baumol Model (for comparison purposes): Minimize (with respect to h/m) the expected cost function

$$E(c) = \frac{\gamma}{h/m} + \frac{mu\, h/m}{2}.$$

It follows that

$$(h/m)^* = \left(\frac{2\gamma}{mu}\right)^{1/2}.$$

We work with γ/mv as the cost ratio, because computer analysis of the very large values necessary for realistic portrayal of γ/v is impossible. The use of γ/mv makes it imperative to normalize h, z, and $E(x)$ (the mean balance) on m, also.
4. See the evidence presented in Table III below.
5. "Splicing" various drift models together on a seasonal basis in general will be non-optimal. It is unlikely, however, that the opportunity costs of doing so will be found large.
6. For an explication of this difference equation technique in evaluating mean passage times, see Feller (1951), chapter xiv.
7. This point is demonstrated in Miller and Orr (1966).
8. For an explicit treatment of this important point, see Wald (1946).
9. Feller (1951), p. 303. His approximation method is developed for the problem of calculating ruin probabilities, a context in which the method works more smoothly (in part because the transition relations lead to homogeneous difference equations). The method of difference equations for the direct calculation of expected passage times is suggested earlier in the same chapter of Feller's book. Because of the intrusion of particular solutions into the passage time problem, we rely more heavily on numerical examples than does Feller.
10. For example, Getoor (1961).
11. Substantially more complicated processes (such as the compound Poisson) must be used to avoid the assumption of uniform transaction size.

V

Sensitivity Analysis and
Analytic Extensions of the Basic
Model: The Objective Function

1. Financial Institutions and the Objective Function

In the development of the basic model (Chapter III), the objective is to minimize a function whose arguments are (a) the probability of a cash balance control transfer and (b) the mean cash balance over time

$$E(c) = \gamma P(T) + \nu E(M).$$

When a control policy of the (h, z) type is used, the equivalent objective is seen to be

(1) $$\min_{h, z} E(c) = \frac{\gamma t}{z(h-z)} + \frac{\nu m(h+z)}{3},$$

assuming that uniform payment and receipt transactions of $\$m$ apiece occur t times per day. Chapter IV presented a sensitivity analysis of those cash flow assumptions. The present chapter examines the structure of the objective function, with two purposes: first, to rationalize the specific form that is employed, by appeal to the institutional constraints on a firm's cash control actions; and second, to determine whether details of the "cost assumptions" underlying the objective (1) play an important

96

part in shaping the money demand predictions that were derived from the basic model. The present section attends to the first of these two purposes.

In the operations research literature, an important taxonomical question is whether a model is of the "discrete time" or "continuous time" variety. The contrast in model type involves issues[1] deeper than the mere convenience of such analytical techniques as the Pontryagin maximum principle or the simplex method, although the issue of convenience is undoubtedly an important one. A somewhat mundane issue arises concerning the discrete time procedure that was employed in deriving Chapter III's basic results. A cash management system (or any other control system) may be reviewed at excessively long intervals, with the result that costly events can occur between the control decisions, escape the attention of the decision maker, and go unrectified. If in fact the control points are spaced too widely in time, the cash balance may wander excessively between control actions, and the objective function will not reflect the true costs incurred in operating the system. Because of economic considerations, the issue is non-trivial. It is usually less costly to take control actions at long intervals rather than at short ones; and "continuous control" must be extremely costly except in the case of a few mechanically regulated systems. Thus, the more effective the control system, the more costly it is to operate. The problem, though widely recognized, has never been analyzed in any particular depth, to my knowledge.[2]

So far as the management of cash and other liquid assets is concerned, several considerations affect the choice of a control interval. There are institutional considerations, such as the fact that a day's interest can be earned by buying a security at the close of one market day, and selling it at the opening of the next; or the fact that most banks make only one daily check, at the close of the day, on the status of its depositors' accounts. There are other considerations of objective fact, such as the nature of cash flows. Finally, there are the costs associated with the full array of states of the system and responsive control decisions; the costs are shaped and determined by the institutional and other objective considerations that lie outside the firm's control, and by the firm's own operating routines and capabilities.

In cash management, the control action is the purchase or sale of earning assets, or alternatively, of the firm's own debt instruments. If the firm has only one cash account (an unlikely event) then it can take a responsive control action after any transaction within a day. With numerous accounts, consolidation will usually be efficient, and daily composite posting of all accounts will probably be significantly cheaper than hourly posting or posting after each transaction. Moreover, a security purchased (or retired) at 10 A.M. earns no more than one purchased at the close of the market (though it may be available at a lower price at the later time); and a cash shortage (overdrawn account) will not be detected by the bank until the close of the day. It seems that there is little advantage in taking cash control decisions more frequently than at daily intervals, unless the price fluctuations of suitable recourse securities, such as treasury bills, are substantial within a day. Other advantages are realized when control actions are taken at daily intervals. Daily control requires less managerial time than continuous control; and if simple standard decision rules, such as those of the (h, z) policy, can be employed, the costs of daily control can be kept low indeed.

A daily control regime, which uses the (h, z) policy, is convenient; and it is feasible because institutional and other considerations beyond the control of the firm assure that an objective function of the form (1) is appropriate so long as control actions are taken at intervals of no more than a day. If daily control actions were impossible, the objective function (1) no longer would be appropriate. For example, if control could be exercised only at intervals longer than a day, then the danger of costly shortages in the cash account would have to be recognized; and this change would complicate the objective function considerably. The operational convenience of control actions taken at intervals of a day is a strong argument for the need of daily cash flow data in empirical research.

Perhaps the compensating balance requirement is the most important institutional consideration that affects the structure of the (h, z) policy. There is disagreement in the literature regarding the motives of banks in requiring that compensating balances be held. A popular view is that compensating balances constitute a means whereby a bank disguises the true rate that it charges, thereby realizing a monopoly return. Davis and Gutentag (1963) have offered a contrary view: they argue that compensating balance requirements seldom exceed the average cash balance that a depositor *wishes* to hold, and so hardly can be regarded as instruments of hidden exploitation. Instead, the balances serve as partial payment under competitive banking conditions for services rendered by the bank to the depositor. Terms on borrowing are, because of competition, most attractive for the large depositor. The compensating balance agreement offers assurance that the large depositor will not move his account.

An examination of banking practice lends support to the view that compensating balance requirements do not constrain or hamper the corporate depositor. In the first place, the requirements are most often stated, for business and corporate depositors, in terms of average balances, rather than minimum balances. Secondly, the averaging period often is open-ended and the requirements are not strictly enforced, as are, say, the reserve requirements that are imposed by the Federal Reserve on its member banks. Were compensating balances viewed as a revenue-generating device, a minimum balance rather than an average balance would be a more efficient requirement, and more careful monitoring of performance would be evident.[3]

For purposes of predicting the demand for money, it is important whether compensating balances are a nominal or an exacting requirement. If the requirements are exacting, as they would be if a minimum balance were specified, then the basic model of Chapter III predicts only a *part* of money demand, namely, the "discretionary" balances in excess of those held to satisfy the bank's requirements. In Miller and Orr (1966), it was suggested that compensating balance requirements, and the practice of holding numerous accounts, might account for some of the discrepancy between the predicted and observed dependency of cash holdings on transaction rates.[4]

Under a minimum balance requirement, compensating and discretionary balances would be additive; that is, money held in fulfillment of compensating balance requirements is available for transactions purposes only at a penalty cost. However, if an average balance must be maintained, the problem is somewhat more complicated. Suppose a firm agrees to hold an average balance of no less than B; the averaging period is open-ended, and an (h, z) policy is adopted. Under these conditions, if the optimal control limit values satisfy the condition

$$m(h^* + z^*)/3 \geq B,$$

then there is no problem; compensating balance requirements are non-constraining. If the inequality is reversed, however, there remains the alternative of solving the constrained problem

$$\max_{h, z} \left[\frac{\gamma t}{z(h-z)} + \frac{vm}{3}(h+z) \right]$$

subject to

$$m(h+z) = 3B,$$

which can readily be accomplished by the use of Lagrange multiplier techniques. An important question then arises: if compensating balance requirements are constraining, does some other policy form offer a superior alternative to the (h, z) policy? If it is further stipulated that the B average balance condition must be met weekly, biweekly or monthly, then the steady-state analytic approach is not sufficiently refined, and decisions based on that approach will not always meet the requirements. If an averaging period is specified, some technique of dynamic optimization must be adopted.

As a first cut, the optimistic view of Davis and Gutentag justifies us in proceeding as though compensating balance requirements are non-constraining, and hence play no important part in the demand for money by firms. The basic model, then, or some variant which makes no allowance for compensating balances, can be used for predictive purposes.

2. Cash-Portfolio Transfer Costs and the Demand for Money

Experience in building models of asset management processes indicates that the specific form of the adjustment cost associated with taking a control action has an important effect on the optimal structure of the control action. Conspicuous examples were discussed in Chapter I, Section 4 above. Consider the dynamic programming objective functional

$$F_t(x_t) = \min_{y_t} \left[\sigma(x_t) + \gamma(y_t) + \alpha \int_{-\infty}^{\infty} F_{t-1}(x_t, y_t, \xi_t) \varnothing(\xi_t) d\xi_t \right],$$

where $\sigma(x_t)$ is the period-t cost associated with the state variable x_t; $\gamma(y_t)$ is the period-t cost associated with the decision variable y_t; ξ_t is an exogenous variable realized in period t; α is a discount factor; and $F_k(\cdot)$ is the minimum present value of cost over k-period horizon.[5] First suppose that the function σ is quadratic in the state variable x. If γ is also quadratic in its argument, $\gamma(y_t) = \gamma_2 y_t^2 + \gamma_1 y_t + \gamma_0$, then an optimal decision rule will be linear in the state variable x and the expected value of the exogenous variable $E(\xi_t)$:

$$a + bx_t + cE(\xi_t),$$

where b and c are constants depending on the coefficients of γ and σ.[6]

Suppose instead that the cost-of-control term $\gamma(y_t)$ is linear in the absolute value of the control variable, i.e. $\gamma(y_t) = \gamma \cdot |y_t|$. That modification of control response cost, innocuous as it appears (Figure X), radically alters the structure of the original policy. Under the modified circumstances, it becomes optimal to use a decision rule of the relaxation response form

$$
\begin{aligned}
y_t &= x_t - D & x_t &> D \\
y_t &= 0 & D &\geq x_t \geq U \\
y_t &= U - x_t & U &> x_t,
\end{aligned}
$$

where D and U are policy parameters in state space.

Given that the optimal policy form is so acutely sensitive to the specific structure of the control cost, it would not be surprising to find that money demand predictions are similarly sensitive. It is little wonder then, that the first aspect of the basic

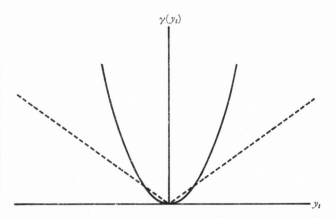

Figure X. Alternative Forms of the Cost of Control

model that attracted analytical attention and comment was the assumed structure of transfer costs. In Miller and Orr (1966), transfer costs were held to be purely "lumpy," that is, invariant with the size and direction of the transfer. The optimal cash management policy under different transfer cost regimes has been analyzed in four papers, two by Eppen and Fama, one by Weitzman, and one by Miller and Orr. Eppen and Fama (1969a) determine the optimal cash management policy under various cash flow conditions, when the cost of transfer is linearly proportional to the transfer size; and they numerically analyze a wide variety of cases involving lumpy and proportional costs (1968). Weitzman (1968) modifies the MO analysis to accomodate the possibility that the "lumpy" cost of transfer may be different depending upon whether a sale or a purchase of securities is involved. The results of Miller and Orr (1968) are the basis of much of what follows in this chapter.

3. PROPORTIONAL COSTS OF TRANSFER: THE EPPEN–FAMA CASE

The economies of scale in cash management that are predicted by the basic model of Chapter III, as well as by the Baumol model, depend in an important way on the postulate of a lumpy cost of cash-portfolio adjustment transfer. Eppen and Fama suggest that a *proportional* cost of transfer, where each unit of earning asset purchased or sold raises the transfer cost by a given amount, and from which lumpy elements are absent, may be a more accurate description than the purely lumpy cost of the basic model. Their view is based on an institutional consideration—the structure of brokerage fees for government securities. It is of course the case that strict cost proportionality can not hold—witness the fact that security purchases in very small denominations, such as $100, or in odd denominations, such as $103,181, are virtually impossible or very difficult. This suggests that the market for treasury bills is far less perfect than the hypothesis of a purely proportional transfer cost implies. Nonetheless, for some purposes pure proportionality may be an approximation superior to pure lumpiness in this crucial cost element, and the results obtained from it are well worth considering. They offer an interesting contrast to the basic model's results.

Eppen and Fama find that if the transfer cost is strictly proportional to the amount transferred, the optimal policy specifies a range $[U, D]$ over which the cash balance drifts freely. When either control limit, U or D, is passed, a control action is signalled and a transfer is made that is just large enough to restore the expected cash balance to the nearest control limit.[8]

A steady-state analysis of a model with proportional cost of transfer is not difficult. The hypotheses follow the basic model's two-asset environment, zero drift in cash transactions (expected receipts = expected payments for any time period), and a proportional opportunity cost v per unit of holding cash. Instead of the lumpy transfer cost γ, a proportional cost τ per unit of transfer between the cash balance and the portfolio is assumed. Shortage penalty costs are infinite—the cash balance never is permitted to become negative. The firm employs the policy that is optimal under the assumed circumstances; when cash falls below $U = 0$, restore it to zero; when it rises above D, restore it to D.[9] Occupancy probabilities are worked out for the case in which cash transactions are generated by a symmetric Bernoulli process in Chapter II, Section 3.

In the steady state the cash balance is uniformly distributed over the integers on the interval $[0, D]$. Consequently, the mean cash balance is $D/2$. The probability that a transfer occurs in any period is $2/(D+1)$. The optimal transfer size is one unit. The firm's expected steady state cost of cash management then is seen to be

$$(2) \qquad E(c) = \nu D/2 + 2\tau/(D+1),$$

which takes its minimum value at $D+1 = (4\tau/\nu)^{1/2}$, a result which, apparently, is identical in form to the one yielded by the traditional type of inventory analysis, exemplified in the Baumol paper (1952), embodying transactions and interest elasticities of $\pm 1/2$ respectively.

Actually, the predicted transaction demand for cash from (2) is quite different from Baumol's, as is seen when the cash transaction structure is taken explicitly into account. In the Baumol tradition, the firm uses m units of cash t times per period; the transaction rate is mt. The cost of cash management is

$$E(c) = \frac{\nu(M+1)}{2} + \frac{\gamma mt}{M},$$

which is minimized by setting M, the "economic lot size," equal to $(2\gamma mt/\nu)^{1/2}$. Here γ is a lumpy cost of transfer, ν is the holding cost, and mt is the mean usage (or receipt) rate for cash.

By contrast, in the structure underlying equation (2), the mean usage rate is zero; the firm receives or disburses one unit of cash once per period. If units are chosen in more general form, so that the firm transacts with m units of cash t times per period, the probability of a transfer is m/D (assuming D to be an integer multiple of m), and the cost of transfer τm is incurred t times as often as in the once-a-day transaction case. Thus the cost function is

$$E(c) = \nu D/2 + 2\tau m^2 t/(D+1).$$

It follows that $D+1$ is optimally set at $(2\tau m^2 t/\nu)^{1/2}$, where τ is the cost per dollar transferred, and ν is the opportunity cost of holding a dollar for one period. The difference, then, between the proportional cost analysis and the Baumol analysis is that the expected net rate of cash flow is the critical dimension of transactions in the latter, while the variance of cash flows is again seen to be the relevant transactions variable in the former. However, the proportional cost case does predict the same interest elasticity of money demand as the Baumol model.

4. THE BASIC MODEL IN LARGE FIRMS

Large firms with heavy cash flows present special problems for the basic model. The optimal policy parameters, which demarcate the range of cash balance fluctuation, may be expressed in the form

$$h = (81\gamma/4\nu)^{1/3}\sigma^{2/3}, \; z = h/3.$$

If the ratio in parentheses is large compared to the daily cash flow variance σ^2, then the range of cash balance fluctuation h, will be large compared to the daily standard deviation of cash flows, σ. A numerical example will help to fix the idea. Suppose that the daily standard deviation of flows in 10,000; let ν and γ be, respectively, .00025 per day (9 per cent per year), and $50. Then

$$h = [(81/4)(200,000)(10,000)^2]^{1/3} = (405)^{1/3}\sigma,$$

and the control range is roughly 7 1/2 times the standard deviation of the daily flow. By contrast, suppose σ is 1 million; then $h = (4.05)^{1/3}\sigma$, and the control range is only 1.7 times the standard deviation. If the actual cash flow process is in the Gaussian domain of attraction, the basic policy will call for an adjustment transfer on approximately half the operating days with such a large variance.

At the level of pure theory, such a narrow control range presents no particular difficulty. However, it must be kept in mind that the traditional sequential-analytic approximation, in which a Bernoulli process is used to represent more complicated cash-flow generating processes, will not work well unless the control range is wide compared to the standard deviation of the random variable. Unless h/σ is large, predictions of adjustment frequency and occupancy probability are subject to large errors.

In practice, another perhaps more important issue arises from the model when cash flows are extremely large. With a transfer size of one standard deviation—about $1 million, say—the idea that the *total* cost of adjustment can be as low as $50 appears absurd *prima facie*. Such a low commission rate is virtually unthinkable—the total charge comes to only 5¢ per thousand dollars. A more reasonable estimate of the cost of transferring one million dollars might be $1000, or $1 per thousand. Yet, if that amount is treated as a purely lumpy cost, the model will be forced to overlook a response that may be desirable—to respond more frequently with smaller asset transfers than is implied by $\gamma = \$1000$; but less frequently, perhaps with larger asset transfers, than is implied by $\gamma = \$50$. A way around the problem is to use the proportional cost of adjustment analyzed in Section 2: transfer costs then vary directly with the size of adjustments. In practice, units can be scaled to avoid the absurd consequences of the optimal policy—a unit of cash can be taken as $10,000, $100,000 or even more; and all adjustments will be made in unit amounts. The suggested scaling strategy, of course, is simply a means of hiding a lumpy cost element. Without lumpy costs, there could be no objections to transfers in "absurdly small" amounts.

A more direct way to portray adjustment costs more realistically, and to obtain more flexible control response, is to use a lumpy plus proportional adjustment cost function. The lumpy cost captures the work of setting up a transfer, while the variable element reflects brokerage charges and similar scale-related considerations. It may be possible to approximate the proportional cost element under a wide variety of circumstances by use of a linear function (Figure XI).

The standard considerations of prediction and control arise once again when lumpy-plus-proportional costs of adjustment are viewed: how does that cost structure affect the optimal control response? What effect does it have on predictions of demand elasticity? These questions are approached in the next section.

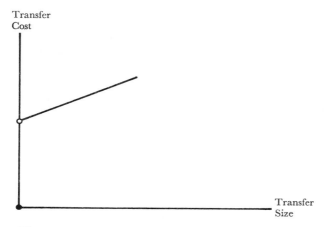

Figure XI. Linear and Lumpy Transfer Costs

5. LUMPY-AND-PROPORTIONAL COSTS OF ADJUSTMENT

In a more general case, in which transfer costs contain lumpy and proportional terms, the optimal policy has not been analytically established. However, the numerical examples of Eppen and Fama (1968) offer extremely strong support for belief in the optimality of this (h, d, u, l) policy. When cash accumulates to the level h, return down to d; when cash falls as low as 1, return up to u, where $l \leq u \leq d \leq h$. In the case of strictly lumpy cost, $l = 0$ and $u = d = 1/3h$, as is seen from the basic model; while in the case of strictly proportional cost, $l = u$ and $d = h$. Thus, the two cases already analyzed are extreme or bounding members of a class or family of four-parameter control policies. If we again assume that cash shortages will not be tolerated, $l = 0$, and the cost function for the mixed lumpy and proportional transfer cost case is

$$(3) \qquad E(c) = \frac{v(h^2 + d^2 - u^2 + hd)}{3(h + d - u)} + \frac{\gamma + u\tau}{u(h + d - u)}$$

$$+ \frac{\gamma + (h - d)\tau}{(h - d)(h + d - u)}.$$

In (3), v is the cost of holding one dollar in cash for one day, τ is the cost of transferring one dollar between the earning portfolio and the cash balance, γ is the lumpy component of transfer cost, and the policy parameters h, d and u reflect the assumption that the transactions parameters m and t (and hence the daily cash flow variance m^2t) equal unity in value.

No novel analysis is entailed in compiling this loss function. It can readily be verified by difference equation methods now familiar that for the zero drift Bernoulli process, the stationary probability density of cash holdings is "trapezoidal," as shown in Figure XII, that is, uniform over (u, d), and triangular over

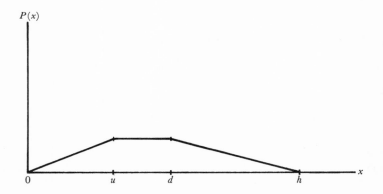

$P(x)$

0 u d h x

Figure XII. Cash Balance Occupancy Probability with
Linear and Lumpy Transfer Costs

$(0, u)$ with mode at u, and over (d, h), with mode at d. In this case, the expected cost of cash holdings is

$$\frac{(h^2 + d^2 - u^2 + hd)v}{3(h + d - u)}$$

and the expected cost of transfers to and from the cash account is

$$\{(\gamma + u\tau)u^{-1} + [\gamma + (h - d)\tau](h - d)^{-1}\}(h + d - u)^{-1}.$$

This expected transfer cost expression also follows from the density function, since the probability of incurring the cost

$\gamma + u\tau$ is equal to the probability of having one unit of cash on hand [or $2/u(h+d-u)$] times the probability of a cash payment (1/2). Similarly, the probability of incurring the cost $\gamma + (h-d)\tau$ is $1/(h-d)(h+d-u)$.

The cost function is next to impossible to crack analytically, but an extensive series of computer "experiments" (constructed numerical examples) provided significant insight into the importance of having a proportional cost term τ in the cost function.

Three questions were considered in the design of the test runs: how much does the presence of a proportional cost-of-transfer term affect (a) the predicted mean cash balance, (b) the interest elasticity of money demand and, (c) the transactions elasticity of money demand. Table VIII lists the values of cost coefficients

TABLE VIII

Values Used in Computer Experiment on Proportional
Transfer Costs and Money Demand*

τ	ν	γ	m	t
.001	.00010	10	1	10
	.00011	50	100	20
	.00020	100	1000	100
	.00021		10000	
	.00030		10100	
			11000	

$5 \times 3 \times 6 \times 3 = 270$ cases

* The units in which the variables are stated are: τ in dollars per dollar transferred; γ in dollars per transfer; ν in dollars per dollar held for one day; m in dollars, and t in events (transactions, not transfers) per day.

and money flow parameters that were combined to obtain 270 test cases.

The cash balance prediction for each case was compared to the mean cash balance prediction that would obtain for identical values of ν, γ, m and t, with $\tau = 0$. Similar comparisons were drawn for demand elasticity predictions. Selected and representative findings from the experimental runs are presented in Tables IX to XII. Several interesting confirmations of the robustness of the predictions drawn from the basic policy model emerge from these numerical results.

As we would expect, the (h, z) policy serves better as a

TABLE IX

Errors in Mean Cash Balance Predictions When (h, z) Policy Is Used to Predict Behavior that Actually Conforms to (h, d, u) Policy*

$m = 100, t = 100$				$m = 1,000, t = 10$			
$\gamma =$ 10	50	100	$\downarrow \nu \downarrow$	10	50	100	$= \gamma$
1.0912	1.0319	1.0201	.00010	1.1973	1.0679	1.0431	
1.0884	1.0309	1.0195	.00011	1.1819	1.0658	1.0418	
1.0730	1.0254	1.0160	.00020	1.1514	1.0542	1.0343	
1.0718	1.0249	1.0157	.00021	1.1492	1.0533	1.0339	
1.0640	1.0222	1.0140	.00030	1.1335	1.0474	1.0300	

$m = 1,000, t = 20$				$m = 1,000, t = 100$			
$\gamma =$ 10	50	100	$\downarrow \nu \downarrow$	10	50	100	$= \gamma$
1.2306	1.0849	1.0541	.00010	1.3671	1.1413	1.0912	
1.2242	1.0823	1.0525	.00011	1.3574	1.1372	1.0884	
1.1873	1.0679	1.0431	.00020	1.3015	1.1137	1.0729	
1.1845	1.0668	1.0425	.00021	1.2973	1.1119	1.0718	
1.1655	1.0595	1.0377	.00030	1.2681	1.1000	1.0640	

	$m = 10,000$	$t = 100$	
$\gamma =$ 10	50	100	ν
2.1908	1.5358	1.3671	.00010
2.1646	1.5224	1.3574	.00011
2.0114	1.4447	1.3015	.00020
1.9997	1.4388	1.2973	.00021
1.9174	1.3978	1.2681	.00030

* Cell entries are (Optimal Mean Balance From (h, d, u) Policy) ÷ (Predicted Mean Balance From (h, z) Policy).

TABLE X

The Predictive Accuracy of Alternative Extreme Transfer
Cost Hypotheses

Y	v	m	t	$M(\tau,\gamma)^*$	$\bar{M}(\gamma)$	$\bar{M}(\tau)$
100	.0001	10,000	10	143,830	121,141	75,711
100	.0002	10,000	10	110,716	96,159	55,000
100	.0001	10,000	100	356,811	260,991	228,607
100	.0002	10,000	100	269,611	207,149	163,114
10	.0001	10,000	100	265,394	121,141	228,607
10	.0002	10,000	100	193,397	96,150	163,114
10	.0001	1,000	10	14,382	12,114	7,571
10	.0002	1,000	10	11,071	9,615	5,500
10	.00011	100	100	5,929	5,447	2,820
10	.0002	100	100	4,788	4,462	1,631

* $\bar{M}(\tau, \gamma)$ denotes mean cash balance when both cost of transfer terms
are taken into account. $\bar{M}(\gamma)$ denotes the mean cash balance prediction
when τ is assumed to be zero but other variables are correctly estimated;
symmetrically for $M(\tau)$. All mean values are in dollar terms.

TABLE XI

Interest Elasticities of Money Demand Under
Different (h, d, u) Regimes

m	t	Y	v	Δv	$\bar{M}/m$	$\Delta\bar{M}/m$	ϵ
100	10	10	.0001	.00001	27.2251	− .8851	− .3251
100	10	10	.0002	.00001	21.4260	− .3927	− .3666
100	20	10	.0001	.00001	34.6634	− 1.370	− .3280
100	20	10	.0002	.00001	27.2250	− .4508	− .3356
100	100	10	.0002	.00001	47.8845	− .8227	− .3687
100	100	100	.0001	.00001	123.5823	− 3.9384	− .3181
100	100	100	.0002	.00001	97.6887	− 1.6006	− .3452
1,000	10	10	.0001	.00001	14.3829	− .5125	− .3563
1,000	10	10	.0002	.00001	11.0710	− .2001	− .3615
1,000	100	100	.0001	.00001	61.3561	− 2.0681	− .3371
1,000	100	100	.0002	.00001	47.8845	− .8226	− .3436
10,000	10	100	.0001	.00001	14.3830	− .5126	− .3564
10,000	10	10	.0002	.00001	26.9611	− .5208	− .3863

Table XII

Transaction Elasticities of Money Demand Under
Different (h, d, u) Regimes*

γ	ν	T	M (10,100)	M (10,000)	ϵ
100	.0003	10	9.5912	9.5207	.7405
100	.0001	10	14.4925	14.3830	.7613
100	.0002	10	11.1537	11.0710	.7470
10	.0001	20	12.9318	12.8181	.8870
10	.0003	20	7.9893	7.9210	.8623
50	.0001	100	32.0841	31.8135	.8505
50	.0002	100	23.9509	23.7529	.8336
50	.0003	100	20.2417	20.0762	.8244
100	.0001	100	35.9725	35.6811	.9167
100	.0002	100	27.1766	26.9611	.7993
100	.0003	100	23.1287	22.9474	.7901

* All elasticity calculations use m as the transaction variable and the value $m = 10,100$ as the calculation base. To determine the transactions elasticity when $\sigma^2 = m^2t$ (the daily cash flow variance) is the transaction base, multiply entries in the ϵ column by .50751.

surrogate in prediction for the (h, d, u) policy, the larger the ratio of $\gamma/m\tau$, i.e. the more important the lumpy cost of transfer compared to the proportional cost of transfer. For example, when $\gamma = 10$, $m = 10,000$ and $\tau = .001$, the lumpy cost of transfer is no greater than the proportional cost of transferring *one* unit of $10,000$. It is unsurprising to find that under these unfavorable circumstances the (h, z) policy predicts the mean cash balance with large error, and in fact, the proportional cost case analyzed in Section 2, with $\gamma = 0$, emerges as a better predictor of mean cash balances for such large ν and m. Table XII compares the predictive powers of the purely lumpy and purely proportional transfer cost assumptions for cases in which the cost mixture actually holds. Save for the cases where the ratio γ/m is extremely low, the error that results from overlooking a proportional element in the transfer cost is much smaller than the error that results from overlooking a lumpy cost component. Thus, the basic model with lumpy adjustment cost offers substantial advantages as a predictive instrument over the simple and analytically tractable rival hypothesis.

We turn to the question of elasticities of money demand. The basic model predicts an interest elasticity of $-.\overline{3}$ and a "transaction" elasticity of $.\overline{3}$ if $\sigma^2 = m^2 t$ is taken as the transaction variable, or $.\overline{6}$ if m is taken as the transaction variable. Tables XI and XII present samples of elasticity information under an (h, d, u) policy regime.

The interest elasticity displays a remarkably stable adherence to values close to $.\overline{3}$, the value predicted from an (h, z) policy. The behavior of transaction elasticities in the (h, d, u) framework is captured only slightly less well by the (h, z) prediction.

From the standpoint of the relevant predictions about money behavior, the (h, z) policy does extremely well, even if business firms recognize and respond to the "fact" that the cost of transfer contains a proportional cost term. It should be kept in mind, also, that the computer experiments embody the "true" value of γ, and no adjustment is made in the value of γ to correct for the omission of τ from the cost function. Any attempt to fit an (h, z) policy to daily cash flow data would almost surely lead to an estimate of γ that would tend to correct partially for the misspecification of an (h, d, u) regime.

So far as control is concerned, it follows that wherever an (h, z) policy predicts an (h, d, u) outcome well, it can be used in control applications with little or no loss of efficiency. Control performance of the (h, z) policy can be improved by fitting a γ to the typical transfer size, rather than using the true γ and arbitrarily setting $\tau = 0$, as was done in the computer experiments reported in this Section. Table XIII compares the control limits that are appropriate in two cases: one with $\tau = .001$ (which leads to an (h, d, u) policy); and one with $\tau = 0$ (which indicates an (h, z) policy).

6. Different "Lumpy" Costs of Purchase and Sale: The Weitzman Case

Weitzman (1968) questions the basic model of Chapter III on the ground that transfer costs involving security purchases are unlikely to be the same as transfer costs involving security

Table XIII

Optimal Control Limits with (h, z) and (h, d, u) Regimes (Selected Cases)*

m	t	γ	ν	h	z	h	d	u
10,000	100	10	.0001	27.27	9.09	59.32	41.15	4.60
10,000	100	100	.0003	30.68	13.56	52.86	25.72	10.12
1,000	100	10	.0001	58.71	19.57	82.08	42.93	13.69
1,000	100	100	.0003	87.72	29.24	94.65	36.17	26.40
1,000	10	10	.0001	27.27	9.09	33.11	14.94	7.21
1,000	10	100	.0003	40.68	13.56	42.28	15.14	12.87
100	100	10	.00011	124.35	41.45	135.69	53.99	35.79
100	100	100	.0003	189.00	63.00	192.44	66.45	61.36

* All units are multiples of m.

sales.[10] If in fact the costs of transfer remain lumpy, the modifications suggested by Weitzman have no significant impact on money demand, which he recognizes.

Let the cost of transfer from cash to bonds be γ, as in (1), but let the cost of transfer from bonds to cash be β. Then the familiar analysis of normalized Bernoulli processes reveals that in the zero drift case, the objective function (assuming the use of an (h, z) type of policy) is

$$(4) \qquad E(c) = \frac{\beta}{hz} + \frac{\gamma}{(h-z)h} + \frac{\nu(h+z)}{3},$$

which can be determined from the basic loss function (1), and the fact that the relative frequency of security sales (conditional on the occurence of a transfer) is given by z/h, while purchases occur with relative frequency $(h-z)/h$.[11]

From the first-order minimum conditions on (4), Weitzman shows that $(h-z)/z$ satisfies this cubic condition

$$\left[\frac{h-z}{z}\right]^3 - (3\gamma/\beta)\left[\frac{h-z}{z}\right] - 2\gamma/\beta = 0.$$

Thus, if $\beta = 44\gamma, z = 2(h-z)$; $\beta = 5\gamma, z = h - z$; and so on. Money demand elasticity predictions are unaltered by Weitzman's extension of the model, despite the fact that variations in the β/γ

ratio will affect predictions about the desired levels of cash balances. Recall that the predicted mean cash balance derived from the basic model (1) was

$$\overline{M} = \frac{3}{4} \left[\frac{3\gamma\sigma^2}{4\nu} \right]^{1/3.}$$

By altering the β/γ ratio, the coefficient of σ^2/ν is altered, but the exponent is not. For example, let $\beta = 5\gamma$. Then the optimal h and z satisfy $h^* = 2z^* = \left[\frac{6\gamma\sigma^2}{\nu} \right]^{1/3}$, and the mean cash balance $M = (h^* + z^*)/3 = z^*$. Thus, in general, the optimal mean cash balance associated with the objective function (4) is of the form

$$\overline{M} = K \left[\frac{\gamma\sigma^2}{\nu} \right]^{1/3,}$$

where K depends upon the ratio β/γ. The relevant measure of transactions is unaffected by the difference between the two costs of transfer, and the relevant interest and transactions demand elasticities similarly are unaffected. Further use will be found for Weitzman's results when three-asset versions of the basic model are considered (Chapter VI, Section 4).

The foregoing analysis lends strong support to two views: (a) even if the control agent is confronted by proportional costs of adjustment, use of the basic (h, z) policy will not entail very large or costly control errors, and (b) the predictions of the basic model of Chapter III, concerning the demand for cash in the corporate sector, are surprisingly robust under a wide range of cost conditions. There remains yet one important and interesting sensitivity analysis to be performed, in which the assumption of homogeneous earning assets is relaxed. That is, we must consider a model in which the possibility of more than two assets is recognized. That investigation is the subject of Chapter VI.

NOTES

1. Telser and Graves (1968) have discovered seemingly pathological circumstances under which discrete time and continuous time approaches should not be regarded as acceptable substitutes.
2. Two helpful references on the problem of control intervals are Kuo (1960),

which deals with the problem of an optimal "data sampling" interval; and Pinkham (1960). Pinkham deals with the effect of the length of the control interval on the appropriate representation of shortage costs.

3. In Miller and Orr (1966) we took the view that compensating balance requirements were typically stated in terms of minimum holdings. That view was based on interviews with bankers, and serves as a nice example of the power of wishful thinking on the part of our informants.

4. After further discussion with bankers and corporate financial officers, I am now of the opinion that compensating balance requirements are an unimportant factor in the demand for money. That same view is implied in the position of Davis and Gutentag (1964).

5. This is a standard formulation of objective for dynamic programming problems.

6. See Theil (1960), Chapter 8, or Holt, Modigliani Muth and Simon (1961), Chapter 6.

7. This is the Eppen-Fama (1969a) and Beckmann (1960) case described in Chapter II, Section 2.

8. Their analysis is more general than is suggested by our descriptive paragraph, since we describe only their analysis of the "infinite cost of shortage" case, in which a lower control limit of zero is appropriate. In other cases involving finite costs of shortage it will usually pay to permit the cash balance to drift below the zero level. These cases are probably of small practical importance since an overdraft privilege cannot be treated as a simple "negative cash balance." Moreover, the "infinite cost of shortage" case is the appropriate one for purposes of comparison with the basic model of Chapter III.

9. Eppen and Fama give an optimality proof in (1969a). See Chapter II, Section 2.

10. "The prospect of running out of cash forces the firm to appropriate managerial attention on a scale of priority far higher than would be the case for the problem of converting excess cash into bonds." One can question Weitzman's intuition on this point: the time delays inherent in security purchases and sales should not be notably different. Moreover, the choices involved are quite similar; in the one case the objective is to purchase the highest prospective yield, in the other case, the choice is to cull out the lowest prospective yield. If these choices are notably difficult or costly to make in either direction some form of the "three asset" model (Chapter VI) is probably appropriate. A major effect of control policies like the ones considered in this book is the elimination of circumstances that "force the firm to appropriate managerial attention" by routinizing operational decisions.

11. This result is established in Feller (1951) chapter 14.

VI

Three-Asset Models of the
Demand for Money

1. Structure and Rationale for a Three-Asset Model

In existing analyses of the demand for cash "inventories," a standard simplifying assumption is that earning assets are homogeneous, or indistinguishable from the standpoint of risk and return.[2] It is important to know whether this assumption has a crucial bearing on such matters as the predicted transactions elasticity of money demand, and so the implications of the two-asset assumption are explored in the present short chapter.

Attention will be confined in this chapter to two different "three-asset" cases; the model involves cash and two distinct earning assets. At first glance these cases seem to represent the most meager conceivable degree of generalization of the results already developed, and from the viewpoint of the portfolio problem it is just that. No attempt is made here to cope with that problem, which seeks a most advantageous tradeoff between riskiness and expected return from a diversified holding of earning securities. In the first three-asset case, we will be concerned with the effect that the existence of portfolio alternatives has upon the demand for cash. The first case involves cash and two earning assets. The earning assets are (a) a low risk, low-return security such as treasury bills (called "shorts"). This asset entails low cost of purchase, and it serves as an automatic first recourse when the cash balance is low or high. (b) All other available securities (called "longs"), no one of which bears less risk, a higher return, and a lower transfer cost than shorts.[3] The firm is assumed to control the level of its cash account by movement into and out of shorts, thereby reducing transfer costs to the bare minimum of paper work and brokerage charges. When holdings of shorts are found to be excessively large or small, correction is made by transfers to or from the "permanent" portfolio of longs. The transfer cost is greatly amplified when any transfer to or from longs is involved, since it then becomes necessary to review a wider range of sale or purchase possibilities, and information of a current and local nature on prices, purchase costs, and returns prospects of the alternatives becomes important to the decision.

The second three-asset case brings the firm's own debt and capital positions into the analysis. Consider first a situation that involves only debt flotation or retirement. The transfer costs involved in reducing or increasing the firm's outstanding debt may be extremely high, because of reasonable or unreasonable internal accounting and control procedures which govern the issue or recall of debt. A more complicated version of the second case deals with the decision process in a firm which accumulates cash to invest in physical capital. The three assets, then, are cash, an earning portfolio, and physical capital. The asset structure presents no difficulty when transfers from liquid assets to capital are considered; but when cash outflows create a drain, it seems unlikely that the response of the firm will be to liquidate physical capital. Instead, the firm can and likely will issue its own securities to provide the needed liquidity. The costs of transfer to and from the more liquid assets, then, may well be different; this problem can be handled by an application of the Weitzman analysis (Chapter V, Section 5). An interesting question to be worked out in the following concerns the appropriate term for such a security issue to meet liquidity needs.

The approach to these three-asset problems will rest upon the same ideas as are embodied in the basic model of Chapter III.

Conditions of environment and motivation are the same as were specified there, except that now two classes of earning asset are recognized. The costs of managing the cash balance and port-folio are (i) opportunities foregone by holding an asset that yields less than the highest available return; and (ii) costs of transfer among the various asset categories. The structure of adjustment transfer costs is of the utmost importance, as will be seen from a comparison of the results obtained under the assumption of a lumpy transfer cost, to those obtained with a proportional transfer cost.

2. Lumpy Costs and Separable Decisions

We first will deal with the simple "heterogeneous portfolio" case, involving assets of different term. In the three-asset case, the structure of the decision rules for cash balance and portfolio management are assumed to be of the same relaxation response type that characterizes the two asset analyses in Chapters III-V; and it is first assumed that transfer costs are purely lumpy. In the first (non-capital goods) case, a portfolio action is taken whenever it is necessary to correct an excess or deficit of cash. If an excess of cash is accompanied by an extremely high level of short holdings, then the portfolio is rebalanced by a purchase of longs. If a deficit of cash is accompanied by an extremely low level of short holdings, then the portfolio is rebalanced by a sale of longs. If the holding of shorts is neither extremely high nor low, correction of the cash position does not create a portfolio imbalance, and the cash adjustment is accomplished by pur-chase or sale of shorts only. A cash balance deficit is signalled when the assumed minimum balance level of 0 is reached, and a surplus is signalled when the upper bound h is reached. Similarly, short holdings are regarded as excessively low when a transfer to cash would put the holding below 0; they are excessively high when a transfer from cash would put the hold-ing above H. The two asset categories, cash and shorts, are respectively returned to z and $\mathcal{Z}$ when corrective actions are taken. The object is to find optimal policy parameters—h, z, H and $\mathcal{Z}$—for the two asset categories.

If the cash balance at an arbitrarily chosen point in time is x, and the shorts balance at the same moment is X, then the form of the control action for that moment in time is

$$(1)\begin{cases} \text{(i)} & \text{sell } z + \mathcal{Z} - X \text{ worth of longs and buy } \mathcal{Z} - X \text{ worth of} \\ & \text{shorts if } x = 0 \text{ and } 0 \le X < z \\ & \text{(increase both cash and shorts)} \\ \text{(ii)} & \text{sell } z \text{ worth of shorts if } x = 0 \text{ and } z \le X \\ & \text{(increase only cash)} \\ \text{(iii)} & \text{do nothing if } 0 < x < h \\ \text{(iv)} & \text{buy } h - z \text{ worth of shorts if } x = h \text{ and } X \le H - h + z \\ & \text{(reduce only cash)} \\ \text{(v)} & \text{buy } h - z + X - \mathcal{Z} \text{ worth of longs and sell } X - \mathcal{Z} \text{ worth} \\ & \text{of shorts if } x = h \text{ and } H - h + z \\ & < X \le H \text{ (reduce both cash and} \\ & \text{shorts).} \end{cases}$$

If these rules are followed, the cash balance and the shorts holding will perform random walks on the intervals $(0, h)$ and $(0, H)$ respectively, and the theory of random walks can be invoked to simplify the process of finding optimal values of the policy parameters, h, z, H, and $\mathcal{Z}$, in much the same manner as in the basic two-asset model. Once the optimal values of the policy parameters are obtained, the firm cannot operate at lower cost unless a better policy than (1, i-v) can be discovered.[4]

We will analyze the operation of these rules and find "optimal" values for the policy parameters z, h, $\mathcal{Z}$, and H for the case in which cash transaction flows are generated by a driftless Bernoulli process. The rates of return on "longs" and "shorts" will be denoted respectively v_l and v_s; the lumpy cost of purchase or sale of longs will be denoted γ_l, and the lumpy cost of purchase or sale of shorts will be denoted γ_s. For obvious reasons it is assumed that $\gamma_l > \gamma_s$ and $v_l > v_s$. The cost of holding cash, then, is v_l, and the cost of holding shorts is $(v_l - v_s)$. As in the basic model of Chapter III, cash shortages are assumed to be very costly and yet easy to avoid, and for that reason the cash balance is never allowed to fall below zero.

Cash flows are structured, and the cash account is regulated in the same manner as in the basic two-asset analysis; hence the behavior of the cash balance depends upon the policy parameters h and z in the same way as in that analysis. The results developed in Chapter III that are useful here are: associated with specific values of h and z, the long run average cash balance is

$$(2) \qquad\qquad (h+z)/3;$$

and the probability in any time period of a transfer to or from cash is

$$(3) \qquad\qquad \sigma^2[z(h-z)]^{-1},$$

where σ^2 is the variance in the cash flow per unit period.[5]

There is in fact a major difference between the basic model and the three-asset variant examined here. The cost consequences of assigning specific values to h and z are more far-reaching in the three-asset case, because the sequence of actions taken to control the cash balance is the process that generates fluctuation and change in the shorts balance. Thus, the frequency magnitude and direction of changes in the shorts account depend on the values given to h and z. If in fact the behavior of the shorts balance (and consequently the cost of managing the shorts balance) is sensitive to the values assigned to h and z, then these cost effects realized in the shorts account must be considered in setting the h and z values.

The flow into and out of shorts, generated by purchases and sales of shorts to control the cash balance, will obviously not be Bernoullian, since transfers between cash and shorts do not occur regularly in time. Nonetheless, remarkably enough, the time series of security purchases and sales will have the same periodic variance as the cash flow, namely σ^2, no matter what values are assigned to h and z.[6] This is readily demonstrated.

Let the cash transactions variance be σ^2, and let the cash account fluctuate between 0 and h with return to z when 0 or h is reached, as is stipulated in the control rules (1, i-v). Security sale transfers to cash will be of size z and security purchase transfers from cash will be of size $h - z$. The probability of a sale, conditional on the occurrence of a transfer, is $(h-z)/h$, the probability that the first passage occurs at 0 and not at h. The conditional probability of a purchase, given that a transfer occurs, is z/h. The probability of a transfer is given in expression (3). Thus the variance of the periodic movement between shorts and cash is

$$\sigma^2[\,zh\,(h-z)\,]^{-1}[\,z^2(h-z)+z\,(h-z)^2\,]=\sigma^2.$$

Since this variance of movement in the shorts account is σ^2, the expected first passage time for the shorts balance from Z to either 0 or H is $Z(H-Z)/\sigma^2$, and the steady-state probability of a first passage, which signals a purchase or sale of longs, is

$$[\,Z(H-Z)\,]^{-1}\sigma^2.$$

This passage probability measures the likelihood that transfers into or out of cash will involve the purchase or sale of longs. *Consequently, the frequency of trade in longs is determined entirely by the values assigned to H and Z, the control levels on the shorts account, and is independent of h and z, the control levels on the cash account.*

Similarly, the mean balance in the shorts account is not much affected by the values assigned to h and z.

The effect of the h and z choices on the mean balance of the shorts account is not easy to establish precisely. However, the magnitude of the effect can easily be shown to be trivial in general, by a combination of analysis and numerical examples. The transition rules governing movements in the shorts account yield the steady state relations

$$P_X = (2/3)P_{X+1} + (1/3)P_{X-2}$$
$$P_Z = 2/3[P_{Z+1}+P_1] + 1/3[P_{Z-2}+P_{H-2}+P_{H-1}].$$

Familiar difference equation methods reveal that the solution structure is of the form

$$(4) \qquad \begin{array}{ll} P_X = A_1 + A_2 X + A_3(-1/2)^X & 0 \leq X \leq Z \\ P_X = A_4 + A_5 X + A_6(-1/2)^X & Z \leq X \leq H, \end{array}$$

where $A_1, \ldots, A_6$ are arbitrary constants, to be assigned values conforming to the boundary conditions

$$P_X = 0 \qquad X \le 0$$
$$P_X = 0 \qquad X \ge H$$
$$A_1 + A_2 \mathcal{Z} + A_3(-1/2)^Z = A_4 + A_5 \mathcal{Z} + A_6(-1/2)^Z$$
$$\sum_x P_X = 1.$$

An explicit solution for $E(X)$ in terms of H and $\mathcal{Z}$ can, with great difficulty, be found from these conditions. That $E(X)$ will be close to $(H+\mathcal{Z})/3$ is seen from the structure of (4) after all but two of the arbitrary constants have been eliminated:

$$P_X = A_1[1 + 3X - (-1/2)^X] \qquad 0 \le X \le \mathcal{Z}$$
$$P_X = A_5\{(X-H) - 2/3[1-(-1/2)^{X-H}]\}\mathcal{Z} \le X \le H.$$

These expressions are "nearly" linear in X and $X-H$, respectively; any error in $(H+\mathcal{Z})/3$ as an estimate of $E(X)$ is due to the departure from linearity. At the extreme values 0 and H, the constant term and terms in $(-1/2)^X$ cancel each other; and when X departs from the extreme values, the effect of the term $(-1/2)^X$ vanishes rapidly.

Numerical examples, presented in Table XIV confirm that

TABLE XIV

1	2	3	4	1	2	3	4
H	$\mathcal{Z}$	True $E(X)$	$\dfrac{H+\mathcal{Z}}{3}$	12	5	5.4631	5.6667
6	2	2.4536	2.6667	12	6	5.7920	6.0000
6	3	2.8462	3.0000	36	3	12.7821	13.
9	3	3.7914	4.0000	36	6	13.7823	14.
9	4	4.1417	4.3333	36	9	14.7825	15.
9	5	4.5555	4.6667	36	12	15.7829	16.
12	3	4.7929	5.0000	36	15	16.7833	17.
12	4	5.1269	5.3333	36	18	17.7839	18.

$(H+\mathcal{Z})/3$ is an extremely good estimate of $E(X)$ in most cases, so long as H is not unreasonably small, and $\mathcal{Z}$ is of the order of $H/3$ or larger. Even with so extreme a ratio of purchase to sale magnitudes as 2:1, the error entailed in estimating the steady state mean balance in the shorts account by use of a symmetric generating process is small.

Since the numerical values of h and z in the cash control process do not affect the passage time or mean balance in the short account importantly, cash will be controlled on the basis of the same considerations as govern in the two-asset model; the cash balance will fluctuate between 0 and $h = 3z$, with returns to z upon passage of either 0 or h; and portfolio effects are not considered in assigning values to h and z. Moreover, asymmetric movements within the shorts account, that stem from shorts purchases of size $h - z$ and shorts sales of size z, will have negligible effect on Bernoullian predictions of the mean shorts balance and the frequency of transfers involving longs.

As a consequence, the steady state expected cost per period of time that will result from the cascaded (h, z) policies that obtain when the rules (1, i-v) are implemented is

$$(5) \qquad E(c) = \frac{\nu_l(h+z)}{3} + \frac{\gamma_s\sigma^2}{z(h-z)} + \frac{(\nu_l-\nu_s)\ (H+Z)}{3}$$
$$+ \frac{\gamma_l\sigma^2}{Z(H-Z)}$$

and the optimal values of the policy variables are

$$(6) \begin{cases} h = 3z \\ z = \left(\frac{3\gamma_s\sigma^2}{4\nu_l}\right)^{1/3} \end{cases} \qquad \begin{aligned} H &= 3Z \\ Z &= \left(\frac{3\gamma_l\sigma^2}{4(\nu_l - \nu_s)}\right)^{1/3}. \end{aligned}$$

Note that the numerator of Z is larger than of z, and the denominator is smaller; consequently and reassuringly the frequency of transfers involving the longs account is smaller than the frequency of transfers involving cash and shorts only.

We conclude that because the cash control rule does not significantly affect the frequency of short-long transfers or the mean level of short holdings, it has negligible effect on the cost of managing shorts. Therefore, the two accounts, cash and shorts, may in effect be managed independently of each other without significant departure from optimality. Because the portfolio problem may thus be "separated" or "decomposed," the money demand predictions of the basic model of Chapter III are not significantly affected when the two-asset assumption is relaxed. The relevant transaction measure is still the variance of cash flows, the relevant interest measure is the "long" or "cost of capital" rate, and the relevant money demand elasticities are $\pm 1/3$. These findings are of major interest, for economists apparently have been concerned for some time over the problem of locating or identifying the appropriate opportunity cost of holding cash.[7] When transfer adjustment costs (or as they are more commonly called, "transactions costs") are systematically brought into the discussion, it certainly appears that the appropriate charge for holding money is (as any economist unschooled in the arcanum of empirical monetary research would suggest) the *greatest* opportunity foregone.[8] The close substitutability for cash of such highly liquid securities as short term treasury bills is of course relevant, but it is appropriately modeled by assigning a low cost of transfer to and from such securities, rather than by taking their low earning rates to be the opportunity rate on money balances. Unfortunately, this triumph of logic and simplicity is short lived, at least in the presence of proportional adjustment transfer costs.

3. Proportional Transfer Costs and Interdependent Asset Management Decisions

If transfer costs are not purely lumpy as posited in Section 2, but are proportional to the amount transferred instead, then the analysis changes significantly and money demand predictions change significantly as well. It has been observed that treasury bills can be purchased (in lots satisfying some minimum size requirement) for a fee that is a small percentage of the total purchase price. If no effort is devoted to a search among available alternatives for a satisfactory tradeoff between price and term to maturity, the structure of these brokerage fees implies that a "purely proportional" formulation of transfer costs offers representational advantages over a "purely lumpy" representation. If the asset management problem is viewed as involving cash, treasury bills, and a third asset class, and if the proportional representation of transfer costs is preferred, then the "variance preserving" properties of the shorts control rule will be destroyed, and the separability of asset management decisions does not hold as in Section 2. Let the cash balance perform a random walk on the interval $(0, h)$. Upon passage of 0, the cash balance is returned to 0; and upon passage of h, the cash balance is returned to h. Thus, the cash control rules that are used are the optimal ones for a two-asset model with purely proportional transfer costs. Additionally, let the shorts balance perform a random walk on the interval $(0, H)$, with returns to $\mathcal{Z}$ $(0 < \mathcal{Z} < H)$ when 0 or H are passed, on the assumption that the cost of transfers involving longs is lumpy. There is of course a real issue as to whether the two kinds of rules should or would ever be juxtaposed in the described combination by a rational operator —in the three-asset milieu, a splicing together of individually sensible policy actions may be nonsense. Our purpose in this exercise is to show that the separability of asset management decisions that "fell out" of the analysis of Section 2 was a special case, albeit potentially an extremely important one.

Under the described regime, and with zero drift in cash flows, the mean cash balance will be $h/2$. The holding cost is ν_l per dollar held. The steady state probability of a transfer from cash to shorts will be $\sigma/(h+1)$; and the same probability holds for a transfer from shorts to cash; σ^2 is the variance per period in cash flows (transactions). The mean shorts balance is $(H+\mathcal{Z})/3$, the holding cost $(\nu_l - \nu_s)$; and the probability of a transfer from longs to shorts or shorts to longs is $[\mathcal{Z}(H-\mathcal{Z})]^{-1}\sigma_s^2$, where σ_s^2 is the variance of changes in the shorts account. The cost of a transfer involving longs is ν.

The objective function associated with the specified regime is

$$\underset{h,\ H,\ \mathcal{Z}}{\min}\quad E(c) = h\nu_l/2 + \tau\sigma/(h+1) + [\mathcal{Z}(H-\mathcal{Z})]^{-1}\sigma_s^2\gamma \\ + (H+\mathcal{Z})\ (\nu_l - \nu_s)/3,$$

where σ_s^2, the variance of movements in the shorts account, is approximately[9] $2\sigma^3/(h+1)$.

The usual first order conditions reveal that

$$H - \mathcal{Z} = 2\mathcal{Z}$$

$$\mathcal{Z}^3 = 3\gamma\sigma_s^2/4(\nu_l - \nu_s) = 3\gamma\sigma^3/2(\nu_l - \nu_s)\ (h+1)$$

$$(h+1)^2 = \frac{2\tau\sigma\mathcal{Z}(H-\mathcal{Z}) - 4\gamma\sigma^3}{\nu_l\mathcal{Z}(H-\mathcal{Z})}.$$

The important fact that emerges from these optimization conditions is that the decision rule parameters for the shorts account and the cash account are interdependent. This interdependence will hold whenever the fundamental variability of cash flows is transformed by the cash control rules, so that the variance of movements in the portfolio differs from the cash flow variance.

The first order conditions also reveal that both the long and the short rates v_l and v_s enter into the determination of the optimal cash balance (since Z affects h and vice versa). Cash will be sensitive to both interest rates whenever the optimal control objective encounters the sort of interdependence among asset classes that characterizes the example dealt with here.

Perhaps the most important message that emerges from Sections 2 and 3 is that conditions which are innocuous by themselves may be critically important when present in combination. We saw, in Chapter V, Section 4, that the existence of proportional costs doesn't confound the basic model; and the presence of three asset classes is not a major source of dislocation, as we saw in Section 2 of this chapter. In combination, however, the two conditions do lead to money demand conditions that the basic model predicts very poorly.

The analysis further underscores one of the main themes of this book—adjustment transfer costs may be of pivotal importance in understanding money demand and other problems of asset management. Apparently, asset management decisions are as profoundly affected by the structure of these cost relationships as by their magnitude.

4. A Three-Asset Model of Capital Accumulation in the Firm

For the sake of completeness, and because of its importance in the analysis of Chapter IX, we will examine the peculiar features of the second important three-asset model, in which the assets are taken to be cash; a portfolio of earning assets; and a "third asset" of heterogeneous structure. When holdings of the first two (liquid) assets are held in excess, some are "laid off" for purchase of physical capital.   When the first two assets are in short supply, the firm issues its own debt.

Care is necessary to avoid unwanted advice from a model with the asset structure just described. Suppose that the rate on the firm's own borrowing is less than the internal marginal rate of return on investment; the model should advise the firm to borrow directly for investment purposes so long as the rate discrepancy prevails, and cash management be damned. That advice can be laid to the excessive simplicity of a three-asset structure, in which important questions, like leverage and the term of security issues, are ignored by the analysis. Most firms avoid the financing of capital undertakings out of security issues of term much shorter than the payout period of the undertaking, and perhaps wisely so. Certainly, short-term security issues, which may be quite suitable to meet temporary liquidity needs, are unlikely to win favor as the basis for capital expansion. In the following model, that unwanted advice is circumvented in a rather crude way. Issues of the firm's own securities are not made to finance expansion; rather, they are made only to meet temporary liquidity needs, as an alternative to liquidation (at distress prices) of physical capital. It is convenient to regard the borrowing decision as a transfer out of the third asset. The model differs from its counterpart of Section 3, then, only in the fact that adjustment transfer costs to and from the "third asset" are different.

For simplicity, all transfer costs are treated as lumpy. The cost of portfolio adjustment is denoted γ_s; and two costs γ_I and γ_B, attend the adjustments that involve investment or borrowing. The earning rate on the portfolio is ν_s, and on capital equipment, ν_l. On the ground that short-term borrowing cuts into the firm's ability to borrow long for investment purposes, the full capital return rate is charged as the opportunity cost of borrowing for liquidity needs.[10]

The firm's objective, under the proposed arrangement, is the same as in the first three-asset case (5), except that the cost of transfer involving the longs account is

$$\left(\begin{array}{c}\text{Probability of a transfer}\\ \text{involving longs}\end{array}\right).$$

$$\left(\begin{array}{c}\text{cost of}\\ \text{borrowing}\end{array} \;.\; \begin{array}{c}\text{probability of}\\ \text{borrowing}\end{array} + \begin{array}{c}\text{cost of}\\ \text{investing}\end{array} \;.\; \begin{array}{c}\text{probability}\\ \text{of investing}\end{array}\right)$$

or

$$\sigma[\mathcal{Z}(H-\mathcal{Z})]^{-1}[\gamma_I \mathcal{Z}/H + \gamma_B(H-\mathcal{Z})/H].$$

The objective, then is

$$\begin{array}{c}\min\\ h,\, z,\, H,\, \mathcal{Z}\end{array} E(c) = \frac{(h+z)\nu_l}{3} + \frac{(H+\mathcal{Z})(\nu_l - \nu_s)}{3} + \frac{\gamma_s \sigma^2}{z(h-z)} + \frac{\sigma^2[\gamma_I \mathcal{Z} + \gamma_B(H-\mathcal{Z})]}{H\mathcal{Z}(H-\mathcal{Z})}.$$

As in the first case (6),

$$h = 3z, \quad z = (3\gamma_s \sigma^2/4\nu_l)^{1/3};$$

predictions about the behavior of the cash balance over time do not change. On the other hand, the shorts balance does behave differently. We have the optimum conditions (letting $\Upsilon = H - \mathcal{Z}$)

$$\partial/\partial \mathcal{Z} = 2(\nu_l - \nu_s)/3 - \gamma_B \sigma^2/\mathcal{Z}^2(\Upsilon + \mathcal{Z}) - \gamma_B \sigma^2/\mathcal{Z}(\Upsilon + \mathcal{Z})^2 - \gamma_I \sigma^2/\Upsilon(\Upsilon + \mathcal{Z})^2 = 0$$

$$\partial/\partial \Upsilon = (\nu_l - \nu_s)/3 - \gamma_I \sigma^2/\Upsilon^2(\Upsilon + \mathcal{Z}) - \gamma_I \sigma^2/\Upsilon(\Upsilon + \mathcal{Z})^2 - \gamma_B \sigma^2/\mathcal{Z}(\Upsilon + \mathcal{Z})^2 = 0.$$

Let $\Upsilon = k\mathcal{Z}$. Substitution in the first-order maximum conditions leads to the simultaneous equations in k and $\mathcal{Z}$,

$$k^3 = (3\gamma_I k + 2\gamma_I)/\gamma_B$$
$$\mathcal{Z}^3 = \frac{3[\sigma^2 \gamma_I(2k+1) + \sigma^2 \gamma_B k^2]}{(\nu_l - \nu_s)k^2(k+1)^2}.$$

It is likely, but by no means certain, that the cost of physical investment γ_I will be significantly greater than the cost of borrowing γ_B. Suppose the cost ratio is of the order $\gamma_I = 5\gamma_B$. Then k will be slightly greater than 4; if $\gamma_I = 10\gamma_B$, then k is slightly more than 6. These values of k, of course, imply a ratio of H to $\mathcal{Z}$ greater than 3:1: When $k = 2$, $\mathcal{Z} = H/3$.

What of the value of $\mathcal{Z}$ for large k? Consider the case $\gamma_I/\gamma_B = 10.8$ which gives $k = 6$. Then,

$$\mathcal{Z}^3 = 3\gamma_B\sigma^2/10(\nu_l - \nu_s) = \gamma_I\sigma^2/36(\nu_l - \nu_s).$$

Notice that $\mathcal{Z}$ is smaller (in terms of γ_B or γ_I) than it would be with $\gamma_B = \gamma_I$; the range $H = (k+1)\mathcal{Z} = 7\mathcal{Z}$ is larger than would be the case with $\gamma_B = \gamma_I$.

It is conceivable, of course, that in some firms a backlog of well-justified investment projects awaits the availability of funds. Certain firms, for example, are known to have rigid policies against long-term borrowing, and they rely heavily on internally generated funds for capital expansion; projects with very high present value await funding. Without commenting on the wisdom of such practice, we offer the observation that the effect on the model will be to make the cost of investment smaller than the cost of borrowing, or $\gamma_I < \gamma_B$. The analysis of the second three-asset case can of course be modified to accommodate that change.

The analysis of the second three-asset case is vague concerning an important question: what is the appropriate term of security issues that the firm floats to meet liquidity needs? The analysis can be viewed as assuming that the firm issues consols, and retires them at a cost γ_I in amount $H - \mathcal{Z}$ per retirement, when available liquidity permits. The sloppiness of this view is apparent, but perhaps it can be justified with the stipulation that an entirely different model must be developed to regulate investment policy on those occasions when the firm has debt outstanding. In other words, the model is a device to regulate the frequency and amount of borrowing to meet liquidity needs; but it is not a suitable device for use at times when there is significant debt outstanding.

The alternative to what may appear as excessive pragmatism in that view is to stipulate a term of issue on borrowings to meet liquidity needs. Once that stipulation has been made, the dynamic consequences must be faced; future issues to cover securities that mature too early are costly; and the maintenance of or refunding of securities that do not mature soon enough is also costly.

These costs must be recognized in the analysis; the advantage of the "consol" view implicitly adopted in the model is that it defines the problem in terms that are easy to comprehend.

With random cash flows, it may be futile to devote much attention to the term of issue in the hope of lowering redemption costs. Unless accurate forecasts can be made of the time when cash inflows will make adequate liquidity available, there can be little benefit from trying to pick a cost-minimizing term of issue. With Bernoullian cash flows, the time until some specified balance is attained is a random variable with a highly skewed density function.[11] Expected values of these waiting times will be sufficient statistics only under very restrictive assumptions about the cost of forecast errors.

Certainly the topic of optimal term for security issue is one that requires analysis. For the purposes of analyzing money demand, a matter that merits closer attention, however, is implication of the second three-asset model when (a) security issues are for *any* fixed term; (b) cost of debt retirement differs from cost of capital investment; and (c) the opportunity cost of debt differs from the return on capital.

NOTES

1. This chapter is a substantial revision and extension of Miller and Orr (1968), Section III.
2. Exceptions are found in Porter's (1961) model of bank portfolio selection, and recent work of Eppen and Fama (1969b). The Eppen-Fama model treats all transfer costs as strictly proportional to the amount transfered, and they give no consideration to the possibility of a lumpy transfer cost.
3. The shorts of category (*a*) thus may or may not belong in an efficient portfolio according to criteria proposed by Markowitz (1959), who ignores transfer costs as a relevant element in portfolio decisions.
4. There are grounds *a priori* to suppose that the policy rules (l, i-v) will be hard to improve upon so long as both transfer costs are purely lumpy. A discussion of the optimality issue for the two-asset case is found in Chapter III, Section 7.
5. The values given in (2) and (3) are exact if the underlying process which generates cash transactions is Bernoullian, as we assume. If the cash transaction process is some other member of the Gaussian family, then both values are approximations which increase in accuracy as $z (h - z)/\sigma^2$ increases.
6. In effect, so long as the policy rules (l, i-v) are used, the flow through the shorts account will have the same variance as it would if the firm held no cash balance, but anticipated every cash payment by a security sale, and immediately followed every cash receipt by a security purchase.
7. See Tong-Hun Lee (1967).

8. There have been frequent occasions in recent years when short-term interest rates have exceeded long-term rates, at least on government securities. We won't go into the reasons underlying this "paradox", but we note that it doesn't vitiate the three-asset analysis developed in this chapter. There remains the hierarchy cash, treasury bills ("shorts"), and the firm's own debt; this is our second "three-asset" case, to be considered in Section 4 below.

9. The mean purchase size of shorts from cash is σ, and the mean sale transaction of shorts to correct a too-small holding of cash is σ. The probability of a purchase and a sale is $\sigma/(h+1)$. This approximation is spelled out in Wald (1946).

10. It should be emphasized that this is a highly restrictive condition, as anyone who tries to construct a model in which the condition is omitted will quickly realize. If the opportunity rate on borrowing differs from the capital return rate, a "four asset" model will be necessary, and some means will have to be imposed to limit the amount of borrowing for direct investment.

11. See Feller (1951), chapter xiv. The number of trials until passage of A, given an origin at z, will be n with probability

$$P_n = \frac{1}{A} \sum_{v=1}^{A-1} \cos^{n-1} \frac{\Pi v}{A} \cdot \sin \frac{\Pi v}{A} \cdot \sin \frac{\Pi (A-z) v}{A}$$

if the generating process is symmetric.

VII

The Household Demand
for Cash

1. SOME CRUCIAL DIFFERENCES BETWEEN FIRMS AND HOUSEHOLDS

F.: "You know, Ernest, corporations' cash flows are different from ours."

H.: "Yes, I know. Firms get and write checks far more often and for far more money than we do."

Had Scott Fitzgerald and Ernest Hemingway been tuned in to problems of money management, their widely quoted[1] exchange might have taken the indicated form. The reader must decide whether the conjectural revised conversation gains on the (apocryphal?) original in incisiveness and relevance what it loses in whimsy. Had Hemingway made the point contained in the revised form, and had the point somehow survived despite its eminently forgettable phrasing, we might have been spared several years of thrashing about on the part of the monetary economists who tried to rationalize the Baumol model as a paradigm for money demand by firms, who searched for subtle differences between Baumol's and the formally identical Tobin version of the (s, S) inventory policy, and who finally inevitably lapsed into the easy but perhaps also incorrect position that the "inventory approach" lacks predictive, and hence analytical, substance.

I hope the analytical material on random walks, and descriptive material on daily corporate cash flows, in the foregoing chapters will convince the reader of two things: that the simple s, S policy (or Baumol-Tobin model) is unsuitable as a device for money demand analysis in the corporate sector, because it overlooks or ignores the importance of the diffusion component in cash flows; and more suitable models have been devised, and afford promising approaches.

If optimizing models are to be taken seriously as potentially useful indicators of asset demand, they should be prescriptively appropriate for the decision-maker whose behavior is under study. In the present chapter, the objective is to show that inventory models of the Baumol-Tobin variety, when properly handled, *may be* useful instruments for the study of money demand in the *household* sector. A priori analysis based on extensions of that model may or may not offer useful and valid insight into the problem of how households handle money. In fact, it may be that no simple optimizing model is appropriate to a sufficiently large group of households to yield good predictions of the sector as a whole. The amount of diversity in cash flows and operating goals may be greater here even than is true in the corporate sector. Such issues must be settled empirically— or by devising such compellingly good models that they are widely adopted for decision purposes once their existence is known.[2] For what it is worth, the analysis that we turn to now suggests that two classes of decision—savings decisions, and decisions regarding the use of consumer credit—may have especially important bearing on household money stocks. These two classes of decision should not be operative in the corporate sector.

2. HOUSEHOLD CASH BALANCE MANAGEMENT

The receipt side of a typical household cash flow probably is dominated by regularly spaced relatively large receipts, representing a monthly, bimonthly, or weekly salary check. Payments, no doubt, are usually smaller in size and more frequent, and perhaps are irregularly timed over the salary period. In considering control policies to monitor such a flow, we suppose that the opportunity cost of holding cash is the rate obtainable on earning assets, or ν per dollar per period. We also let $\gamma + m\tau$ be the cost of transferring m dollars between cash and "bonds," the earning assets. Initially for analytical purposes it is assumed that there is only one type or class of earning asset that can serve as an alternative to cash; this condition is relaxed in Section 4 below.

Existing analyses of money management based on the s, S control policy suggest that the household, upon receipt of $\$M$ in the form of a salary check, uses a part of the receipt to purchase a bloc of bonds. As time passes, the cash retained from the salary receipt is used up, and then $\$M/n$ of the bond holding is liquidated at cost $\gamma + \tau M/n$ to replenish the cash balance. It is convenient and customary further to assume that the household's salary receipt exactly equals its total flow of payments during the salary period, and that the payments flow is uniform throughout the period.[3]

The household's decision problem then is conventionally described this way: find the optimal value of n, the number of bond purchases and sales during the salary interval, when the objective function is

$$
(1) \qquad C(n) = \begin{cases} n\gamma + M\nu/2n + 2\tau M(n-1)/n & n = 2,\ 3\ \ldots \\ \\ M\nu/2 & n = 0. \end{cases}
$$

The case $n = 1$ is ruled out as a possibility, since it would entail making a purchase of bonds, with no provision for their subsequent resale within the same period. In (1), γ, τ and ν are the cost coefficients as defined above, and M is the magnitude of receipts and total payments during the salary period. $C(n)$ then is the cost of cash balance management during one of a sequence of identical salary periods; and a choice of n that is optimal for one period is optimal for any and all periods, since conditions affecting the decision are assumed to be stationary. The first cost term is due to the fact that n transfers are made during the period: a security purchase followed by $n - 1$ sales.[4] The second cost term reflects the assumption that payments are a uniform flow over time, and attaches the opportunity cost ν to the average cash balance $M/2n$. The third term assumes that all security sales during the period are of the same size, and each sale is equal in dollar amount to the cash balance withheld from the purchase of bonds at the start of the period.[5] The fraction $(n-1)/n$ of the salary payment M then is transferred into and out of earning assets during the period, and each time the cost τ per dollar is incurred.

The expression (1) is locally minimized where n is an integer satisfying the difference conditions on (1)

$$(2) \qquad \Delta C(n) = C(n+1) - C(n) \geq 0$$
$$\Delta C(n-1) = C(n) - C(n-1) \leq 0.$$

To find a global optimum, it is necessary to make a comparison of the $C(n)$ for all positive N satisfying (2), and the boundary case $C(0)$. The conditions (2) are

$$(3) \qquad (n-1)n \leq M(\nu - 4\tau)/2\gamma \leq n(n+1).$$

First, note that $\nu > 4\tau$ is requisite if a meaningful (positive) solution is to be found. This is not a trivial requirement. Suppose $\nu = 1/2\%$ per month; then τ must be on the order of .1% or less on the amount transferred to make the temporary investment of transactions balances thinkable.

Even if $\tau = 0$, however, there are obstacles to the short-term investment transfer program. Suppose again that the opportunity rate is 6% per annum, or .005 per month. Suppose further that γ is on the order of \$2, which is not excessively high even when considered only as a brokerage charge, in light of the magnitudes of transfer that will emerge. With cost coefficients τ and γ of those magnitudes, in order that it be economical for the household to engage in *any* transfer activity, the value of the monthly salary M must be about \$1,600; which means that the household in question must be in the top 5 per cent or so of the income distribution, questions of non-salary income and saving out of salary aside.

With a zero value of τ, the proportional cost of transfer, the condition (3) implies that

$$(4) \qquad n^* \approx (M\nu/2\gamma)^{1/2}.$$

If the order-of-magnitude problems that affect the relevance of the analysis are ignored, we will be led to the prediction that households have a transaction demand elasticity for cash of $1/2$; that is, if a household's income (and its volume of payment transactions) quadruples, the average cash balance held by the household should double. This prediction is based on the expectation that the average cash balance $\overline{M}$ would be about $m/2n$, or

$$(5) \qquad \overline{M} \approx \left(\frac{\gamma M}{2\nu}\right)^{1/2},$$

which in turn hangs on the condition that payment transactions be more or less regularly spaced in time. Similarly, the interest elasticity of the household demand for cash would upon too-literal interpretation of (4) be taken to be $-1/2$.

However, acknowledging the relevant magnitudes of cost coefficients, we are led to suggest that these elasticities are respectively more nearly 1 and 0; the order of magnitude of the relevant variables dictate that the "corner solution" involving zero transfers is optimal for most households.[6] We conclude, reluctantly, that short-term asset management decisions have little importance in shaping household money demand; we must turn instead to such variables as the propensity to save in search of good predictions about household cash balances.

There are, of course, possibilities which if realized would mean that this conjectural and theory-based conclusion is wrong. In some areas, there is an apparent aversion to demand deposits in the household sector. Time deposits are the repository of personal income, and currency is the dominant medium of exchange. If fear of loss surmounts the other less rational impulses underlying such an arrangement, then we can expect that the elasticity of money balances with respect to the transactions rate will be substantially less than unity, so long as time deposits are not defined to be part of the money supply.

3. Saving and Household Cash Balances

It is obvious that regular saving in the amount S per period will reduce transactions balances in the household sector. For instead of an average transaction balance of $M/2$ without saving, the average balance will be $(M - S)/2$. Happily enough, the obvious conclusion as stated may be completely wrong, and in fact, a typical household's cash balance may rise when the household saves. The conclusion that saving diminishes average cash balances is always true so long as the cash account is not used as a temporary repository for savings; but when adjustment transfer costs are significant, it may be economical to purchase securities for saving at intervals of several periods, and to hold "idle cash" between savings purchases.[7]

Suppose, then, that once every k periods the household purchases $\$kS$ worth of earning assets for saving, and the fraction $(n - 1)/n$ of the transaction balance $M - S$ also is invested on a short-term basis; during the period, these short-term holdings are restored to the cash balance by $n - 1$ security sales. However, in the intervening periods $1, 2, \ldots k - 1$, no cash balance management transfers are made, since to do so without making a transfer for saving purposes involves excessive costs of transfer. The costs of cash balance maintenance encountered in this savings program are fairly simple in structure. Through the first $k - 1$ periods, only the opportunity cost of idle cash is incurred. In the kth period, transfer costs arise as well. In the first period, the average transaction balance is $(M - S)/2$, and the savings balance is S. Thus, opportunity cost is $(M + S)/2$. An amount $\$S$ per period is added to this balance in every period through the $k - 1$st. In the kth period the average balance falls to $(M - S)/2n$, but $\$n$ in transfer cost also arises. The k-period cost is

$$\frac{v(M + S)}{2} + \frac{v(M + 3S)}{2} + \ldots + \frac{v[M + (2k - 1)S]}{2}$$
$$+ n\gamma + \frac{v(M - S)}{2n}; \ k > 1,$$

which implies an average cost per period of

$$(6) \quad C = \frac{1}{k} \left[\frac{(k - 1) vM + (k - 1)^2 vS}{2} + n\gamma + \frac{v(M - S)}{2n} \right] k \geq 1,$$

since the sum of the first $k - 1$ odd integers is $(k - 1)^2$.

In this first view, the level of saving S is assumed to be exogenously determined. The objective of the household is to minimize C with respect to k and n. The first difference conditions

(7) $(n-1)n \le \nu(M-S)/2\gamma < n(n+1)$
      $(k-1)k \le [2n^2\gamma + \nu(M-S) - n\nu M]/n\nu S < k(k+1)$

are necessary to the objective. The conditions (7) permit us to demarcate the alternatives open to the household. If $k=1$, then we can take any integer value for n. That is, if a saving transfer is made in every period, any number of cash balance management transfers conceivably can accompany it. If $k>1$, then n is limited to the values 1, 2. If it is uneconomical to make saving transfers in every period, it will not be economical to let more than one cash management transfer go for a "free ride" at the time when transfer costs are incurred for savings purposes. Conditions determining the various possible outcomes are tabulated in Table XV; they are derived from the inequalities (7).

TABLE XV

$n \diagdown k$	1	2	>2
1	$2\gamma < 3\nu S$	$4\gamma > \nu(M-S)$ $3\nu S \le 2\gamma \le 7\nu S$	$7\nu S \le 2\gamma$
2	$8\gamma - \nu M < 5\nu S$	$12\gamma > \nu(M-S) \ge 4\gamma$ $5\nu S \le 8\gamma - \nu M < 13\nu S$	$13\nu S \le 8\gamma - \nu M$
>2	$18\gamma - 2\nu M < 7\nu S$	$\nu(M-S \ge 12\gamma$ $7\nu S \le 18\gamma - 2\nu M \le 13\nu S$*	$13\nu S \le 18\gamma - 2\nu M$*

* Note contradictory conditions for $n>2$, $k>1$; when $k>1$, it is necessary that $n\le 2$.

The household's average cash balance, when savings transfers are made less often than once per period, will be (by the same calculations that let to (7)),

(8) $[M + (k - 2)S]/2 \geq \overline{M}_S \geq [(2k - 1)M + (2k^2 - 4k + 1)S]/4k,$
$$k > 1.$$

The upper bound on $\overline{M}_S$ holds when there are no cash management transfers, and the lower bound holds if one transfer (the maximum allowable number) is made for cash management purposes during the period when the savings transfer is made. When $k = 1$, savings transfers are made in every period, and the average cash balance is reduced to $(M - S)/2$ instead of $M/2$. For $k > 1$, $n = 1$, average cash holdings are increased by saving. For $k = 2$, $n = 2$, they are reduced; for $k > 2$, $n = 2$ the comparison depends on the magnitudes (of M, S, k, v and γ) specific to the case.

4. DEMAND ELASTICITIES WITH SAVING

The introduction of a savings decision into the discussion of household cash balances befogs the interesting question of transactions and interest elasticities. Suppose, as is customary, that the rate of saving is held to depend on disposable income and the rate of interest,[8] i.e.

$$S = S(M, v).$$

For households that engage in no cash management transfers, the mean cash balance in the presence of saving is

(9) $\overline{M}_S = [M + (k - 2)S]/2$

from (8), where

(10) $k \sim \left(\dfrac{2\gamma}{vS} - 1\right)^{1/2},$

obtained by setting $n = 1$ in the second expression of (7). Combining expressions (9) and (10),

$$\overline{M}_S = M/2 - S + [(2\gamma S - vS^2)/4v]^{1/2}.$$

Naturally, v is taken as the appropriate interest rate in a derivation of interest elasticity. Although $M - S$ is probably the best transactions measure, M will be used in the derivation of transactions elasticity. These elasticities are respectively

$$\epsilon_\nu = \frac{\partial \overline{M}_S}{\partial \nu} \cdot \nu/\overline{M}_S = \frac{2}{M - 2S + [2\gamma S - \nu S^2)/\nu]^{1/2}}$$

$$\cdot \left\{ -\nu S_\nu + \frac{\nu\gamma S_\nu - \nu S S_\nu - \gamma S}{2\nu[(2\gamma S - \nu S^2)/\nu]^{1/2}} \right\}$$

$$\epsilon_M = \frac{\partial \overline{M}_S}{\partial M} \cdot M/\overline{M}_S = \frac{2}{M - 2S + [(2\gamma S - \nu S^2)/\nu]^{1/2}}$$

$$\cdot \left\{ \tfrac{1}{2} - S_M + \frac{\gamma S_M - \nu S S_M}{2\nu[(2\gamma S - \nu S^2)/\nu]^{1/2}} \right\},$$

where S_ν and S_M are respectively the partial derivatives $\partial S/\partial \nu$ and $\partial S/\partial M$. Obviously, the transactions and interest elasticities no longer have simple constant values, and each depends critically upon the response of saving to either income M or interest ν. Notice that symmetry present in the simple Baumol model: $\epsilon_M = -\epsilon_\nu = 1/2$: disappears when saving is going on.

The foregoing analysis is completely deterministic; that is, it embodies no element of randomness in the cash flow or elsewhere. Two avenues for generalization to stochastic cash flows can confidently be suggested: the cash flow can be depicted as a non-zero drift Bernoulli or other random process, which is appropriate when there is uncertainty regarding both receipt and payment flows; or a stochastic version of the s, S policy can be analyzed, which is appropriate when receipts are certain but there is uncertainty concerning the volume of payments in each period (and hence, when the volume of savings is randomly determined).[9] Neither line will be pursued explicitly in the remainder of this chapter, since reinterpretation of existing literature in the context of household money management should be a straightforward matter. Elasticity predictions probably will not change significantly from those of this section in the presence of either generalization about cash flows, but the "regular sawtooth" pattern envisioned in the Baumol model and still present in the version with savings will no longer characterize the cash balance.

It is extremely simple and perhaps descriptively fruitful to make the payments flow non-uniform over time in the foregoing non-stochastic model. For example, a household may make its major monthly payments (on credit accounts, installment purchases, and rent or mortgage) coincide with the monthly salary receipt. If the "first-of-the-month" payments volume is P, then $(M - P)$ can be substituted for M throughout the analysis of Section 1.

5. A THREE-ASSET ANALYSIS

Another avenue of generalization does offer the possibility of finding significant results beyond those already reported or available elsewhere in the literature. The analysis can readily be extended in the manner of Chapter VI, in which three distinct classes of asset are analytically incorporated. While such an extension cannot be looked upon as a solution of the household's portfolio problems, it does offer a framework in which to investigate whether anything happens to money demand when, for example, it appears economical to make accumulations in a time account until the volume is "adequate" to make a purchase of common stocks. The objectives and decisions of a household operating in such a three-asset environment are formalized as follows: Every k periods a savings transfer from cash to a "short" account is made. The transfer cost is γ_s. Then every K periods a transfer is made to the permanent savings repository or "long" account, with $\$S$ coming from cash, and $\$(K-1)S$ from the short account.[10] A cost γ_s is incurred in liquidating the short account and γ_l in making the purchase of longs. The average cash balance will be $\bar{m}_S$ (9), and the average balance in the "shorts" account will be $(K-1)S/2$ (since the account is empty in the first period after a transfer to longs; and contains $\$jS$ in period $j+1$ after a transfer). The opportunity costs per dollar held in cash and shorts are respectively v_l and $(v_l - v_s)$. Transfers into or out of the short account occur once every k periods, and transfers into the long account occur once every K periods. The household, then, seeks

$$(11) \quad \min_{k,\ K} \left\{ \frac{M + (k-2)Sv_l}{2} + \frac{v_s}{k} + \frac{(v_l - v_s)(K-1)S}{2} + \frac{v_l}{K} \right\}.$$

The necessary conditions are

(12) $(k-1)k \leq 2\gamma_s/S\nu_l \leq k(k+1)$
            $(K-1)K \leq 2\gamma_l/S(\nu_l - \nu_s) \leq K(K+1).$

The formulation (11) assumes that no intraperiod transfers between cash and the short account are made for the purpose of cash balance management; in the notation of Section 2, $n = 1$ by assumption.[11]

From the optimality conditions (12) the approximations

$$k^* \approx (2\gamma_s/S\nu_l)^{1/2}$$
$$K^* \approx [2\gamma_l/S(\nu_l - \nu_s)]^{1/2}$$

are derived.

As an alternative to (11), the household should consider the possibility that it will be economical to bypass the short account entirely, and to accumulate an economical transfer quantity in the cash account before moving directly into longs. The objective in so operating, with a transfer interval of J periods, is

(13) $$\min_{J} \left\{ \left[\frac{M + (J-2)S}{2}\right] \nu_l + \frac{\gamma_l}{J} \right\},$$

as in the two-asset analysis of Section 2. The optimal J turns out to be

$$J^* \approx (2\gamma_l/S\nu_l)^{1/2}.$$

By substituting J^*, k^* and K^* in the appropriate objective functions, we find that (12) is a preferable objective to (13) so long as

$$[2\gamma_l S(\nu_l - \nu_s)]^{1/2} < \frac{S}{2}(\nu_l - \nu_s) + (2\nu_l S)^{1/2}(\gamma_l^{1/2} - \gamma_s^{1/2}).$$

The mean cash balances associated with the two cases are respectively

$$M/2 - S + (\gamma_s S/2\nu_l)^{1/2}$$
$$M/2 - S + (\gamma_l S/2\nu_l)^{1/2}.$$

In either case, the cash balance is sensitive only to the long rate, the rate on the permanent part of the portfolio, as in the "purely lumpy γ" case of Chapter VI; unless the rate of saving depends on the short rate. Given the customary formulation of saving objectives, it is inoffensive to proceed as though the saving relation were

$$S = S(M, \nu_l).$$

If the formulation holds up empirically, the analysis implies simply that the long rate is the appropriate opportunity rate on household cash balances. Another point on which the formulation and finding may be vulnerable is noted in the next section.

6. CONSUMER CREDIT: CONJECTURAL REMARKS

Consumer credit may have an extremely important determining influence on cash balance demand. Consumer credit makes the payments flow less uniform and the average cash balance smaller if households tend to make payments on installment purchases and credit card accounts synchronously with the salary receipt. This effect of consumer credit on cash balances can be handled in the manner described in the last paragraph of Section 4.

To the extent that interest rates affect installment buying, there is empirical merit in using consumer credit rates to predict money demand. Empirical objectives would be served best by the choice of a period in which the consumer credit rates don't move with long-term asset returns; for conventional savings objectives are probably most closely related to the latter rate. If returns on long term assets are closely related to terms on consumer credit, then the interest effect on cash balances may be hard to identify, for interest should affect money directly through normal saving objectives and through the opportunity cost in the objective function, and inversely through the cost of consumer credit.

Consumer credit also offers an alternative to precautionary holdings of the "short" security. In Section 5, the three-asset analysis pegged the shorts holding only on consideration of adjustment transfer costs. It would seem that the shorts balance is also an excellent place to hold an emergency fund against medical emergencies, automobile failures, or other unforeseeable cash needs. Liquidations of longs in the face of such contingencies can mean high cost of transfer; and further problems arise if values are depressed in the long portfolio at the time of an emergency. Consumer credit, of course, offers an alternative to the liquidation of longs when liquidation would be expensive.

Depending on how emergencies are anticipated, the precautionary motive may not show up as a perpetual buffer stock in the cash account. In a three-asset world without consumer credit, emergency needs will be met out of cash and shorts holdings—the lower the transfer cost γ_s, the more likely is the shorts account to be the repository. If consumer credit is available, and the "transfer costs" of gaining access to it are small, then neither the cash or shorts account will be as large as otherwise. Cheaply accessible consumer credit thus has a twofold impact in diminishing money holdings: less cash will be held for precautionary purposes, and as noted before, greater "fixed" payment demands will be made on the cash account early in the payment period. The effect of credit on money demand, in fact, is well captured in two questions, for which a three-asset analysis is unnecessary: Do we hold currency or demand deposits to meet emergencies and to buy the "big things" we want? Or do we borrow for these purposes, and make repayment out of future income receipts?

NOTES

1. By Paul Samuelson, in the several editions of his best seller.
2. Surprisingly often, operations research-oriented writers take this ambitious and optimistic view.
3. The model in this standard formulation doesn't provide for the expenditure of interest earned on the invested portion of the cash balance. This is a trivial oversight in dollars-and-cents terms; to correct it will not affect the conclusions drawn here in a significant way, and will entail substantial analytical effort.
4. In his independent derivation and extension of Baumol's results, Tobin shows that no bonds purchases will occur optimally except at the time cash is received. See Tobin (1956).
5. These conditions on the size and timing of securities-to-cash asset transfers also follow optimally from the assumed cost and cash flow conditions which in particular abstract from speculative considerations. See Tobin (1956).

6. This prediction is qualitatively supported, so far as transactions elasticities are concerned, in the empirical work of J. J. McCall (1960).

7. A point much like this is made by George Akerlof (1969) ; and Duesenberry (1963) makes much of the same idea. The point gains in force when "daily interest" is not available on time deposits or saving and loan shares. Daily interest (*pro rata* interest payment, from arbitrary date of deposit to arbitrary date of withdrawal) makes those interest-bearing alternatives very attractive as places to hold the sums out of which securities purchases are to be made. Costs of transfer into and out of cash probably are quite low for most people.

8. A useful byproduct of reliable empirical tests of this model, with implications beyond the question of money demand, is further information about the response of personal saving to the interest rate. Empirical evidence on the relation between savings and interest is not very conclusive, so far as aggregate saving behavior is concerned. See Tobin (1968).

   Evidence at the individual household level is, so far as I can find, nonexistent.

9. The second alternative offers a genuine opportunity to examine the relevance of a distinction between "transactions" balances and "precautionary" balances. In a cash flow regime of complete drift, where inflows and outflows both are completely predictable, cash balances will be held solely for the purpose of economizing on transaction costs. Thus, a necessary condition to the existence of precautionary balances is diffusion or uncertainty in the cash flow. But diffusion is not a sufficient condition. Suppose that whenever the household's balance fell to zero, cash could be obtained instantly by sale of bonds. It is conceivable that cash balances would have the same average value as in the case of wholly predictable flows, and there would be nothing that could properly be regarded as a precautionary holding. Finally, suppose there is some delay in implementing a decision to replenish the cash account. (Such a delay may stem from the need to wait for a run-off in the earning portfolio, or the absence of an earning portfolio and the need to wait for a new receipt.) With delays and uncertain flows, it is wholly rational to hold more cash than would be held in their absence. The extra balance held may be called a precautionary balance, but there is no point in this taxonomical indulgence unless the balance responds in a way different from the transactions balance to shifts in transactions flows or interest rates.

   It should also be noted that an attempt to predict the two effects independently will generally result in an overestimate of cash balances, for the two effects are non-additive. To see a simple inventory model that captures this "interdependence" between transactions and precautionary balances, turn to T. M. Whitin (1957). Finally, observe that random cash flows, in conjunction with savings accumulation in the cash balance, will cause the cash balance to depart widely in its behavior over time from the regular sawtooth configuration made familiar by Baumol and Tobin.

10. Appropriate measures of the "short" and "long" rates might be respectively the rate on saving and loan deposits, and an average return over an expected lifetime on a randomly selected New York Stock Exchange portfolio.

11. From (7) and Table VII–A we see that $n = 1$ follows optimally in the two-asset case so long as $4\gamma > \nu(M - S)$.

VIII

Application to Business Practice

1. BACKGROUND

About twenty-five years have passed since the "new wave" of managerial technique first lapped at American business. An applied science, which called itself operations research, began to attract talent from various mathematical, scientific and engineering disciplines, with the central goal of comprehending practical problems in models. This discipline soon boasted at least three technical journals, and some of the contributions that appeared in *Management Science, Operations Research* and *Naval Research Logistics Quarterly* have been durably influential and interesting. Most of the contributions to the new discipline have been concerned with economics in the Robbins sense— the allocation of scarce resources among alternative uses.[1]

In conjunction with, or perhaps as a result of, the hoopla accompanying operations research there emerged the view that operations research "software" and computer hardware would succeed in replacing human decision and judgment to a great extent—much of the management process could be automated. This has proved to be possible only in a few specialized contexts, such as in the management of oil refinery operations, and even in these cases, the extent and significance of the achievement may be overstressed. It is more realistic to view these modern hardware and software developments as tools of management. Paper and pencil models, and computer-based numerical analyses and simulations can help the manager who is skilled in their use to locate potential bottlenecks before they become actual bottlenecks, to avoid destabilizing decision rules, and to identify crucial relationships within or overlapping the span of his control.

Cash management is a problem that escaped extensive treatment in the OR literature during the early years. Extravagant attention was devoted to other similar problems of asset management, especially inventory management; and even difficult problems of capital theory were occasionally tackled. But on the question of cash balances, the first gun was fired by an economist, in an economics journal, and the vocabulary and issues were from Keynes.[2] Perhaps the reason for this lack of attention can be found in the then prevalent earnings rates on liquid debt instruments—by the standards of 1965–70, the interest rates of the accord period and beyond were absurdly low, and the opportunity cost of holding cash hardly merited notice.

The purpose of the present chapter is to examine the ways in which admittedly crude models such as the basic model of Chapter III, can serve as management tools in the specific context of cash management. Case studies can be instructive, for a number of reasons—they reveal much about the nature of cash flows and the problems of cash management; they tell us something about the importance of having good solid "inside" information, and they re-emphasize the complementarity between the problems of prediction and control.

2. Approaches to the Problem of Liquidity in the Firm

It would be delusion to suggest that there is significant uniformity in the practice of cash management in business firms. Two polar extremes, and a range of behavior in between, seem to capture most approaches to the problem. The first extreme reflects an attitude, sometimes fostered at the highest level of corporate management, that "it isn't our business or in our stockholders' interest to play the treasury bill (or short-term paper) market." In such situations, the opportunity to earn interest on idle cash is not viewed as an opportunity at all, and a high cash-sales ratio is taken as an important benchmark of sound operation. Lines of credit in commercial banks, if they exist at all, are short and little used, and short-term indebtedness is frowned upon as a manifestation of recklessness or lack of foresight. The operating mode in this case, then, is to maintain a *positive* cash balance, and to expend little effort on controlling the balance.

The opposite extreme is characterized by an attitude that money is a scarce and costly productive resource. In such companies, projects with short payout periods and prospective rates of return in the vicinity of 30 per cent await the availability of investable funds. Compensating balance agreements with banks are negotiated to do double duty—they cover a reasonable volume of ordinary transaction activity, and they serve as payment, in whole or in part, for lines of credit. These credit lines are seldom used (especially if additional compensating balances are required when the credit is taken down). Rather, they serve as security for short-term debt flotations— the presence of bank credit enhances the marketability of the firm's issues, and permits flotation at lower rates than would be paid if the credit lines themselves were used. Thus, the ready availability of bank credit is a crucial and pivotal element in obtaining acceptance for short term securities issues; but actual cash on hand may typically be small (50 per cent or less) compared to short term debt outstanding.

This highly committed short-term debt position enables the firm to cover its transaction needs with very little reliance on internally generated capital. In effect, the firm is operating with a *negative* cash balance, reflecting the view that the internal rate of return justifies the investment of liquid capital and the reliance on short-term borrowings to meet liquidity needs. Borrowed capital also is the basis of much of the firm's expansion, but this activity usually is funded by longer term debt issues.[3]

So far as flow maintenance is concerned, a variety of measures are available for economizing on cash. Receivables collection is speeded up by locating special bank accounts around the country, within one day's postal service range of heavy concentrations of customers. These banks automatically clear the firm's balances (above and beyond some level to compensate for service) into more heavily-used repository accounts. The firm then makès its payments out of the several repository accounts so as to maximize float time: New York payments are drawn against Los Angeles banks, and vice versa. A further refinement is the use of sight drafts, rather than checks, for some large payments. These drafts must await the payer's approval, and by approving once per day, in the morning, float time is in effect stretched out an average of 18 hours or so. Interest payments to banks that hold the outstanding sight draft balances overnight are routine; these balances are tantamount to a line of credit that is unsecured by compensating balances.[4]

Several questions are raised by this "sharp pencil" approach to cash management. (a) Does the frequency of dealing and trading lead to a large volume of adjustment costs that could be avoided if a more relaxed approach were taken? (b) Does extensive short-term borrowing, for purposes of meeting peak net outflows of cash, weaken the market for the firm's long term issues? (c) Perhaps most crucial of all, is the firm forced to borrow unnecessarily often or in unnecessarily large volume as a result of operations with cash balances that appear low in light of compensating balance agreements? Such borrowing actions may be based upon forecast information, and the problem of excessive or unnecessary borrowing may be diagnosed as a need for better forecasting. That diagnosis is correct only if better forecasts are a cheaper solution than the alternative solution, of adopting a looser control regime that is less vulnerable to forecast misinformation. In cash management, as in all operations involving the control of randomly fluctuating systems, the danger of over-control is always present.

Varying degrees of confidence can be attached to the answers to these questions. The first question, concerning the firm's susceptibility to adjustment costs, is the hardest to answer of the three. Adjustment costs are elusive. The managerial effort and time involved in an incremental purchase of treasury bills or sale of the firm's own paper may look small, precisely because the firm has adapted its organizational structure to assure that adjustment costs will not be a major nuisance. Managerial functions are so defined that the cash-debt responsibility is compartmentalized; the man in charge would simply be less busy were he to loosen his grip on those matters. Further, it can be argued that with high interest rates, a man, or even a small group, that can enable the firm to reduce its average cash holding by $2 million or so, more than pays for itself on a full-time basis. Where, then, are the adjustment costs? The firm's short-term debt is sold through a bond house which makes its money on a spread. Moreover, the spread pricing arrangement means that the cost of placement is a proportional cost, paid out over the term of the issue. If the problem is to farm excess money out, adjustment costs are softened by the fact that treasury bills are proportional cost instruments, at least they appear so at first glance. These objections to concern over adjustment costs, particularly lumpy adjustment costs, are hard to answer—however, a case study reported in Section 5 is instructive.

The second question, concerning the effect of heavy short term debt issues on the ability of the firm to borrow long, is almost as hard to answer. Two effects must be weighed if tight financial management enhances the firm's profitability. Higher profitability means that new equity capital will cost less. On the other hand it has been conventional to regard a high cash position as a mark of soundness, and consequently, a low cash position might damage credit ratings. The issue hangs on the extent to which tight management is profitable, and the speed with which that news of profitable practice finds its way into the murky recesses of the financial rating services, which play such a large role in determining the cost of new debt to a firm.

3. EFFECTS OF FORECAST ERRORS

The last question, concerning the possibility of excessive response in the form of too-frequent borrowing, is easier to answer.

Consider a cash management decision rule of the form

$$(1) \qquad C_t = \hat{A}_t + \alpha(M_t^* - M_{t-1}) \qquad 0 < \alpha \le 1,$$

where C_t signifies the magnitude of a control action in period t (either short-term borrowing to increase cash, or a short-term security purchase to "put cash holdings to work"); $\hat{A}_t$ is the forecast of net cash flow activity (payments and receipts) during period t; α is an adjustment smoothing coefficient; M_{t-1} is cash on hand at the *end* of the period $t - 1$; and M_t^* is the target cash balance for period t. In such a scheme, the decision involves three critical internally controlled variables, $\hat{A}_t$, the forecast; α, the speed of adjustment; and M_t^*, the target cash balance level for the end of the period. The cash balance varies in accord with the transition rule

$$(2) \qquad M_t = M_{t-1} + C_t - A_t,$$

where A_t is actual cash account activity during period t (payments less receipts), and C_t is the net control action during t (borrowing less lending). In the present section, our objective is to see the effects that various combinations of the variables $\hat{A}$, M^* and α have on the stability of cash balances and control decisions.

A decision rule of the form (1) may be worthwhile (depending on how well the discretionary values $\hat{A}$, α and M^* are set) so long as adjustment costs do not contain a large or significant lumpy component. Should lumpy costs of adjustment be present, the strategy of adjusting every period is unattractive compared to the alternative offered by some form of relaxation response rule.[5]

In the context of the rule (1), we can say that the firm is exercising tight control of its cash balance if (a) serious effort is devoted to the flow forecast, so as to reduce each term of the sequence of differences between forecasted and realized values $\{|A_t - \hat{A}_t|\}$; (b) if adjustment to target cash balance levels is rapid (α is near 1 in magnitude); and (3) if M^* is low, which must be judged in terms of the ability to forecast and the speed of corrective responses. Note that it makes little or no sense to forecast accurately and to adjust rapidly to a *high* cash target level: the three kinds of cost involved (of forecasting, of adjusting, and of holding cash) are all high in that case.

Cash receipt and payment flows, designated A_t in the preceding paragraph, are subject to a fundamental variability that effectively is uncontrolled by the firm. The variability of receipts can be *increased* by the firm—it has but to bunch the due dates on the bills it sends out. On the payments side, there usually is little leeway—fixed obligations such as payroll must be met on time; there is little merit in paying a bill a week before it is due, and a discount may be sacrificed if payment is delayed past the due date. While it may be possible to force a higher degree of synchronization between receipts and payments, it is not likely that it will be economical to do so.

If the decision rule (1) is well structured and operating smoothly, the fundamental variability of cash flows will not be greatly amplified by the control process. Harlan D. Mills (1967), in an interesting and important paper, establishes a definitive criterion of control performance in terms of the amplification of variability. Mills shows that regardless of the decision rule employed, there are constraints on the firm's ability to cut down on the variability in its cash balances and its borrowing-lending control decisions. In fact, there is a fundamental "conservation of variability" that affects any control decision process under uncertainty.

Mills' analysis proceeds as follows. In any cash flow system, a *stable* control process is defined as one in which the expected level of cash balances is not increasing over time, i.e.

$$\overline{M}_t = \overline{M}_{t-1} \qquad V_t,$$

where the overbars denote expected values. For a stable process with stationary, independent random activity flows, (2) can be rewritten

$$(M_t - \overline{M}) = (M_{t-1} - \overline{M}) + (C_t - \overline{C}) + (A_t - \overline{A})$$

(if the sequence A_t is composed of independent, identically distributed random variables, $\overline{A}$ is invariant over time as shown).

We can square both sides and take expectations, obtaining the expression

$$\sigma_M^2 = \sigma_M^2 + \sigma_A^2 + \sigma_C^2 + 2\rho\sigma_M\sigma_C,$$

where ρ is the correlation coefficient between the sequence of cash balance levels and the sequence of net borrowing and lending control actions. Transposing, and using the condition $-1 \le \rho \le 1$, we see that

$$\sigma_M\sigma_C \ge -\rho\ \sigma_M\sigma_C = [\sigma_A^2 + \sigma_C^2]/2,$$

which implies the condition

(3) $$\frac{\sigma_M}{\sigma_A} \ge \frac{1}{2}\left[\frac{\sigma_C}{\sigma_A} + \frac{\sigma_A}{\sigma_C}\right].$$

A plot of the relation (3) reveals a surface or boundary which delimits the "smoothing capacity" of control policies under the assumed conditions describing cash flows (Figure XIII); it is impossible to design a policy that will yield values of the critical variances such that the system operates below the curve FF′, unless some information about specific values of the $\{A_t\}$ sequence is obtained.

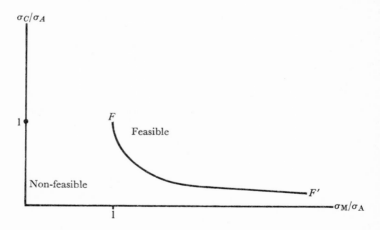

Figure XIII.   Mills' "Smoothing Capacity" Frontier

Mills' result can be used as a benchmark against which control performance is judged. If actual performance yields ratios σ_M/σ_A and σ_C/σ_A substantially to the right and above the "smoothing capacity frontier" FF', then significant variability is being introduced into the system by the decision process.

This variability can be a good manifestation—as when lumpy adjustment costs are present. With lumpy costs it will be desirable to utilize a relaxation response policy; and if the costs of adjustment are *purely* lumpy (no proportional element is present) then an (h, z) policy will be used. As it is applied in the basic model of Chapter III, the (h, z) policy yields the values (given $h = 3z$)

$$\sigma_A^2 = 1, \ \sigma_M^2 = \sum_x [x - \tfrac{4}{3}z]^2 P_x, \text{ and } \sigma_C^2 = 1,$$

where in σ_M^2,

$$Px = \begin{cases} 2x/3z^2 & 0 \le x \le z \\ (3z - x)/3z & z < x \le 3z. \end{cases}$$

It follows that whenever $z > 1$, σ_M^2 is greater than 1. Hence, the left side of (3) will be greater than the right side. However, the variability is magnified because the control activity shows a pattern of large, infrequent adjustments, and that pattern is justified on the ground that it avoids excessive adjustment costs.

Suppose, by contrast, that control adjustments are frequent and small compared to those generated by a relaxation response adjustment regime. This suggests that concern over lumpy adjustment costs is not an underlying cause of poor smoothing performance. The trouble may lie in excessive reliance on poor forecast information. For example, borrowing or lending adjustments may be made frequently in anticipation of high cash outflow or inflow. If the cash flows do not materialize on some occasions, the result will be avoidably high variability of both cash balances and borrowing-lending activity.

Some of the pitfalls of bad forecasting can be made clear upon examination of the decision rule (1). Mills (1967) demonstrates that if the firm uses the mean activity level as a forecast, $\hat{A}_t = \bar{A}$, and for any α, $0 < \alpha \le 1$, and any M^*, it will be the case that

$$\bar{C}_t = \bar{C} = \bar{A}, \; \sigma_{C_t}^2 = \sigma_C^2 = \frac{\alpha^2 \sigma_A^2}{1 - (1-\alpha)^2}, \text{ and } \sigma_I^2 = \frac{1}{1 - (1-\alpha)^2} 2\sigma_A^2.$$

Thus, if $\alpha = 1$, then $\sigma_C^2 = \sigma_I^2 = \sigma_A^2$ (Figure XIII), and the decision process operates on the smoothing feasibility frontier. The entire frontier can be generated by varying α continuously through the interval $(0, 1]$. Note how little information is required to achieve smoothing efficiency. In fact, with $\hat{A}_t = \bar{A}$, we see, substituting in (1), that the policy

$$C_t = \bar{A} + \alpha(M^* - M_{t-1})$$

involves no forecasting—it is, if you will, a simple *tracking* device that makes no attempt to anticipate movements in cash flow activity over time.

But also note that if perfect information is available, the firm can operate to the left of the feasibility frontier as, for example, at the point $(0,1)$ (Figure XIII).

What are the pitfalls in an attempt to move the smoothing feasibility frontier leftward by devising more accurate forecasts? First and foremost, there is the danger that forecast procedures will systematically overestimate demands, and move the control system well to the *right* of the smoothing efficiency frontier. Suppose, for example, that the rule (1) is used, and that the mean level of activity is no longer taken as the activity forecast in every period; further, suppose that the forecasted activity value $\hat{A}_t$ differs from the expected activity level $\bar{A}$ in *every* period. These results will emerge, for example, if the forecaster tries to guess on *which side* of $\bar{A}$ that A_t is more likely to fall on in a given week.

Further, suppose the decision policy (1) is used so as to achieve the tightest possible control, that is, forecast information is relied on heavily, and past forecast errors are fully adjusted out in each period:

$$(4) \qquad\qquad C_t = \hat{A}_t + M^* - M_{t-1},$$

i.e. $\alpha = 1$.

For simplicity, suppose that the successive values $A_1, A_2, \ldots$ are uncorrelated. Let the expectations $E(A_t) = \bar{A}$ and $E(A_t - \bar{A})^2$

$= \sigma_A^2$ be constant over all values of t. There is a real problem of how forecasts can be developed for an independent and stationary series, but that needn't detain us—let it simply be that forecast information, of a degree of quality measured by the correlation $\rho\ (\hat{A}, A)$, exists concerning the sequence A.

The decision rule (4) and the balance relation (2) can be combined to obtain

$$M_t = \hat{A}_t - A_t + M^*$$
$$C_t = \hat{A}_t - \hat{A}_{t-1} + A_{t-1}.$$

It follows that if $\bar{M}$ is finite $E(\hat{A}) = \bar{A}$, which further implies that $\bar{C} = \bar{A}$. By taking expectations on terms like $(M_t - \bar{M})^2$, we obtain

$$\sigma_M^2 = \sigma_{\hat{A}}^2 + \sigma_A^2 - 2\rho\sigma_{\hat{A}}\ \sigma_A$$

and

$$\sigma_C^2 = 2\sigma_{\hat{A}}^2 + \sigma_A^2 - 2\rho\sigma_{\hat{A}}\sigma_A.$$

Correlations exist between $\hat{A}_t$ and A_t, but $\hat{A}_{t+1}$ and A_t are uncorrelated.

The value of the forecast information that is used is seen to depend on the size of $\sigma_{\hat{A}}$ compared to σ_A, and on the value of ρ. For example, when $\hat{A} = A$, forecasting is perfect, $\sigma_C^2 = \sigma_A^2$, and $\sigma_M^2 = 0$. In the case $\hat{A} = \bar{A}$, the forecasting role is abdicated. In this case, $\sigma_M^2 = \sigma_A^2 = \sigma_C^2$, as illustrated in Figure XIII. For forecasting to make sense, the system must better the level of performance that is achieved when $\hat{A} = \bar{A}$. We immediately see that two crucial break-points are involved, assuming non-negative values of ρ, the correlation coefficient:

(5) $\sigma_{\hat{A}} < \rho\sigma_A$: C and M are more stable than with $\hat{A} = \bar{A}$:
                forecasting definitely pays
          $\rho\sigma_A \le \sigma_{\hat{A}} < 2\rho\sigma_A$: C is less stable, and M more stable,
                than with $\hat{A} = \bar{A}$.
          $2\rho\sigma_A \le \sigma_{\hat{A}}$: the attempt at forecasting harms operating performance.

Thus, we see that a forecast can go sour in two ways: it can induce excessive variability in the system ($\sigma_{\hat{A}}/\sigma_A$ not small enough); or it can fail to find good enough correlations (ρ too close to zero). Should the forecast routine lead to negative values of ρ, the forecasting activity is certain to be quite costly.

The criteria (5) are easy to develop and interpret, mainly because of the simplicity of the policy rule (4). We will not spend much effort on the questions of the optimality of the policy (4);[6] instead, we simply note that (4) makes reasonable sense whenever the objective is tight control of the cash balance, and there are no lumpy costs of adjustment to contend with, even though (4) it may not be an optimal choice of policy.

We turn now to two case studies, that illustrate the potential value of the (h, z) policy as a control instrument, and the potentially costly consequences of reliance on bad forecasts.

4. THE UNION TANK CAR CORPORATION, 1965–66[7]

It obviously is non-economical for a firm to permit its cash balances to wander freely, with no attention given to short-term lending opportunities. It is less obvious whether extremely tight forecast-oriented control is economical behavior: in Section 3 we saw that much depends on the firm's ability to forecast, and the view that the firm takes toward adjustment costs. It is instructive, then, to see how the basic model of Chapter III fares as a device for management control. With the advent of tight money in the mid 1960's the Union Tank Car Corporation instituted a cash management regime which had certain important features in common with the (h, z) control policy that emerged from the basic model of Chapter III.[8] The routine, with one important exception, was essentially an (h, z) policy. The exception was attributable to a policy of long standing in the firm, not to trade in marketable securities. That restriction effectively eliminated the lower control limit signal to sell securities; runoffs from the portfolio were the device by which liquidity needs were met.[9] Moreover, in part because of that constraint, the upper decision limit h, and the return point z varied over time, in response to current and forecast information. Thus, for example, the company transferred virtually its entire cash balance into notes, to pick up three days' interest over the weekend, whenever an issue of appropriate maturity was available on a Friday. The Assistant Treasurer had to devote much attention to the selection of maturities, to coincide with foreseeable peak cash needs. Finally, as is typical, the company's compensating balance agreements were negotiated on an average balance basis. The banks interpreted the agreement to imply that the running average cash balance from the inception of the agreement would not fall below some agreed level; however at times the firm took a somewhat more relaxed attitude, and on several occasions, the cash balance ran below the stipulated average for several days at a stretch. During several periods when cash was low, the Assistant Treasurer waited for a runoff, and thereby avoided the cost of borrowing on a short-term basis to meet liquidity needs.

Accompanying those important differences from the rigid control specifications of the (h, z) policy were a number of significant similarities. First, during the period we examined, the firm did little or no short-term borrowing, either on bank lines of credit or through bond houses. Thus, liquidity needs were met out of past cash accumulations, rather than out of future flows, the procedure envisioned in the basic model. Second, the cash accounts of the firm were consolidated into one balance for purposes of decision-making. Obligations existed with regard to each account—compensating balance requirements, agreements with subsidiaries to avoid peremptory withdrawals, and the like. Net of these obligations, available cash was regarded as a single sum, regardless of its distribution—and sometimes, as was indicated earlier, the obligations themselves were shaded briefly during periods of low cash availability. Finally, a substantial lumpy cost of adjustment was recognized in the process of going from cash to securities. (A similar cost would hold in going from securities to cash, if the firm permitted security sale transactions.) Some of the important factors underlying this portfolio adjustment cost can be seen in the steps involved in a security purchase: (a) two or more long-distance phone calls to a short-term securities specialist, plus up to a half-hour of decision time, as the Assistant Treasurer weighed terms and yields of various alternatives; (b) typing and checking over an authorization letter for the signature of the Treasurer (in quadruplicate); (c) obtaining the Treasurer's signature; (d) transmitting the copies to the Controller's office, where special accounts are opened, entires are posted, and final checks on arithmetic are made. It is difficult to put a precise dollar figure on these costs; and in fact, due to the amount of managerial discretion involved in the process, the cost is probably highly variable, depending on the press of other business. For purposes of analysis, it seems reasonable to suggest that the cost seldom is less than $20 per event, and may occasionally be more than $50 per event.[10]

Given data on cash balances, security purchases and runoffs, it was possible to construct a series of daily net cash changes.[11] The zero-drift hypothesis was descriptively acceptable (Table III, Chapter IV), so the (h, z) policy control limits were established with $h = 3z$; the discretionary control range was operated above and beyond a minimum balance level, based on the firm's total cash-holding obligations. With z set at some arbitrary level, the cash flow data were run through the control system. The frequency of adjustment and the mean balance depended on z. By varying z, the firm's frequency of adjustment could be approximated.[12] With z set so that the hypothetical policy yielded the same transfer frequency as was realized in practice, the two systems could be compared on the basis of the mean holdings of idle cash that would result from each. It is instructive and enlightening that the (h, z) policy would have produced a mean cash balance some 40 per cent lower than was realized in practice ($160,000 vs. $275,000). In a similar test, the model was run to match the realized mean cash balance. It achieves this performance level with 80 transfer adjustments, instead of the 112 actually made.

Other details and dimensions of comparative performance are interesting. Figure XIV shows the frequency distributions of portfolio purchases, as the (h, z) policy would have made them, and as they were actually made. The total number of adjustments have been forced into a match, but the (h, z) policy purchases average $600,000 in size, while the firm's average purchase actually was only $440,000. The (h, z) policy never purchases in amounts less than $266,000 at the desired adjustment frequency; in practice, nearly a fourth of the purchases

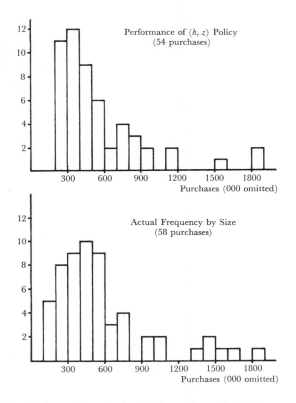

Figure XIV. Hypothetical vs. Actual Performance
(Purchase Size and Frequency)

were smaller than that amount, and five were less than
$100,000.[13]

Even allowing for the fact that some of these small transactions were for weekends, the total impression of the history
of actual performance is one of excessive small-lot purchasing.
This impression is reinforced by the low implicit transfer cost
that caused the model to make 112 transfers—more than 90 per
cent of the total interest earnings achieved by the model with
112 transfers could have been attained with about 50 total

transfers. Of the 50, moreover, only 20 or so would be purchases, and all purchases would be of fairly large size.

Equally revealing is Figure XV which shows the distribution of the closing cash balance on days when no portfolio action was taken. Because of its rigid upper limit the model never lets the cash balance go above h which in this case is about $400,000. The actual practice was much less consistent in this respect. No less than twenty-three buying opportunities of this amount or larger were foregone, including three of over a million dollars. In part these omissions were due to the fact that the Assistant

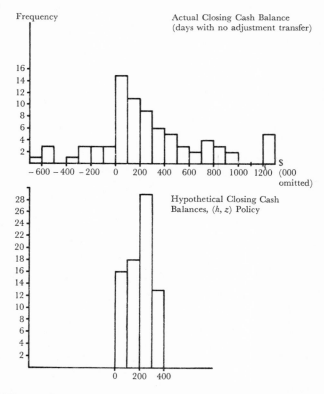

Figure XV. Actual vs. Hypothetical Daily Closing Cash Balances

Treasurer had many other responsibilities, and could not always be at his desk when a decision had to be made. Without actually constructing his worksheet, there was no way for him to determine whether an interruption of his other work would be profitable. By making his limits more explicit (in the spirit of the model) and by delegating to others the purely mechanical task of monitoring these limits, he was subsequently able to achieve a significant reduction in the size and frequency of lost opportunities.

In comparing these performance levels, the constraint imposed by the firm's policy of not dealing in marketable securities must be kept in mind. The policy may have kept the firm from making purchases on occasion when cash was high, but no securities of sufficiently short maturity were available. Similarly, the policy may have forced the firm to be conservative with respect to average term held—fewer purchases of longer-term issues might have been made, had sales been an alternative to runoffs. Furthermore, the actual cost of adjustment no doubt was raised considerably on occasion, because of the imposed need to hunt down an appropriately short maturity. Operating to offset these disadvantages, it must be remembered, is the fact that the firm never actually incurred any transfer cost on the sale side. In comparing the hypothetical control system to the historical record, we got around these difficulties by imputing the same cost of adjustment to actual purchases and the model's purchases and sales; moreover, an adjustment cost was charged to the actual operating regime whenever a maturity was allowed to run off, instead of being rolled over. Whether the actual control performance would have varied considerably had the non-marketability constraint *not* been operative, we can never know.

Despite the non-marketability constraint, which may have handicapped actual operations, the comparative study is instructive with respect to the value of forecasting and other information of a current and local nature. The (h, z) policy can be structured on the basis of information about the moments of past cash flows. Limits are set in accord with deposit obligations, mean and variance of flow, and estimates of adjustment cost and opportunity cost; if the limits do not perform as the theory predicts (perhaps because of non-Gaussian cash flows), they can be adjusted on an ad hoc basis. Once the limits are established, the cash balance can be monitored routinely; the limits themselves will require regular review and updating, but that is a simple process. There is little danger of making a big, costly kind of error in such a system. The principal disadvantage of the approach would seem to be that it does not recognize or accommodate relevant information about foreseeable crucial events, whether these events be regular, like payroll obligations, or unique, like a one-shot opportunity to invest long at very attractive rates and low risk.

Whether or how a basic operating regime such as the (h, z) policy should be modified to accommodate special information is another (very difficult) problem. Analytical techniques now available to decision theorists are not very helpful, in the sense that optimal policies for controlling systems embodying a mix of systematic and random components are non-existent, and hence each instance must be taken as a special case. What our analysis seems to suggest is that a systematic and well rationalized response to sketchy but unbiased information will often yield a higher level of performance than more intuitive responses to inside information. Strong support for that conclusion can be found in our second case study.

5. A LARGE UNNAMED CORPORATION, 1968–69[14]

The emergence of this company in the period since 1955 as a diversified billion-dollar giant, is one of the interesting stories of American business history. The firm has aggressively expanded into new lines, and has consistently sought better methods for generating capital, especially from within the firm. Accordingly, considerable effort has been devoted to the management of cash, in the attempt to make it do double duty—to meet normal liquidity needs, and to serve as a source for funding new investment. The data clearly indicate that the firm was overly zealous in pursuit of these objectives, and in fact, a more relaxed approach to control would have been exceedingly beneficial.

The data sample included daily payments and receipts (broken down into several categories, including wages and salaries, dividends, and transfers to and from subsidiaries), purchases of short-term securities, overdraft activity, and sales of the firm's own short-term paper, all for the period January 1968—June 1969. It is quite possibly the most detailed data base ever made available by a private concern for purposes of academic research. It is to be hoped that several similar series can be constructed over longer time periods, for the purpose of inter-firm comparison, and to permit the study of responses to dramatic shifts in the rate of interest. Even the data that are available can be used further to obtain instruction on such conventional questions as the underlying form of the distribution, serial independence, and periodicity of movement of daily cash account changes. The wealth of detail reported will permit the testing of hypotheses on pooling effects (Chapter IV, Section 5). Those enticements, however, must await future development. For now, our purpose will be the modest one of showing that the basic model can serve as a useful control device, even when the objective is tight control.

That there is room for improvement on actual performance is suggested by application of Mills' smoothing theorem (Section 3). Let M_t denote the actual cash balance, C_t the control action, and A_t the cash flow activity, all as of or during day t. The control C_t is composed of borrowing minus repayment, plus short-term security maturities minus purchases. The variance of the several flow rates and levels over time are

$$S_M^2 = 116.538 \times 10^{12}, \ S_A^2 = 4.786 \times 10^{12}, \text{ and } S_C^2 = 5.775 \times 10^{12}.$$

Mills' inequality

$$S_M \geq \tfrac{1}{2}(S_A/S_C + S_C/S_A)$$

takes the numerical values

$$4.9345 \geq 1.0044.$$

The two sides of the inequality are "far apart," the left side being nearly five times as large as the right side. That suggests much room for improvement in smoothing performance.

There are many approaches that will smooth efficiently, including various linear adjustment rules like (1). Since the management of the company expressed strong skepticism about the importance of lumpy adjustment costs in their own operations, such linear rules might well be considered. However, the illustrative value of this exercise is increased if the linear adjustment approach is ignored, and instead an (h, z) policy is used, with a nominal value imputed to γ, the adjustment transfer cost. The chosen approach served to make a couple of important points: big values of γ are not a precondition for the (h, z) policy to work reasonably well; and in fact, the policy can be useful even in the firm that prides itself on tight and aggressive cash management. With the value $S_A^2 = 4.786 \times 10^{12}$, and with interest rates near 9% on short-term corporate borrowing, a value of γ in the neighborhood of $7. yields the limits

$$z = 2 \times 10^6 \text{ and } h = 6 \times 10^6.$$

Performance under these limits would have been considerably better than actual performance, as is seen in Table XVI. To

TABLE XVI

Comparative Performance, Actual vs. Hypothetical Control Limits

	Actual	Hypothetical (h, z)
Number of Adjustment Transfers	147	69
Mean Cash Balance	$10.8 million	$ 2.9 million
Mean Debt Outstanding (Net of short-term asset holdings)	$20.4 million	$10.8 million

conform more closely to the firm's actual practice, we assume that the firm borrows or retires its own debt whenever adjustment transfers are called for.

Thus, the hypothetical system significantly improves on actual performance on all three of the dimensions of performance that affect cost: the mean cash balance and mean debt position are reduced, and the number of adjustment transfers also is reduced. A policy systematically designed to reflect optimality considerations can of course improve on the ad hoc hypothetical system;

nonetheless, it is clear that the (h, z) policy serves as a useful benchmark for judging performance, and may serve as a guide in the design of control policies as well.

6. CONCLUSION

One rose does not a summer make, nor two case studies a conclusive demonstration of the operational virtues of a model. The principles that are tentatively suggested by the two studies, however, are clear—first, simple models offer a helpful and sometimes revealing benchmark against which actual performance can be judged. Second, stripping away and discarding detail that is typically involved in model building may be a more useful activity, if the goal is higher payoff from decisions, than is the converse activity of getting all the relevant details in sharp focus—an activity that often is the first response when one is newly confronted with complex decision problems. This is just to say that an emphasis on better and more systematic *use* of information will have a higher payoff, usually, than an emphasis on greater detail, accuracy, and speed of delivery of information. At the present time, many decision-makers probably already have "more, better, and faster" information than they know how to use effectively.

The case studies are ambiguous when we ask what they show about the presence of scale economies in cash management. On the one hand, they suggest a concern over effective use of cash; on the other, they reveal that the knowledge of analytic techniques (so useful in the service of that concern) are far from ubiquitous. The issue, then is: is the concern over the effective use of cash widespread; and if so, is the concern (on the average) well-served by actions taken because of it? The available data simply aren't adequate to support an opinion on these questions. So much for the firms that are cash conscious. But what of those that operate at the passive extreme? Even if they are large in number, they probably don't contribute net *diseconomies* to the picture—at worst, probably, their cash balances vary in proportion to the transaction volume.

Firms who behave as Union Tank Car does, and attempt to

"put idle cash to work" without forcing themselves into a position of short-term borrowing, will find the job easier as their transaction volume grows. Costs of adjustment are easier to absorb quickly as the size of an adjustment transfer increases, and hence it will pay to increase the frequency of adjustment transfers. As such firms find the payout from cash management increasing, they will seek and find guides to better decisions—models like the ones discussed in this book, perhaps. Moreover, they will be led to abandon obstructive policies, such as Union's self-imposed rule against selling marketable securities, when those policies are found to cloud the issue and make the job harder.

All of these remarks about arbitrarily categorized corporations are, of course, conjectural. It is premature to suggest that the basic model is a widely applicable normative guide for corporate cash managers, and even more so to suggest that the model points out the route to knowledge concerning money demand in the corporate sector. There are gaps in the theory structure, and there is little supporting evidence from relevant and credible empirical tests. Yet there are reasons to feel encouraged that the approach is worth further development effort, as a tool of management, and as a basis for predicting the effects of monetary policy (an issue that we turn to in the next chapter). Perhaps the most encouraging consideration that can be pointed to at this stage of the subject's development is that economic theory seldom if ever has seen a simple analytic structure that holds significant promise as a useful predictive device, and at the same time makes reasonable sense as a tool for managing or controlling the variables that it is designed to predict.

NOTES

1. Indeed, some of the most important contributions to operations research have been the work of such economists as K. J. Arrow, T. C. Koopmans, F. Modigliani and H. Theil; and some of the articles that appeared in economics journals in the 1950's (notably in *Econometrica*) had greater impact upon operations research than economics.
2. Baumol (1952).
3. We frequently encounter the operating rule that debt issued to fund an investment project should be for a term commensurate with the duration of the

project. That rule may yield real economy on transaction cost. Whether the rule makes sense under the prospect of falling interest rates depends on how well prices (yields) reflect that prospect.

4. The lack of uniformity in corporate cash management practice is accompanied by a lack of uniformity in the pricing of banking services and the application of compensating balance requirements. There apparently is much room for negotiation on such points as the maintenance of minimum vs. average balances, on the duration of the period over which balances will be averaged, on the amount of check clearing activity that will be tolerated before a bank feels that an agreement is being abused, and on the use of an average balance as compensation to the bank for both clearing activity and credit line maintenance. Hard bargaining, skillful negotiations, and warm personal relations with the bank's customer man all play a part in determining the cost of a financial service and credit availability mix—or so firms believe.

5. It is well known that a rule of the form (1) will be an optimal response, if the objective function is quadratic, of the form

$$\sum_t \gamma(C_t - \hat{A}_t)^2 + \eta(M_t - M^*)^2 \qquad (\gamma, \eta \text{ constants})$$

over a finite planning horizon. A large literature on the subject exists, notably Holt, Modigliani, Muth and Simon (1960) and H. D. Mills (1967). Both these sources contain further bibliographical material on the subject.

6. It is not a simple matter to find conditions that imply the optimality of the rule (4), where $a = 1$. If the firm's objective function is quadratic, of the structure

(a) $$\sum_{t=1}^{\eta} \gamma(C_t - C^*)^2 + \eta(M_t - M^*)^2$$

(where γ and η are constants, and C^* and M^* are target levels) then the optimal first-period control decision is

(b) $$C_1 = \overline{A} - a(M_0 - M^*),$$

where

$$a = \{\eta/\gamma[4 + (\eta/\gamma)^2]^{1/2} - (\eta/\gamma)^2\}/2.$$

To obtain $a = 1$ requires imaginary values for the cost coefficient ratio η/γ. There are, of course, other possible specifications of the objective function (a) which may imply the optimality of the control response (b), and which may avoid this problem.

7. The Union Tank car study of this section was also joint work with Merton Miller. It is reported in somewhat greater detail in Miller and Orr (1967).

8. In 1965, a series of fortunate events put Merton Miller in touch with D. B. Romans, then Assistant Treasurer, now Treasurer, of the Union Tank Car Corporation. Romans' generosity in making data available and revealing the bases of his decisions is gratefully acknowledged.

9. As we will see, this type of "policy constraint" on operating behavior may be a costly thing to live with.

10. If we are willing to impute flawless rationality to the firm, it is quite clear that the transfer cost typically lies nearer $50 than $20, for with the rates of interest prevalent at the time of the study, earnings were about ten cents per thousand dollars per day loaned out; the average size of a loan transaction was about

$440,000 and such transactions occurred at less than daily intervals. If the transfer cost were $20, the implied profit in the very first day of security holding would be *double* the transfer cost. The firm could profit from daily trading, under those circumstances, while in fact, over the 189-day sample period, the firm bought securities only 58 times. The transfer cost estimate did not play an important part in the subsequent comparative analysis, however, so little attention was devoted to the problem of pinning down its exact magnitude.

11. Our original data series of 189 daily observations was subsequently extended, and some of the properties of the firm's cash flow rate are reported in Chapter IV.

12. In the early stages of the comparison, some difficulty was anticipated because the (h, z) policy calls for security sales, while the firm relied exclusively on portfolio runoffs. However, a reconstruction of experience showed that on some 54 occasions, runoffs occurred when cash was low, and there was no immediate security repurchase. Those occasions were held to correspond to security sales in the (h, z) regime. Hence, we first sought a value of z such that the (h, z) policy would yield $58 + 54 = 112$ portfolio-cash adjustment transfers.

13. Variations in the size of security transfer are due to the fact that the (h, z) control system was operated on a "daily review" rather than a "continuous review" basis. During some days, the cash balance passed well beyond the limits (o, h) before a corrective action was taken.

14. The data sample used in this study was assembled from company records with the explicit purpose in mind of studying cash management performance. A desire for anonymity was expressed by the corporate officer who made the numbers available.

IX

Implications for Aggregative
Analysis

This chapter is an attempt to develop a perspective on the usefulness of the foregoing analysis to macroeconomists. Clearcut
difficulties confront an effort to use the money demand relation
of the basic model for such "conventional" purposes as large-
scale model-building, or predicting the effects of policy actions.
A central difficulty at the level of the individual enterprise is
our lack of knowledge concerning linkages between daily cash
flows and such widely observed activity indicators as sales or
profits; the same difficulty confronts the further effort to translate the basic model's demand relation into predictions about
aggregate cash holdings. Section 1 is concerned with these
problems. Section 2 examines a variety of empirical results on
money demand, and suggests ways in which the asset management approach can be useful in conventional macroeconomic
research. Together, sections 1 and 2 constitute a view of asset
management theory as it relates to empirical research. Those
sections deal with these and other questions: How consistent are
the predictions of the theory with well-documented empirical
research results? What direct or indirect contributions can the

basic model make to work in empirical research? What are the major problems that obstruct the empirical testing of the model?

Sections 3, 4, and 5 attempt to relate the results of earlier chapters to macroeconomic models of income determination. The asset classes used in asset management analysis are seen to have the same implications as the aggregative structure used in conventional analysis—the interpretation of results, and indeed even the results themselves, depend on the taxonomical choices made in model-building. An evaluation of the speculative motive for money demand is offered, based on considerations of optimum choice by individual firms. Analyses based on risk aversion motives are held to be less useful than older ideas that focus on price change expectations. In this connection, yet another view is offered of the liquidity trap.

Section 6 is a commentary on the homogeneity postulate, the view that money demand is proportional to the general price level. The response of adjustment costs to price level changes is seen to be important; it is suggested that adjustment costs vary over different phases of the cycle, and variations in adjustment cost will affect the observed interest and transactions elasticities of money demand.

Section 7 is an examination of the idea that cash is a highly conventional capital good. The "long run asset preference" idea found in the work of Friedman (1959), Chow (1966), Brunner-Meltzer (1963), Pesek-Saving (1967), and Nadiri (1969) among others is challenged, and the empirical evidence, that serves as the major support for that long run view of money demand, is reconciled with cash-holding motives of the inventory-theoretic type.

1. Aggregation, and Representation of Transaction Flows

Throughout the analysis of individual asset management decisions in earlier chapters, heavy emphasis was placed on relaxation response control rules. These rules imply delays and discontinuities in the adjustment of cash balances to the levels desired by individuals, even in the presence of changes in such critical determining variables as interest rates and transaction rates. However, those delays and discontinuities pose no threat to the existence of regular and orderly macroeconomic relationships. This is true just as surely, and for the same reasons, as the fact that irregular and infrequent purchases of refrigerators by individuals is consistent with an orderly and regular demand function in the refrigerator market.

The problems associated with money demand estimation do not differ widely from those encountered in commodity estimation, except for the important issue of how to correct for the response of demand to changes in activity levels. Income is the logical and conventional variable to represent activity levels in most demand studies, but the analysis of foregoing chapters suggests that the first two moments of the cash flow process are the directly relevant activity variables for the study of the money stocks of individuals. There is then a problem of finding an empirically observable surrogate for the cash flow moments, whether the mean be the dominant one, as the Baumol model suggests, or the variance, as the basic model indicates.[1] Once past the difficulty of an activity level measure, things are easier. The interest rate fills the role of own price in ordinary demand studies;[2] and the dependent variable, individuals' mean cash holdings over time, causes no problems of aggregation.

Thus, in the demand relation from the basic model (Chapter III, Section 5),

$$\overline{M} = (16\gamma\sigma^2/9\nu)^{1/3},$$

the main difficulties of estimation attach to the cash flow variance σ^2. Various surrogates can be and have been tried, notably sales and income, both at the level of the individual enterprise and at aggregated levels. An identification problem emerges from those estimations, due to the speculative element of money demand.

Sales, of course, is only one possible representative of cash flow variability. For the whole business sector, check-clearing data may serve well, despite obvious problems of separating inter-firm transactions from transactions involving only one firm or no firms; determining the extent to which payments and receipts synchronize at the individual firm level; and determining the way that cash flow variance aggregates across firms. Clearing data also will reflect the possibly non-trivial volume of activity that is generated to adjust portfolios and cash balances.

Cash flows do not seem to vary in any coherent way with sales and income. As a point of departure, it is inviting to guess that sales is the positive component of cash flows, and sales net of undistributed profits is the negative component. If this were true, it would at least be possible to infer cash balance drift from income statement data. Unfortunately, various charges, notably depreciation, are made against profits, and some of these charges have no actual counterpart in the cash flow process; because of them, nothing reliable can be inferred about cash flow drift along the suggested lines. Moreover, the size and frequency of transactions will vary widely among firms of the same sales volume, due to differences in the nature of their products, differences in bookkeeping practices, different degrees of vertical integration and capital intensiveness, and different arrangements for storing inputs and storing and distributing outputs.

2. Empirical Findings on Money Demand Elasticity

Partly as an outgrowth of predictions drawn from "inventory theory" models, transactions and interest elasticities of money demand have attracted substantial attention from empiricists. Various empirical studies examine real or nominal balances; they explain the entire money stock, or cash holdings of the business sector, or cash holdings of individual firms; they take a simultaneous equations or a single equation estimation approach; they use quarterly or annual data; they use a variety of proxy variables for transactions; and they use both short and long term interest rates to represent the cost of holding idle cash. The results of those tests for the most part can be classed in two groups; those which find transaction elasticities of roughly unity; and those which find a positive transaction elasticity of less than unity. No attempt will be made here to summarize the state of the literature, nor is it suggested that highly suggestive tests of the basic model are to be found in it. The variety of ideas and hypotheses that serve to motivate the various investigations are simply too diverse, and the data used are inappropriate, to constitute good evidence on the basic model. So far as the important question of interest elasticity is concerned, there does appear to be a steady accumulation of evidence that it is of sign and magnitude consistent with the predictions of the basic model (or one of its variants considered in Chapters IV, V, or VI.[3]) But, for the transaction elasticity, the problems associated with the various proxy measures discussed in Section 1 seem to have been intractable up to now. There is indirect evidence to support the basic model from a number of studies on economies of scale in cash management, with attention to the relation between cash balances and various measures of firm size. Those findings are mixed, but there is sufficient positive evidence so that it is reasonable to accept the existence of scale economies, given the theoretical arguments that can be brought forward on their behalf.[4] Any theory in which the law of large numbers operates on cash flows will sensibly predict scale economies in cash holding at the individual enterprise level.

The inability to observe cash flows in sufficient detail on a wide scale would be less of a handicap in empirical testing if more were known about the relations among cash flow and various observable series. The bothersome fact is our lack of knowledge about the nature (or even the existence) of "linkages" among financial series. Those linkage problems stand in the way of applying the predictions of the basic model to conventional macroeconomic questions and evaluation of policy.

There do seem to be strong empirical relationships between money holdings and various aggregate variables, such as income, sales, and wealth. These relations can themselves be used in conventional macroeconomic applications, if they are found to be sufficiently regular over time, even if they are not understood in terms of individual behavior. It remains desirable, though, to explain good curve-fitting results in terms of a descriptive theory of optimizing behavior, for to understand the demand process at that level both enhances the ability to generate good fits under changed or different circumstances, and justifies greater confidence in the predictions that the mechanism yields. The limited amounts of disaggregated cash flow data that can be obtained through consulting and other forms of personal contact can be used to identify and confirm the linkages between cash flows and more widely reported data at the individual enterprise level. Even then, there will remain the usual difficulties of aggregation: attention must be paid from the beginning to the aggregative properties of different "linkage rules." Only by good fortune will a non-linear relation between cash and transactions in the firm translate well into a relation of simple aggregative structure between cash and sales or income. Direct and indirect evidence is accumulating that the basic model, or a variant, will be useful as a normative guide to cash management in the firm,[5] and it can be anticipated then that the model will be increasingly useful as a predictive device if a suitable proxy for cash flows can be found.

3. Monetary and Fiscal Policy in a Simple Economy

Simple empirical fits may provide worthwhile insight into the equilibrium properties of the monetary sector, but the literature on adjustment lags induced by monetary policy suggests that it may be utterly futile to rely on empirical fitting for insight into the dynamics of money demand. It is for the understanding of dynamic processes that the basic model or models like it are potentially the most useful and hard to replace.

Macroeconomic theory contains numerous "scenarios" that purport to describe the sequence of events in an adjustment from one equilibrium to another in a static model. There are good and bad scenarios;[6] at best, working one out can illuminate the way that crucial variables behave during the equilibration process. Such scenarios form the content of this section. They are not held to be realistic descriptions of the adjustment process, but are useful in bringing out a variety of crucial institutional and behavioral conditions that affect asset holders' response. It will be seen that reference to the basic model does not affect the conventional view of how stabilization policies work. The analysis relies on a three-asset extension of the basic model, along the lines of Chapter VI. The three assets are cash, bonds and physical capital. Physical capital enters as the conventional bridge between the money supply or government expenditure and the macroeconomic target variables.

Consider an economy in which there is no banking system. Private individuals (including firms) hold either cash or bonds, and the central authority engages in open market operations— the purchase or sale of bonds—as its major instrument for stabilization.

Equilibrium in this economy requires that

$$MS \equiv \Sigma_i M_i = \Sigma_i \bar{M}_i$$

where MS is the money supply, M_i is the cash holding of the ith individual, and $\bar{M}_i$ is the *desired mean* cash balance of that individual. If the monetary authority bids away $\$K$ worth of bonds, individuals' portfolios are changed by a transfer of that amount from bonds to cash, and the financial markets respond with higher bond prices and lower interest rates on bonds. The three-asset models of Chapter VI suggest that an individual firm will control its asset balances in accord with the objective function

$$(1) \quad E(C) = \nu_l E(M) + \gamma_s P(\tau_b) + (\nu_l - \nu_s) \, E(B) + \gamma_l P(\tau_{b,k}),$$

where ν_l and ν_s are respectively the earnings rate on capital equipment and bonds; ν_s is cost of a portfolio transfer involving cash and bonds; γ_l is the cost of a transfer involving cash, bonds and capital; $E(M)$ and $E(B)$ are the expected holdings of money and bonds; and $P(\tau_b)$ and $P(\tau_{b,k})$ are the probabilities of the two types of portfolio transfer, the first involving money and bonds, the second involving money, bonds and capital. The analysis of Chapter VI suggests that an increase in the money supply will stimulate bidding for bonds, lowering ν_s. The desired mean cash holding

$$(2) \qquad\qquad \bar{M} = (16\gamma_s \sigma^2 / 4\nu_l)^{1/3}$$

will be unaffected, but the desired mean holding of bonds

(3) $\overline{B} = [16\gamma_l\sigma^2/4(v_l - v_s)]^{1/3}$

will *decline* due to the increase in $v_l - v_s$. Accompanying the
desire to hold fewer bonds is the desire to hold more physical
capital. In this case of purely lumpy adjustment costs, at least,
monetary policy does not lead to the desired outcome by
changing the demand for money; monetary policy simply makes
physical capital more or less attractive relative to holdings of
other more liquid assets. The increase in the money supply, in
fact, cannot be accommodated by asset holders unless the
marginal efficiency v_l declines with the increase in capital stock.

Apart from the last mentioned feature, which is mildly novel,
the adjustments in response to monetary policy are not changed
much by explicit reference to the basic model of money demand.
Inclusion of the basic model, then, doesn't affect the attainment
of equilibrium in any significant way. It remains only to ask
whether the *maintenance* of equilibrium is significantly affected
by the basic decision-making process for asset control. In equilibrium, cash and bonds change hands in the private sector,
with individuals who pass their upper cash control limits de-
manding bonds, and individuals who pass their lower limits
supplying them. In short time intervals, purchase and sale offer-
ings may not balance within the closed system, but the central
monetary authority can intervene to maintain stable security
prices if it is desirable to do so.[7] Even without stabilizing inter-
vention, the likelihood of wide price movements in bonds is
small, if private holders are numerous and the market is
sufficiently well organized to bring buyers and sellers together
quickly.

In reference to relaxation response control rules for optimal
cash management, George Akerlof (1969) called the set of upper
and lower bounds on the cash holdings of individuals the
"money box." Whenever one or another of the bounds is
crossed, an asset adjustment is signalled. If most of the adjustments that are called for are security purchases, then interest
rates fall, and the money box expands. If most are sales, the box

contracts. If the interest rate changes on bonds are translated by business firms into borrowing and investment decisions, then monetary policy functions effectively.

One potentially important point is underscored when open market operations are analyzed in an asset management framework. The effect of a monetary policy action on income is a one-shot effect; once asset holdings have shifted from bonds to cash and physical capital, only second order stimulii, which may stem from the higher productivity associated with the new capital, will persist. Further, if it is anticipated that bond sales may follow soon upon bond purchases, the incentive to respond to the purchase is reduced. Expectations can operate to defeat monetary policy in the manner suggested by the familiar liquidity trap argument (see Section 5 below). For monetary policy to have a persistently stimulative effect, security purchases must continue over time; investors will base their responses on their estimate of a normal and persistent spread between marginal efficiency v_i and the bond rate v_s. If this view of individuals' response is correct, much of the day-to-day adjusting that goes on by order of the Federal Open Market Committee may be wasted effort.

Fiscal Policy. As an alternative means to stimulate the flow of income, suppose the central authority collects taxes from individuals and buys goods that the individuals produce.[8] A greater volume of payments and receipts will occur in the private sector, accompanied, let us suppose, by an increase in the cash flow variance σ^2. Individuals will obtain liquidity by selling securities; security prices will drop and the bond rate v_s will go up. Equations (2) and (3) tell us that the indicated changes in σ^2 and v_s will lead to lower investment in the private sector, which will tend to defeat the fiscal policy action. Note that the increase in the bond rate is not necessary to the argument: an increase in σ^2 is sufficient to produce the added demand for liquid assets. That demand has a depressing effect on income, whether resources are fully employed or not.[9]

These simple interpretations of the workings of monetary and fiscal policy look more classical than Keynesian—monetary policy works in the desired direction, while fiscal policy tends to be defeated by offsetting changes in the private desire to hold liquid assets. The analysis confirms that "constant velocity" (vulgarly viewed as fundamental to the "classical" position), can be interpreted in terms of the desire of individuals to avoid the costly excesses of too much cash or too-frequent trips to the securities market to restore transactions balances. In the process of adjusting balances to avoid the excesses of one extreme or the other, the private sector will respond to the central authority in a manner that confirms the quantity theory, as it was worked out by Fisher and others.[10]

Before chalking up another faint mark in favor of the "modern quantity theory" and its proponents, however, it is necessary to extend the analysis a bit, to see whether a commercial banking system, with its powers of credit expansion, has important effect, and to consider some of the effects of speculative money demand, an important subject about which writers in the asset management tradition have had little to say. To obtain classical results from a model that abstracts from liquidity preference (as we have above) is, after all, no important new achievement.

The first of the two supplementary considerations can be disposed of quickly. Commercial banks have no important effect in either the monetary or the fiscal policy scenario. The purchase of securities by the central authority increases the stock of "high powered money" in the system—reserves and free reserves are expanded, and banks can extend new loans. Deposit "creation" provides loanable funds, reduces interest rates which stimulates investment, and furnishes the added cash balances that are demanded for transactions purposes during and following the expansion. Fiscal policy (of the restrictive tax-funded variety), by contrast, has no impact on bank reserves—unless it is accompanied by transfers from privately held time deposits to Treasury (tax and loan) demand deposits, in which case the impact is non-expansionary. In a world free of speculative asset-holding decisions, then, it appears that the only favorable effects of fiscal policy stem from "incidental" expansions or contractions of the money supply. In the next two sections a clearer perspective will be developed on that conclusion.

4. SPECULATIVE AND RISK-AVOIDING PORTFOLIO ACTIONS AND THEIR IMPLICATIONS

This section offers an attempt to rationalize and trace the effects of the "speculative motive," and to see whether (in the same framework of *a priori* reasoning as was used in the preceding section) the motive can accomplish the things that are demanded of it in modern income and employment theory.

Speculative Balances in the Firm. All wealth in a private economy ultimately is held by individuals. But this does not mean that decisions regarding the form in which wealth is held are made only by individuals acting on their own behalf. The assets of a business firm are allocated by the management of the firm, on behalf of the firm's owners, a process that is economical because it avoids tax losses and transaction or adjustment costs, and because the managers have a skill advantage in making such allocations. Other intermediaries can and do participate in allocating the wealth of private individuals; banks, investment trusts (mutual funds), and savings associations are probably the most important of these. All of these intermediaries are constrained in different ways, and all have different perspectives. We can therefore expect their behavior, and hence their demand for cash balances, to differ. In this section and the next, attitudes toward the prospect of capital gains, and the variance of prospective return, are discussed from the viewpoint of a manufacturing enterprise or *firm*, which is concerned with the production of physical goods for sale.

Probably the most important idea that arises in a discussion of speculative money-holding is that cash may be held by firms for reasons that have very little to do with the productive services that it renders: under some circumstances it may be demanded as a component of wealth, and not just as an input into the process of generating income. When speculative balances are viewed in this way, an issue of property rights emerges. On what basis is a firm justified in withholding cash from stockholders (the owners of the asset) unless that cash is used by the firm in a direct way, with positive marginal product?

Viewed somewhat differently, why should speculation in cash ever be through the intermediary of a firm, rather than directly by the owners of the cash? An answer to these questions can be cast in terms of adjustment costs. If it is expected that the price of non-cash productive assets will fall in the near future, then the firm can hold cash for later investment, and thereby avoid costly transfers of cash back and forth between the firm and the owners of the cash. The argument hinges on the expectation of a price drop; its status is unclear under the "zero mean price level change" postulate found in Tobin's strong version of liquidity preference, considered in Section 5 below.

Even with this transactions-oriented construal, conceptual problems are attached to the idea of speculative balances in the firm. Suppose an earning asset no riskier than cash can be found—why then would cash be held? Various government and private interest-bearing securities of arbitrarily short maturity generally are available. "Keynesian" (or expectation-of-change) liquidity preference theory, provides a satisfactory explanation of demand for such assets, which afford nearly fixed yield, and fixed values at the end of a very short term to maturity; but the theory hardly explains the demand for cash, narrowly defined, within the category of those assets, so long as others with positive nominal returns (and hence higher real returns) are available. If such interest-bearing monetary assets did not exist, it would be necessary for man to invent them; or more precisely, to provide the service which they provide, for which there is significant demand. Even in the presence of low-risk, short-term earning securities, conventional (Keynesian) liquidity preference may lead to an expanded demand for cash, as will be shown in the next few paragraphs.

Expectation Differences as a Driving Force. In the standard view, speculative demand[11] implies a highly interest-elastic money demand function at low rates of interest, and explains the failure of interest rates to respond to expansionary actions directed at the money supply or free bank reserves. One explanation holds that at low interest rates, individuals will expect the rate to rise to "normal" levels. Consequently, because of the pervasive fear of capital losses on bonds, expansion of the money supply only adds to the idle balances that are held, and does not drive interest rates down any further.

Steady-state analyses of the type developed in Chapters III–VI are not entirely suitable for use in the analysis of expectations and expectation-associated behavior. Steady-state analysis is well suited to the analysis of repetitive events in an unchanging environment. Expectations, to be of any importance to asset demand, must be changing or subject to change—in response to current and local information, or special and nonrecurrent circumstances, for example. A graphical analysis similar to the one developed in Chapter III, Section 7, can be useful in seeing how expectations affect cash holdings.

The firm holds M in cash and B in bonds at the beginning of a decision period. The decision involves mapping of M and B into b, an adjustment in the bond holding; the conditions $M \geq b \geq 0$ and $0 \geq b \geq B$ hold on bond purchases and bond sales, respectively. The returns realized and costs incurred over the decision horizon, that affect the choice of b, are (a) opportunity costs on cash balances held (returns on bonds purchased); (b) transfer costs of portfolio adjustment incurred whenever b takes a non-zero value; (c) capital gains or losses on the bond holding $B + b$; (d) costs of maintaining the cash balance and portfolio from the beginning of the next decision period.

These costs are formulated analytically in a dynamic objective function (Chapter II, Section 1). The cash holding cost (a) is taken to be a linear function of the cash balance, or a linear return on bonds held; the rate is v. The transfer costs (b) are of the purely lumpy variety; that is,

$$\gamma\{b\} = \begin{cases} 0 \text{ if } b = 0 \\ \gamma \text{ if } b \neq 0 \end{cases}.$$

The capital gain (c) is in proportion to the interest rate change (which is assumed to occur at the end of the period). If the interest rate is expected to change by Δv, then the expected capital gain on bonds is $(B + b) [- \Delta v/(v + \Delta v)]$.

The three cost categories (a), (b), and (c) include all the costs incurred during the current decision period. The dynamic objective functional is

(4) $$\Pi_T(M) \overset{\min}{=}_b \left[\nu b - \gamma\{b\} - b\Delta\nu/(\nu + \Delta\nu) + \int_{-\infty}^{\infty}\Pi_{T-1}(M + b - m)\phi(m)dm \right],$$

where m, a random variable with density function ϕ, is the cash flow during the current period; and $\Pi_j(k)$ is the minimum expected cost of operation over j periods when the initial cash-balance is k. The cost category (d) is represented by the expression $\int_{-\infty}^{\infty}\Pi_{T-1}(M + b - m)\phi(m)dm$. During the T-period dynamic decision process, no more than one interest rate change is expected in any period.

Graphical Analysis: The "Normal" Case. The simplest way to explore the properties of a solution for the decision problem (4) is with a graphical analysis. The horizontal axis of Figure XVI represents the possible initial cash balances to which the firm can adjust, $0 \le M + b \le M + B$. The function labeled ν is the cost component (a), holding cost; the function labeled Π is the cost component (d), the minimum expected costs of operation in periods beyond the current one. The effect of the cost component (c), capital gains or losses, is to rotate the ν function to a position such as $\nu + \Delta$ or $\nu - \Delta'$. The sum of these three cost components is denoted $\Gamma(M + b)$; it is drawn to represent the case $\Delta = \Delta' = 0$, and it takes its minimum value at z^*. The decision rule, then, is:

(5)   If $\Gamma(M) > \Gamma(z^*) + \gamma$, set $b = z^* - M$
        If $\Gamma(M) \le \Gamma(z^*) + \gamma$, set $b = 0$.

Thus, for any $M \ge h$, or ≤ 0, it will pay to adjust to z^*. For $0 \le M \le h$, it will pay to stand pat at M.

The effects of "speculative" considerations on the cash position of the firm can be seen clearly from the graph. If interest rates are expected to rise, the function Γ becomes less steeply inclined, moving to a position like $\{1\}$, and the range of values of M which induce no adjustment widens, as from $(0,h]$ to $(0,h']$. It follows that average cash holdings increase. A similar effect in the opposite direction can be anticipated when the interest rate is expected to decline. From the standpoint of

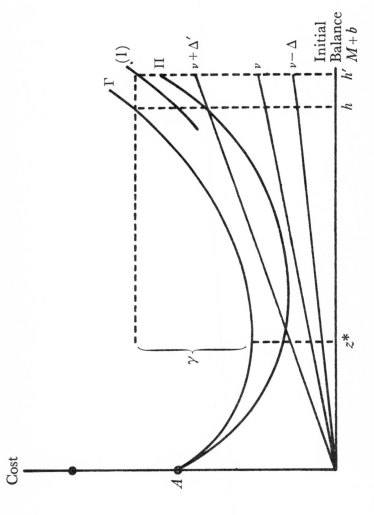

Figure XVI. Effects of Speculative Demand on the Cash-holding Decision

the (h,z) policy, the effect of the expected change in interest rates is an adjustment of the *top* of the "control range," that is, a change in h, so long as the cost components have the properties assumed in Figure XVI. It will not be optimal to provide speculative balances in the form of a "cushion," by adjusting to z^* or any other level *before* the cash balance falls to zero, unless the coordinate of the point A is greater than $\Gamma(z^*) + \gamma$; or unless points along Γ slightly to the right of A lie above A. Neither possibility is especially plausible; it is a good exercise for the reader to reason why. The convexity of the function Γ over positive values of the cash balance certainly depends on the shape of the cost component (d). Literature exists on this question;[12] since our concern is with the effects of speculative behavior, we will simply assume that the cost components are approximately as we have drawn them in Figure XVI. Even significant violations of that assumption do not affect the basic argument much.

Graphical Solution: The "Keynesian" Case. In the preceding paragraphs, speculative considerations had no especially profound impact on money demand. In the "normal" case described there, expected changes in the capital values of securities over the decision horizon period were converted to a rate of return, and considered on an equal footing with interest yields. The effect on money demand is about the same as would be realized by changing the opportunity rate ν in the analysis of Chapter III. In the present section the approach remains the same, but the cases considered are rather more extreme— speculative considerations can affect the analysis dramatically if the expected capital value changes are sufficiently large relative to interest income.

In Figure XVII several crucial relationships illustrate the effects of extreme expectations regarding changes in capital value. The several functions are labeled in the same way as their counterparts in Figure XVI. The critical feature is the slope of the $\nu - \Delta'$ function, composed of interest earnings plus expected capital losses, expressed in rate terms. In position $\{1\}$, the firm will never buy securities from a monetary asset base of $M + B$ or less. It will add to its cash balances when they fall to

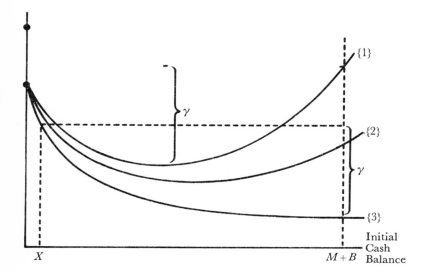

Figure XVII. Effects of Extreme "Keynesian"
Speculative Demand

the level zero. As in the "normal" case, adjustment will be to
a cash balance z^* that is *less than* $M + B$.

However, should the $\nu - \Delta'$ function fall to the level {2}, the
firm will no longer engage in securities purchases. Finally, when
the critical return function falls to a position like {3}, the firm
will sell *all* its earning assets when the cash balance falls below
x; the stimulus of a cash balance drop to zero is not necessary
to trigger an adjustment. There will be no subsequent purchase
of assets with the return function in the position {2} or {3}, until
expectations and coupon rates of return shift the function to {1}
or some level above. Thus, whenever the return function is at or
below {1}, the conditions of a liquidity trap are fulfilled by an
individual—he will refuse to buy securities, because the earnings
rate fails to offset expected capital loss.

Differences in Individuals' Expectations. In his description of the
Keynesian version of the liquidity trap (1958), Tobin posits an
abrupt "discontinuity" in the responses of individuals to
changes in the rate of return on securities. That discontinuity

was held to be a small weakness of the Keynesian view (perhaps on Marshallian grounds).[13] To review Tobin's analysis, consider the relation between two rates of interest on homogeneous earning assets—the current rate ν and the expected future rate, ν_e. Suppose that the expected future rate is a proper function of the current rate: $\nu_e = \phi(\nu)$. If the expected return on securities, including capital gains, exceeds zero, then the entire fund of speculative assets is held in bonds; if the expected return is *less* than zero, then the fund is held in cash. Because the expected return ν_e is a function of the current return ν, it follows that there will be no investment in securities unless

(6) $$\nu > \nu_e/(1 + \nu_e),$$

which is obtained from the condition of positive total returns

$$\nu + \nu/\nu_e - 1 > 0.$$

In the event that (6) holds, the entire fund of speculative

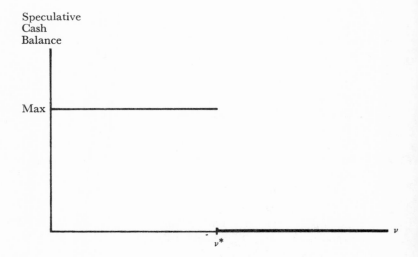

Figure XVIII. Discontinuity Associated with Distinct Treatment of Speculative and Transactions Balances (Tobin)

balances will be held in bonds; if (6) is reversed, then the fund is held in cash. Because of the discontinuity in cash holdings implied by the condition (6), and illustrated in Figure XVIII, it is necessary that the ϕ-function that maps current returns into expected returns differ among individuals. With everyone having the same expectation, no equilibrium could be found, except perhaps fortuitously with $v_e v = v_e - v$, when everyone would be indifferent between cash and bonds.

Our graphical analysis of the more extreme cases (indicated by {2} and {3} in Figure XVII), suffers from a similar condition: without differences among individuals' expectations, nobody would want to hold bonds, and an upward shift in the return on bonds would be inevitable. However, there are no circumstances in our analysis under which nobody is willing to hold cash; this, of course is the product of our "failure" to distinguish between transactions and speculative balances. Note that in the normal case, individuals will hold a mixture of bonds and cash; equilibrium is assured so long as commonly held expectations leave the $v + \Delta$ function at or above {1} (Figure XVII); and so long as the interest rate v that underlies the expectations will clear both the money and the securities market.

5. LIQUIDITY PREFERENCE AS RESPONSE TO RISK

In the foregoing analysis, the holding of cash balances for speculative purposes (by individuals or in the whole economy) is in anticipation of interest rate changes. The first effort to break this connection between expectations and speculative holdings won wide acceptance very quickly, and that analysis of Tobin's (1958) is now securely established as a standard theoretical construct in the macroeconomics literature.

Tobin's paper analyzes the process whereby individuals allocate their *speculative balances* among different *monetary* assets. The decision to hold a particular asset is based on two criteria: expected return, and risk. Every decision-maker is assumed to attach a probability distribution to the set of possible return rates on every available asset. The mean of that distribution measures expected return. As a measure of risk, the standard deviation (or the variance) of the distribution is used. Decisions are based on the first two moments, then, of the distribution of expected returns: in effect, the mean and variance enter as arguments of a utility function; the mean is always given positive weight, while the variance is usually thought to take negative weight.

The ranking of securities by reference to the first two moments of the expected returns distribution can be shown to be an optimal decision policy, so long as the underlying conditions of the analysis hold. The conditions include: (1) There is an investment period, such that (a) no securities have maturities before the end of the period,[14] and (b) no transactions to change the composition of the portfolio can occur, *except* at the ends of periods.[15] (2) A fixed and exogenously determined fund of speculative balances is to be allocated. (3) Either (a) the decision-maker's utility function is quadratic in expected returns, of the form

$$U = \alpha_1 + \alpha_2 \bar{R} + \alpha_3 \bar{R}^2;$$

or (b) the probability distribution of anticipated returns is fully characterized by its mean and variance, that is, the distribution is normal.[16]

An apparent weakness of the Tobin analysis is that it emphasizes cash to the exclusion of other assets of positive return, but of short maturity and very low risk. Such securities, as we have already had occasion to emphasize, serve admirably as temporary abodes of purchasing power. It was pointed out long ago that the dispersion of prospective returns can be countered by reduced average term to maturity in the portfolio, as well as by an increased proportion of liquid assets in cash. The advantages of shortening the average term of the earning portion of the portfolio compared to increasing the cash holding, will depend on the adjustment costs encountered by each method. Hence, if cash is increased to reduce returns dispersion in the portfolio of liquid assets, the action can also be imputed to adjustment costs.[17]

Risk Aversion and Aversion to Ruin. When the basis of speculative money demand is held to be aversion to variance of prospective return on securities, very little is cleared up. But suppose the asset alternative to cash is physical capital and not bonds. In deciding whether or not to invest, a firm may indeed be sensitive to risk. It may well be, however, that risk aversion in the investment decision is manifested not by sensitivity to the variance of non-monetary assets, but rather, by sensitivity to a large probability mass at large negative rates of return. The probability measure relevant to the firm's decision then is not the dispersion of returns, but the probability of the total failure of an investment program—if you like, firms are ruin-averse rather than risk-averse.

If it is in the nature of physical investment that success or failure may hinge on one or a small number of contingencies, as is *a priori* plausible, then the distribution of returns can be bimodal, with significant probability attached to rates of return indicative of failure. The variance will be a very poor and insensitive measure with which to capture this crucial probability number. It is easy to construct hypothetical cases in which attractive prospects will have high variance, and unattractive ones, low variance, once the definition of ruin has been established. How do firms respond to the danger of ruin in their choice of capital assets? They diversify in their choice among these assets. It becomes particularly attractive and easy to hedge if an important contingency, such as a piece of pending legislation, has opposite effects on different asset alternatives.

Does the possibility of ruin lead a firm to hold larger average cash or liquid security balances in the course of its operations? If no adequate opportunity for diversifying its holding of physical capital is available, the firm may become a candidate for acquisition or merger. It is not easy to see, however, how an increase in ruin probabilities on investment programs, let alone an increase in the dispersion of prospective rates of return will cause a firm to increase its holding of liquid assets, instead of paying out dividends—barring the possibility that transaction flows have a systematically higher variability in situations where prospective returns are more widely dispersed.

The argument, so far as monetary assets are concerned, then, may be summarized as follows. Most business firms will not expend great effort in considering a wide range of securities for their portfolios. Instruments of low risk and positive return are available, and are made even more attractive as alternatives to cash by the low adjustment costs of transferring to and from them. Risk (as measured by variance or in any other way) doesn't have much of a role in this scheme; to the extent that price level changes are foreseen or feared, the maturity structure of the portfolio is shortened. Because of the opportunity afforded by shorter maturities, it is not necessary that the response to risk is higher average holdings of cash on the part of the firm.

It may be argued that a relevant application of risk aversion is to investment in physical capital: in seeking to avoid ruin, firms do measure the risks that attend investment in different physical assets. If the definition of "money" is extended broadly to encompass bonds, then a case may be made that increases in the riskiness of physical capital leads to increased holdings of "money." Such an argument, it would seem, must be avoided on aesthetic grounds. For note that monetary policy is specifically intended to operate on cash, and often the policy instrument is the purchase or sale of the securities in question. To tell us more about how policy works, our theories must maintain consistency of definition. Thus, a narrow definition of money in the description of policy alternatives, and a broader definition in the specification of demand relations, is confusing because of its inconsistency. There is no rule that says we must define money narrowly in studying demand for it; but if we do not define it narrowly, our findings will be inappropriate to the study of open market operations and other policy measures affecting a narrowly-defined monetary base.

Individual Portfolios and Mutual Funds: A Digression. The foregoing discussion offers the hypothesis that speculative money holdings are unlikely to be important as a persistent part of the portfolios of firms. But what of individuals, or firms whose primary function it is to deal in the debt and equity issues of other firms? Such cases offer the prospect of substantial liquidity demand for money along lines discussed by Tobin (1958), for it is a primary activity for them to maintain portfolios. One of the most important differences between a mutual fund and a more conventional type of business firm lies in the contractual commitments that emerge from the capital investment decisions of the latter. A mutual fund can move large amounts of "capital" into or out of an industry with little in the way of contractual commitment or adjustment cost. Should the firm decide to reverse its decision it can often do so over relatively short periods of time, with little or no penalty or loss.[18] When a conventional firm commits its assets to an industry, a variety of contractual obligations accompany the action, and a transfer of assets out of the industry can seldom be made at low cost, even over fairly long periods of time.

Given the objectives of mutual funds, and the institutional constraints under which they operate, how likely is it that the picture of liquidity preference as risk-averse behavior is descriptively useful? Again, we must consider motivation, and alternative responses to the holding of cash. Are mutual funds systematically attracted to or repelled by risk, as measured by variance? As in the case of "firms," we can wonder whether the important dimension is not the prospect of a large gain or loss contingent on one or a small number of events. If mutual funds also are ruin-averse, it is legitimate to extend the argument developed for firms; the variance is again a poor measure of the dispersion of outcome possibilities. So far as alternatives that are open to them are concerned, mutual funds have the same low risk—positive return monetary asset alternatives as are available to firms. Moreover, diversification of portfolio asset holdings will occur, in the presence of adjustment costs, as a normal consequence of changing prospects over time; and that diversification assures that liquidity will be available and serves further as a hedge against large loss or gain.

As with firms, we would expect the portfolios of mutual funds to be more heavily weighted toward cash and Treasury bills when lower future security prices is a highly probable prospect; but this is again conventional Keynesian liquidity preference, and not "behavior toward risk."

Tobin's analysis rationalizes the sensitivity of money balances to interest rates, even when expected price changes are zero; the view offered here is that the effort is unnecessary—transactions demand is sufficiently interest-sensitive to do the job by itself. The positive theoretical case for the interest sensitivity of trans-actions demand is well documented in this book and elsewhere; the negative case against money holding to avoid risk as measured by variance is less well developed as it appears in this section, and is supported only by the flimsy device of *a priori* argument. It is customary to conclude discussions of this type with the comfortable view that such issues are not resolvable at the level of theory—that a resolution can come only by em-pirical research. As is too often true, that conclusion begs the issue, for the techniques and data to do respectable empirical research on expectations-related phenomena simply aren't avail-able. While awaiting a conclusive resolution of the question, we are left with our tastes, and Occam's razor.

6. Monetary Policy Once More

In modern income-expenditure theory, the classical view of monetary policy as a depression remedy frequently is criticized on two counts: (a) it overlooks the possibility of a speculative-demand induced "liquidity trap," in which the elasticity of demand for money becomes infinite at low rates of interest; (b) it overlooks systematic shifts in the efficiency of investment function, which destroy the incentive for investment that other-wise would be brought forth by low interest rates.[19] Thus, the story as it stands is fuzzy as to the reasons why low interest rates fail to produce recovery. The asset management analysis sketched in the preceding sections will, if it is found to have substantial predictive content, be of some help in pointing to the reasons for failure. Do individuals passively hold large sums of cash, or (perhaps more realistically) do banks passively sit on large holdings of free reserves, with no effort to service bor-rowers? This would imply fear of capital loss, or non-neutrality toward risk, which attitudes are hard to justify in the presence of short-term securities. At times of low interest and abundant credit, it should not be too difficult for debtors to market issues of short maturity, and at very low rates. Only creditors' fear of default, and costs of managing a debt of very short average term, stand between borrowers and large sums of low-cost funding. The failure to tap this source of funds implies either anemic prospects for return on new capital formation, or concern over the ability to refinance at similarly attractive rates over the lifetimes of investment projects. If firms accumulate significant excess capacity during downturns, then the prospective return on new investment may be zero—unless it be in a technology-advancing, cost saving type of capital.

The issues to be unraveled, then, are: during depressions, does the marginal efficiency of capital (as a result of excess capacity or otherwise) fall to zero or below? Or is the problem one involving the terms for financing new projects, rather than their prospective rate of return?

A three-asset analysis can help to illuminate the effects of a downward shift in the marginal efficiency schedule. Let the three assets be physical capital, short-term securities and money in the objective function of a firm:

$$(7) \quad E(C) = v_l E(M) + \gamma_s P(\tau_b) + (v_l - v_s) E(B) + \gamma_k P(\tau_{b, k}),$$

where the various symbols and terms are defined in Section 3 above. If the adjustment costs are purely lumpy in form, the analysis of Chapter VI reveals that with $v_l = 0$, v_s becomes the relevant opportunity cost on money balances. We are in a two-asset world—with added considerations imposed in the form of supply and demand conditions for the earning asset. If the market supply elasticity of bills is zero, v_s will be progressively bid down, and equilibrium will be reached in a division of asset balances between cash and bills. At very low yields on bills, the constant elasticity money demand relation

$$\overline{M} = \frac{4}{3}\left(\frac{3\gamma_s \sigma^2}{4 v_s}\right)^{1/3}$$

will look quite flat.[20]

The model does less well in clarifying the effects of a liquidity trap. Let the asset-holder whose decision process is considered be an individual or a mutual fund and not a firm.[21] Let the three assets be cash, short-term bills, and longer-term commitments (bonds). The strong expectation of future interest rate increases will create a preference for bills, since they involve a much smaller likelihood of capital loss than do bonds. Indeed, the return rate on bonds may be low—not much above zero. The result will be, predictably, a heavy downward pressure on the bill rate, to a point that very large increases in the cash holding are necessary to induce responsive purchases of bills, and virtually no change, no matter how large, in the holding of cash or bills can induce bond purchases. Consider what happens in (2) and (3) when v_l and v_s are virtually equal, and both are very small.

Although the three-asset modeling approach does not suggest a conclusive answer as to whether monetary policy fails in a depression because of weakness in the demand for new capital or weakness in the supply of long-term investable funds, the approach does suggest a crude empirical test that may be helpful in unraveling causal movements.[22] Before following up on such tests with any degree of care, it would of course be useful to verify conclusively that monetary policy in fact does tend to break down in the presence of depressed income and substantial unemployment.[23]

The Cyclical Behavior of Adjustment Costs and the Homogeneity Postulate. In discussions of money demand relationships of the type developed in the basic model, or earlier by Baumol (1952) and Tobin (1956), attention usually centers on two major forces affecting desired cash holdings. They are the rate of interest (the opportunity cost on cash holdings) and the transactions rate.

The money demand relations from the Baumol model and the basic model are respectively

$$\overline{M} = (2\gamma\mu/v)^{1/2}$$

and

$$\overline{M} = (16\gamma\sigma^2/9v)^{1/3}.$$

The interest rate is denoted v in both relationships; in the Baumol model the transaction variable is μ and in the basic model the transaction variable is σ^2; μ and σ^2 are the first two moments of the daily cash flow process that the decision-maker seeks to control.

Both models are consistent with the classical homogeneity postulate; money demand is proportional to price levels. In the first instance, a doubling of all prices and costs confronting the firm (including the cost of portfolio adjustment γ, but not the money rate of interest ν) would lead to doubling in the value of μ, and hence to a doubling of $\overline{M}$. In the second instance, recall that σ^2 embodies the total number of daily transactions t and the mean transaction size m; in the symmetric binomial process used in developing the analysis (Chapter III, Section 3), $\sigma^2 = m^2 t$. A doubling of price levels $\overline{M}$ will *ceteris paribus* lead to doubling of m; with γ also doubled, $\overline{M}$ is doubled. It follows in both cases that if the homogeneity postulate fails, the theory suggests that it is because of changes in institutions governing the frequency and pattern of payments, and not because of the way that individuals respond to fixed institutions at different price levels.

The homogeneity of money demand with respect to price levels thus depends on adjustment costs responding as ordinary prices. By contrast, the money demand predictions drawn from the basic model are based on the view that adjustment costs will remain fixed at different phases of business activity, despite different transaction frequencies and sizes, and different interest rates.

In fact, the cost of portfolio adjustment γ is but one of many prices, and it may well move in a cyclical pattern similar to that of general price indices. For example, we observe that during periods of tight credit, the cost of securing a loan is extremely high, and stringent terms may be imposed to discourage the liquidation of loans before they mature. Brokers' spreads on short-term business financing may be systematically higher with tight money, and brokers may be considerably less flexible in accommodating borrowers' desires for inconvenient maturity dates. Bond issues sell only at substantial discounts (if at all), and so on. Conversely, under easy credit conditions, lenders are less well off in terms not only of the rate they can obtain, but also in terms of other conditions fixed at the time of the deal. One example is the elimination of "daily interest" on time or savings and loan deposits—when credit is easy, interest is payable only at quarters' end, and on deposits held for more than twenty days, for example. In addition, compensating balance requirements may be more stringent and more rigidly enforced during times when credit conditions are tight. This increased tightness has the effect of making discretionary balances a smaller fraction of total cash holdings, and leads to a large (absolute) value for the elasticity of money demand.

The effect of such manifestations may well be twofold and significant: (a) costs of borrowing differ systematically from costs of refunding or lending, and (b) the costs vary in opposite ways in response to different credit conditions. All of this is tantamount to a variable cost of transferring into and out of longs, in a three-asset model in which longs are the firm's own debt; and effects analyzed by Weitzman may be important in shaping the realized values of money demand elasticities (Chapter V, Section 5, and Chapter VI, Section 4).

That analysis showed that for a given interest rate ν, as the ratio

$$\frac{\text{Transfer cost of flotation}}{\text{Transfer cost of refunding}} = \frac{\gamma_B}{\gamma_I}$$

increases, the mean cash balance also increases.[24] Tight money causes an increase in this ratio, if the foregoing conjectural remarks are correct, as well as in the interest rate ν. Consequently, the model's predicted interest elasticity of money demand will be biased downward in absolute value; money holdings will decline *less* relative to interest rate increases than the model predicts.

It would be presumptuous, without the requisite additional effort devoted to observation and analysis, to push the discussion of cyclical changes in adjustment cost beyond the preliminary and tentative level reached here. Because the structure and magnitude of adjustment costs may be very important in dynamic analysis, it is worth characterizing and measuring them carefully. Meantime, the undue rigidity in elasticity predictions, thought to be inherent in "inventory" models, may in fact stem from the uncritical acceptance of constant adjustment costs.

7. Theories of Long-Run Asset Preference

Up to this point, the focus of the analysis has been on money as a financial instrument. The objective functions that we have used have embodied the view that money-holding costs can be measured in terms of opportunities foregone on other earning assets. The approach, clearly visible in foregoing three-asset analyses, is based on the view that certain assets (other than currency and demand deposits) afford an advantageous temporary abode of purchasing power.

Command over purchasing power—the ability to arrange and complete transactions with minimal difficulty and effort—is undoubtedly an important input into every production process. This suggests taking the direct approach of searching for an optimal cash balance in the same way as an optimal labor force—by the use of production function analysis. If successful, that approach would reflect and measure the productive contribution of purchasing power, at the margin. Cash could be separated from the general category of capital, and its special role evaluated. That approach seems to be suggested in the early empirical paper of Milton Friedman (1959), when he asks whether cash balances behave more like inventories or like fixed capital: whether they fluctuate more over the cycle than does production, or less.[25] If cash fluctuates less than production, says Friedman, it is because its level is optimally regulated by reference to the average operating rate of the firm over long periods.

Putting the matter as Friedman does may involve serious error in the interpretation of the elasticities of finished goods inventory, cash and physical capital with respect to output rates; and his construction also overlooks the different orders of magnitude of the costs encountered in adjusting the third compared to the first two asset categories. In the asset management view, by contrast, cash is a buffer against the portfolio adjustment costs that would otherwise accumulate heavily in the presence of payment-receipt uncertainty; and finished goods inventory plays a similar buffer role. If this plausible (but perhaps excessively simple) interpretation is grounded in fact, why should finished goods fluctuate more than outputs, while cash fluctuates less?

First notice the results developed by H. D. Mills (1967) that are presented in Chapter VIII, Section 3. Mills measures fluctuations in finished goods inventory, output and sales by their steady-state standard deviations, σ_I, σ_p and σ_s. He proves that under specified conditions,[26]

$$\frac{\sigma_I}{\sigma_s} \geq \frac{1}{2}\left(\frac{\sigma_s}{\sigma_p} + \frac{\sigma_p}{\sigma_s}\right).$$

Suppose we normalize by setting $\sigma_s = 1$, and as a result of the choice of production scheduling rule, σ_p is near the rational-behavior upper bound of 1 also. Then it follows that $\sigma_I \geq 1$; inventory fluctuates *no less than* output. Next, suppose the production scheduling rule leads to the condition that output fluctuates less than sales: then σ_I must necessarily be greater than σ_s, and still greater than σ_p (as we see, for example when $\sigma_p = \frac{1}{2}$ and $\sigma_s = 1$). If the variability of sales changes in the same direction as the mean sales level over the cycle, the effect seen by Friedman is explained.

Cash balances (especially *real* cash balances, corrected for price level changes) can by contrast fulfill their smoothing role without fluctuating more than sales. An increase in sales implies an increase in cash flow activity; some parts of this activity may be in the form of a *larger number* of payments and receipts. An increase in transaction frequency implies an opportunity (via the law of large numbers) for movements to "cancel each other out;" accordingly, we might expect that as sales increases, the daily net of payments over receipts also increases in absolute value, but more slowly. Viewed from the standpoint of standard deviations, we have the mappings

$$\sigma_s = k\sigma_c \rightarrow h,\ z,$$

where σ_c is the variability of the daily cash *flow* (*not* the cash *balance*); k is a scalar greater than 1; and h and z are the control parameters of the cash control policy. Tedious calculation reveals that the variance of the cash balance is $7z^2/18$; and z is proportional to the 2/3 power of σ_c. Hence, the cash balance standard deviation is $\kappa\sigma_s{}^{2/3}$, where the value of κ is $\kappa = (7/18)^{1/2}$ $(4\gamma/3\nu k^2)^{1/3}$; even if $\kappa > 1$, the effect will be swamped by the effect of the exponent 2/3 as σ_s maps into cash balance variability. If the basic model is broadly predictively correct, and if sales variability is substantially reduced as it maps into cash flow variability, then cash balances will indeed fluctuate less than sales. Even though production almost surely will fluctuate less than sales, cash balances can still fluctuate less than production.

Empirical studies may find that cash does indeed vary less than output over time. If the foregoing ratiocination is correct, it is nonetheless a mistake to interpret such findings as saying that cash is "more like" plant and equipment than it is like finished goods stocks. It is less like the former than the latter in the reasons for which it is held, the considerations that enter into its control (most notably the time horizon over which planning takes place), and the costs of adjusting its level.

We can speculate whether it is worthwhile to estimate production functions in order to investigate elasticities of substitution of cash for other productive inputs, including labor and other forms of capital. Such estimates have been presented by M. I. Nadiri (1969) who has found that increases in capital user cost (c), wages (w), and the ratio c/w all are associated with higher cash balances, which presumably suggests that cash is a gross substitute for other inputs, including labor. His finding is hard to rationalize in any simple and direct manner—it seems unlikely that higher wage rates or capital rates leads the firm to substitute money for labor in liquidity—conserving activities such as attention to accounts receivable, or special payment scheduling procedures. Rather it seems possible that higher wages and capital costs imply greater payment obligations, and hence higher cash balances. In fact, it may be that those real prices of inputs are a better surrogate for activity in the cash account than the more commonly used sales figures. If input prices do mirror cash flow variability, their inclusion with sales in the estimation of money demand should yield systematically higher explanation of variance than can be obtained from the use of sales alone, which seems to be the case—Nadiri's R-squares are very high.

The production function approach, then, gives information that is hard to interpret. It has an additional important drawback for money demand estimation: if cash balances are held mainly as buffers against cash-flow uncertainty, then some representation of the forcing stochastic process is all but indispensable to capture the effects that determine cash holdings. Dynamic effects have usually been omitted from production function analyses in the past; those analyses have focused on long run averages, and have omitted the explicit consideration of uncertainty.

Finally, there are conceptual problems associated with the production function approach, that stem from the fact that liquidity is not an all-or-none proposition, and several earning assets may serve well as "temporary abodes of purchasing power." Thus, the entire portfolio of cash and securities (exclusive of the possibly large holdings that are legally committed to pension funds or are untouchable for other reasons) may be the proper variable to capture the substitution, if any exists in the narrow limits traced by routine operating conditions, between purchasing power and other productive inputs.

8. REPRISE ON THE PART AND THE WHOLE

Looking back on this chapter, an idea that emerges is that the quantity theory, as it is stated in the Cambridge tradition, but more importantly, as it is developed by such American writers as Simon Newcomb and Irving Fisher, needed only a vocabulary and some analytic technique to become established in the way Hicks suggested, on a sound decision-theoretic basis. The requisite vocabulary and analytic technique, it appears, can be found in what has variously come to be called the "inventory theory" or "asset management" approach to money demand. Interestingly, the dovetail between old-fashioned velocity analysis and modern optimization theory is made more snug by empirical studies in the tradition of the "modern quantity theory." Those studies, in their findings on interest elasticities of money demand and "scale economies" of cash holding, offer no contradiction to important inferences from the optimization approach.

It is of course of interest to ask where or whether Keynesian money demand theory fits into the picture. In Section 4, it is suggested that Keynesian theory is the classical quantity construct, with important modifications necessary when expectations of change in interest rates are widespread, or when the efficiency of investment schedule is depressed. Because expectations are nonstationary, then, Keynes' is not an equilibrium theory, but rather the classical theory with an appended mechanism for generating occasional powerful disturbances.[27] There remains, of course, the currently canonical version of Keynesian theory, which certainly is a true equilibrium analysis of money demand. Tobin's analysis took speculative demand out of the category of occasional perturbations, and established it as a persistent element that rests on a choice-theoretic foundation. A rather weak challenge to Tobin's construct is offered in Section 5; the dissent is not well rationalized or grounded in solid theorizing, but there does appear to be room to doubt that "liquidity preference as behavior toward risk" is consistent with the kind of optimizing behavior analyzed elsewhere in this book when the term to maturity of assets held is considered as an important variable in the analysis. The central issue, it appears, is whether available financial instruments are sufficiently diverse with respect to return, risk, and term, and whether the cost in transacting in them is sufficiently low, to rule out the holding of money for the purpose of avoiding risk.

Finally, there is the "modern" quantity theory, which in the view of some critics is more Keynesian than quantity. The Keynesian designation is probably misplaced despite an acknowledgement by modern quantity theorists of the possibly important influence of interest rates. The chief novelty of that new approach is its emphasis on the relation of money holdings to permanent components of individuals' "activity level" variables, such as income or sales. Here, again, a rather impressionistic demurral is sounded in this chapter, but this time it is based on the question of the appropriate structure of the decision problem. The issue is whether the principal productive role of money balances is as a buffer against unforeseen cash flow fluctuations of very short period. If that indeed is money's chief role, then long-term asset preference theories will have little to say about money demand.

Apart from this chapter, which turns out to be an attempt to demonstrate the virility of old ideas, this book has two main themes: the asset management approach to money demand analysis can be extended, with richer predictive applications, far beyond the simple "square root lot-size" model in which form it originally was embodied; and simple asset management models have a potentially important role as decision tools in the control of business and other cash flows.

Notes

1. The problem of moving from transactions to observed and recorded activity variables has not escaped the attention of the profession. Keynes devotes much of chapter 14, volume 1 of his *Treatise* (1930) to the problem, and refers to earlier work by Irving Fisher, among others. More recently, Pesek and Saving (1967) p. 319 have noted Keynes' classification (in the *Treatise*) of quantity equations as "Cambridge" (income) and "Fisher" (transactions) types.

2. There is some controversy as to which interest rate is appropriate, on long- or short-term asset alternatives. See the remarks in Chapter VI, Section 2, 3, and the references attached to that discussion, especially the paper of T. H. Lee (1967).

3. Significant interest rate effects are found by Meltzer (1963b) Brunner and Meltzer (1963), (1964), Teigen (1964), Maddala and Vogel (1969) and Nadiri (1969) to cite a few. Friedman's (1959) is the best known suggestion that interest rates do not matter. Keep in mind that some of these analyses use economy-wide data, while others test at the level of the individual corporation.

4. Meltzer's (1963a) has been the most important finding against the presence of scale economies. Contradictory to his results is the evidence of Maddala and Vogel (1967) (1969), Nadiri (1969) and Teigen (1964). Scale economies, of course, are implied by a transactions demand elasticity of less than 1, assuming that the measure of transactions activity is highly correlated with the scale variable.

5. A limited amount of such evidence is offered in Chapter VIII. It also may or may not be significant that the basic model has caught on among finance specialists as a device for orienting discussions of cash management. Two recent examples are the textbooks of Van Horne (1968) and Peterson (1969).

6. See the comments of Tobin (1947) and Leijonhufvud (1968), chapter III, to this effect.

7. The need for occasional security purchases and sales by the central monetary authority to stabilize interest rates can be visualized by considering movements within the "money box" of an economy with two private individuals. The

point is most dramatically illustrated if we assume that the two individuals' money demand relations are identical. Their transactions will be entirely with each other; in the process of exchange, cash can accumulate in one balance and drain out of the other. Each will wish to hold maximum of $h = h(\sigma^2, \nu)$ dollars in cash.

Suppose the money supply is exactly h. Cash eventually will accumulate with one individual, which will result in a desire on the part of both to adjust their balances—one individual holds $\$h$, the other holds zero. Both will wish to adjust to $z = 1/3\ h$, and this is impossible without intervention by a third party. No other choice of value for the initial money stock eliminates this difficulty, either. With three or more individuals in the economy, "synchronization failure" problems of the same sort can be encountered, but the happy coincidence of two security purchases to offset one security sale remains as a possibility which averts the need for intervention.

8. Other methods of support for government spending, such as issuing bonds or "printing currency" will have money supply effects that the analysis seeks to avoid.

9. There are stock-flow pitfalls to avoid in these little stories. In this story, the increase in σ^2 stimulates the demand for M and B, and reduces the desired level of K. The reduced level of investment is temporary; once capital has adjusted to its new desired level, net investment returns to zero, barring a responsive change in the efficiency of investment ν_k, which will operate to reduce both $\bar{B}$ and $\bar{M}$ as we see in (1) and (2).

10. The most important difference between the picture of money demand drawn here, and the transactions demand theory that Keynes (in the *Treatise*) attributes to Fisher is the explicit incorporation here of an objective function. Earlier discussions, if my readings of Keynes and Fisher (1911) are reliable, were based on *ad hoc* motives for money-holding.

11. As speculative demand is discussed by Hansen (1953), Dernburg and McDougall (1968), or Tobin in his summary of Keynesian theory (1958).

12. See for example, Dvoretzky, Keifer and Wolfowitz (1953), Karlin (1958a) and Scarf (1960).

13. *Natura non facit saltum.* As we will see, if the sometimes convenient, sometimes misleading artifice of separate transactions and speculative balances is abandoned, then the jumpy responses predicted by Tobin don't look quite so jumpy.

14. The analysis in Tobin's paper is carried out in terms of two assets, cash and consols. He later extends and generalizes to holdings of several assets that may vary with respect to maturity.

15. The fixed investment period constraint is a means of representing transaction costs. By confining portfolio decisions to separated points in time, the danger of continuous adjustment is avoided, as is the need to attach costs to continuous adjustment.

16. On the necessity of the normal distribution in the absence of a quadratic utility function, see Feldstein (1969) and Tobin (1969).

17. On this point, we should note that if the firm deals heavily in treasury bills, no adjustment costs are incurred if a maturity occurs at a time when cash is not needed. For the Treasury typically offers to replace a matured issue with a new issue. To accept such an offer, of course, lengthens the term of the portfolio. But if the firm owns a large assortment of bills with staggered maturities, then lengthening should not prove to be a problem. Treasury bills may be the only instrument for which this is true, at least for large-sized transfers. Some

savings and loan associations provide an alternative for small transactions at the present time, by paying full daily interest from date of deposit until date of withdrawal.

18. Note that if all firms paid out their entire earnings to their owners, all capital allocation decisions would be made by individuals or investment trusts. The contrast drawn between "firms" and "mutual funds" is meaningful because of retained earnings, and because of the very low propensity of the management of one firm to make long-term loans directly to the management of another.

19. The marginal efficiency schedule can shift because of the expectation of continued depressed conditions, or because of excess capacity (capital accumulated prior to the depression that is for some reason not used during the depression). The excess capacity view is predicated on a degree of non-substitutability between labor and capital; otherwise the productive input available at zero marginal cost (capital) would be fully utilized when wages are positive, and at some low interest rate, new investment would immediately be forthcoming.

20. A drop of .1% when the rate of interest is 5% implies that cash holdings increase by 1/150, or about .66%; when the rate is 1%, a drop of .1% implies that cash holdings increase by 1/30 or about 3.3%; and the base to which the 3.3% increase applied is considerably larger—5 1/3 times as large—as the base to which the .66% increase applies at the higher rate of interest.

21. Recall the use of the terms "mutual fund" and "firm" in Section 5 above.

22. The test is an historical examination of the term structure yield curve. If short-term government and corporate securities were higher in price (lower in yield) during periods of unemployment, compared to long-term issues of equivalent risk, then the suggestion is that a "liquidity trap" failure of demand for issues long enough to underwrite capital investment is the answer: the difficulty is a weakness in the supply of credit. By contrast, if the yield curve shifts during recession toward higher returns on short-term issues, we can conclude that the demand for long-term securities is relatively high, and the difficulty can be laid to a weak demand for credit.

An extremely casual glance at some data in Meiselman (1962), Appendix C, suggests that the liquidity trap (failure of the long term credit supply) is the more empirically plausible explanation of the two considered.

23. The findings of Friedman and Schwartz (1963) and Morrison (1966), among others, suggest that the income-expenditure criticisms of monetary policy considered in this section are without substance. The question is a controversial one, and the effect of constant demand elasticity (exemplified in footnote 20) may be important.

24. Weitzman (1968) shows that with $\gamma_B = 5\gamma_I$, the mean cash balance is $1/2\ h$; and with $\gamma_B = \gamma_I$, the mean balance is $4/9\ h$, where h is the upper control limit on the cash balance in a simple (h, z) policy. The cited result is valid when γ_I remains fixed in value over the cycle, and only γ_B increases; should γ_I increase also, h increases in proportion to $\gamma_I^{1/3}$.

25. Friedman (1959), p. 334.

26. Most important among these conditions is that sales is a serially independent random variable, and the first two moments of the probability distribution of sales must exist.

27. I would hesitate to offer such a view, were it not for the strong stand taken by Leijonhufvud (1968) to the same effect. My reading of that book has had a pronounced influence on the focus of this chapter and the interpretations arrived at in it.

Bibliography and Reference Index*

AKERLOF, GEORGE (1969), "The Demand for Money: A General Equilibrium Inventory—Theoretic Approach" (unpublished multilith). *146, 178.*

ARROW, KENNETH J. (1957), "Decision Theory and Operations Research," *Operations Research* 5, 1957 (765-774). *43.*

ARROW, KENNETH J. (1958), "Historical Background" in Arrow, Karlin and Scarf (ed.), *Studies in the Mathematical Theory of Inventory and Production*, Stanford, Stanford University Press, 1958. *69.*

ARROW, KENNETH J., THEODORE HARRIS, and JACOB MARSCHAK (1951), "Optimal Inventory Policy," *Econometrica* 19, 1951 (250-272). *12, 43.*

ARROW, KENNETH J., SAMUEL KARLIN, and HERBERT SCARF (1958), "The Nature and Structure of Inventory Problems" in Arrow, Karlin and Scarf (eds.), *Studies in the Mathematical Theory of Inventory and Production*, Stanford, Stanford University Press, 1958. *43.*

BAILEY, MARTIN J. (1962), *National Income and the Price Level*, New York, McGraw-Hill Book Co., 1962. *22.*

BAUMOL, WILLIAM J. (1951), *Economic Dynamics*, New York, Macmillan, 1951 (2 ed. 1959). *44.*

BAUMOL, WILLIAM J. (1952), "The Transactions Demand for Cash: An Inventory Theoretic Approach," *Quarterly Journal of Economics* 66, 1952 (545-556). *13, 33, 45, 104, 168, 196.*

BECKMANN, MARTIN J. (1961), "Production Smoothing and Inventory Control," *Operations Research* 9, 1961 (456-467). *34, 43, 116.*

BRUNNER, KARL, and ALLAN H. MELTZER (1963), "Predicting Velocity: Implications for Theory and Policy," *Journal of Finance* 18, 1963 (319-354). *172, 204.*

BRUNNER, KARL, and ALLAN H. MELTZER (1964), "Some Further Investigations of Demand and Supply Functions for Money," *Journal of Finance* 19, 1964 (240-283). *204.*

*Italicized page numbers indicate where references appear in the text.

CHARNES, ABRAHAM, JACQUES DRÈZE, and MERTON H. MILLER (1966), "Decision and Horizon Rules for Stochastic Planning Problems: A Linear Example," *Econometrica* 34, 1966 (307-330). *43.*

CHITRE, VIKAS, "A Dynamic Programming Model of Demand for Money" (unpublished multilith). *69.*

CHOW, GREGORY C. (1966), "On the Long Run and Short Run Demand for Money," *Journal of Political Economy* 74, 1966 (111-131). *172.*

DAVIS, RICHARD G., and JACK M. GUTENTAG (1963), "Balance Requirements and Deposit Competition," *Journal of Political Economy* 71, 1963 (581-585). *99, 116.*

DERNBURG, THOMAS, and DUNCAN MACDOUGALL (1968), *Macro-Economic Theory* (3 ed.), New York, McGraw-Hill, 1968. *205.*

DUESENBERRY, JAMES (1963), "The Portfolio Demand for Money and Other Assets," *Review of Economics and Statistics* 45, 1963 Supplement (9-24). *146.*

DVORETZKY, ARYEH, JACK KEIFER, and J. WOLFOWITZ (1952), "The Inventory Problem," *Econometrica* 20, 1952 (187-222). *43.*

DVORETZKY, ARYEH, JACK KEIFER, and J. WOLFOWITZ (1953), "On the Optimal Character of the (s, S) Policy in Inventory Theory," *Econometrica* 21, 1953 (586-596). *43, 205.*

EDGEWORTH, F. Y. (1888), "The Mathematical Theory of Banking," *Journal of the Royal Statistical Society* 51, 1888 (113-127). *43.*

EPPEN, GARY D., and EUGENE F. FAMA (1968), "Solutions for Cash Balance and Simple Dynamic Portfolio Problems," *Journal of Business* 41, 1968 (94-112). *37, 67, 102, 107.*

EPPEN, GARY D., and EUGENE F. FAMA (1969a), "Cash Balance and Simple Dynamic Portfolio Problems With Proportional Costs," *International Economic Review* 10, 1969 (119-133). *34, 37, 44, 67, 102, 116.*

EPPEN, GARY D., and EUGENE F. FAMA (1969b), "Three Asset Cash Balance and Dynamic Portfolio Problems" (unpublished multilith). *131.*

EVANS, G. C. (1930), *Mathematical Introduction to Economics*, New York, Macmillan, 1930. *25.*

FAMA, EUGENE F. (1963), "Mandelbrot and The Stable Paretian Hypothesis," *Journal of Business* 36, 1963 (420-429). *18, 23.*

FELDSTEIN, M. S. (1969), "Mean-Variance Analysis in The Theory of Liquidity Preference and Portfolio Selection," *Review of Economic Studies* 36, 1969 (5-12). *205.*

FELLER, WILLIAM (1951, 1966), *An Introduction to Probability Theory and Its Applications*, New York, John Wiley & Sons. Vol. 1 (discrete sample spaces) 1951, Vol. II (continuous sample spaces) 1966. *22, 23, 44, 70, 92, 95, 116, 132.*

FISHER, IRVING (1911, 1913), *The Purchasing Power of Money*, New York, The Macmillan Co., 1911 (rev. ed. 1913). *205.*

FRIEDMAN, MILTON (1956), "The Quantity Theory of Money—A Restatement" in Friedman (ed.), *Studies in the Quantity Theory of Money*, Chicago, University of Chicago Press, 1956. *6, 22.*

FRIEDMAN, MILTON (1959), "The Demand for Money: Some Theoretical and Empirical Results," *Journal of Political Economy* 67, 1959 (327-351). *172, 199, 204, 206.*

FRIEDMAN, MILTON, and ANNA J. SCHWARTZ (1963), *A Monetary History of the United States*, Princeton, Princeton University Press, 1963. *206.*

GEORGESCU-ROEGEN, NICHOLAS (1951), "Relaxation Phenomena in Linear Dynamic Models" in Koopmans (ed.), *Activity Analysis of Production and Allocation*, Cowles Commission Monograph 13, New York, John Wiley & Sons, 1951. *43.*

GETOOR, RONALD K. (1961), "First Passage Times for Symmetric Stable Processes in Space," *Transactions of the American Mathematical Society* 101, 1961 (75-90). *95.*

GNEDENKO, B. V., and A. N. KOLMOGOROV (1954), *Limit Distributions for Sums of Independent Random Variables* (Trans. K. L. Chung), Reading, Mass., Addison-Wesley Publishing Co., 1954. *22.*

GOLDBERG, SAMUEL (1958), *An Introduction to Difference Equations*, New York, John Wiley & Sons, 1958. *44.*

HAAVELMO, TRYGVIE (1959), *A Study in The Theory of Investment*, Chicago, University of Chicago Press, 1959. *42.*

HADLEY, GEORGE (1964), "A Comparison of Order Quantities Computed Using Average Annual Cost and Discounted Cost," *Management Science* 10, 1964 (472-476). *30.*

HANSEN, ALVIN (1953), *A Guide to Keynes*, New York, McGraw-Hill, 1953. *205.*

HAYEK, FRIEDRICH A. (1955), *The Counter-Revolution of Science*, Glencoe, Ill., The Free Press, 1955. *21.*

HICKS, J. R. (1935), "A Suggestion for Simplifying the Theory of Money," *Economica* (New Series) 2, 1935 (1-19). *5, 13, 22, 69.*

HICKS, J. R. (1950), *The Trade Cycle*, New York, Oxford University Press, 1950. *43.*

HOLT, CHARLES C., FRANCO MODIGLIANI, JOHN F. MUTH, and HERBERT SIMON (1961), *Planning Production, Inventory and Work Force*, Englewood Cliffs, N.J., Prentice-Hall, Inc. 1961. *116, 169.*

JOHNSON, HARRY G. (1962), "Monetary Theory and Policy," *American Economic Review* 52, 1962 (335-384). *22.*

KARLIN, SAMUEL (1955), "The Structure of Dynamic Programming Models," *Naval Research Logistics Quarterly* 2, 1955 (285-294). *28.*

KARLIN, SAMUEL (1958a), "Optimal Inventory Policy for the Arrow—Harris—Marschak Dynamic Model" in Arrow, Karlin and Scarf (ed.), *Studies in the Mathematical Theory of Inventory and Production*, Stanford, Stanford University Press, 1958. *205.*

KARLIN, SAMUEL (1958b), "Steady State Analyses" in Arrow, Karlin and Scarf (ed.), *Studies in the Mathematical Theory of Inventory and Production*, Stanford, Stanford University Press, 1958. *43.*

KEYNES, J. M. (1930), *A Treatise on Money*, Vol. I, London, Macmillan & Co. 1930. *5, 204.*

KEYNES, J. M. (1936), *The General Theory of Employment, Interest and Money*, New York, Harcourt-Brace & Co., 1936. *5*.

KUO, T. C. (1960), *Automatic Control Systems Engineering*, New York, Prentice-Hall, Inc., 1950. *115*.

LEE, TONG-HUN (1967), "Alternative Interest Rates and the Demand for Money—The Empirical Evidence," *American Economic Review* 57, 1967 (1168-1182). *131, 204*.

LEIJONHUFVUD, AXEL (1968), *On Keynesian Economics and The Economics of Keynes*, New York, Oxford University Press, 1968. *204, 206*.

LUCE, R. D. and H. L. RAIFFA (1957), *Games and Decisions*, New York, John Wiley & Sons, 1957. *43*.

McCALL, JOHN J. (1960), "Differences Between The Personal Demand for Money and The Business Demand for Money," *Journal of Political Economy* 68, 1960 (358-368). *146*.

MADDALA, G. S., and ROBERT VOGEL (1967), "Cross-Section Estimates of Liquid Asset Demand by Manufacturing Corporations," *Journal of Finance* 22, 1967 (557-575). *204*.

MADDALA, G. S., and ROBERT VOGEL (1969), "Estimating the Lagged Relationships in the Corporate Demand for Liquid Assets," *Review of Economics and Statistics* 51, 1959 (53-61). *204*.

MANDELBROT, BENOIT (1963a), "The Variation of Certain Speculative Prices," *The Journal of Business* 36, 1963 (394-419). *22, 23*.

MANDELBROT, BENOIT (1963b), "New Methods in Statistical Economics," *Journal of Political Economy* 7, 1963 (421-440). *23*.

MANNE, ALAN S. (1961), *Economic Analysis for Business Decisions*, New York, McGraw-Hill Book Co., 1961. *43*.

MARKOWITZ, HARRY (1959), *Portfolio Analysis*, New York, John Wiley & Sons, 1959. *22, 131*.

MARSCHAK, JACOB (1951), "Why 'Should' Statisticians and Businessmen Maximize 'Moral Expectation'?" in Neyman (ed.), *Proceedings of the Second Berkeley Symposium on Mathematical Statistics and Probability*, Berkeley, University of California Press, 1951 (493–506). *43*.

MASSÉ, P. B. D. (1946), *Les Réserves et la régulation de l'avenir dans la vie économique*, Paris, Hermann, 1946. *12, 143*.

MEISELMAN, DAVID (1962), *The Term Structure of Interest Rates*, Englewood Cliffs, N.J., Prentice-Hall, Inc., 1962. *206*.

MELTZER, ALLAN H. (1963a), "The Demand for Money: A Cross-Section Study of Business Firms," *Quarterly Journal of Economics*, 1963 (405-422). *204*.

MELTZER, ALLAN H. (1963b), "The Demand for Money: The Evidence From the Time Series," *Journal of Political Economy*, 1963 (219-247). *204*.

MILLER, MERTON H., and DANIEL ORR (1966), "A Model of the Demand for Money by Firms," *Quarterly Journal of Economics* 80, 1966 (413-435). *14, 15, 22*.

MILLER, MERTON H., and DANIEL ORR (1967), "An Application of Control Limit Models to the Management of Corporate Cash Balances," in

Robichek (ed.), *Financial Research and Management Decisions*, New York, John Wiley & Sons, 1967. *169*.

MILLER, MERTON H., and DANIEL ORR (1968), "The Demand for Money by Firms: Extensions of Analytic Results," *Journal of Finance* 23, 1968 (735-759). *14, 95, 102, 131*.

MILLS, EDWIN S. (1962), *Price, Output and Inventory Policy*, New York, John Wiley & Sons, 1962. *43*.

MILLS, HARLAN D. (1962), "Inventory Valuation: An Analytic Technique," *Management Science* 8, 1962 (58-68). *43*.

MILLS, HARLAN D. (1967), "Smoothing in Inventory Processes" in Shubik (ed.), *Essays in Mathematical Economics in Honor of Oskar Morgenstern*, Princeton, Princeton University Press, 1967. *153, 155, 169, 200*.

MORRISON, GEORGE R. (1966), *Liquidity Preferences of Commercial Banks*, Chicago, University of Chicago Press, 1966. *206*.

NADIRI, M. I. (1969), "The Determinants of Real Cash Balances in the Total U.S. Manufacturing Sector," *Quarterly Journal of Economics* 83, 1969 (173-196). *172, 201, 204*.

NELSON, RICHARD R. (1962), "Uncertainty, Prediction and Competitive Equilibrium," *Quarterly Journal of Economics* 75, 1961 (41-62). *29*.

OPPENHEIM, PAUL, and HILARY PUTNAM (1958), "Unity of Science as a Working Hypothesis," in Feigl, Scriven and Maxwell (eds.), *Minnesota Studies in the Philosophy of Science:* Vol. II, Concepts, Theories, and the Mind-Body Problem, Minneapolis, University of Minnesota Press, 1958. *21*.

ORR, DANIEL (1962), "A Random Walk Production-Inventory Policy: Rationale and Implementation," *Management Science* 9, 1962 (108-122). *43*.

PATINKIN, DON (1956, 1965), *Money, Interest and Prices*, Evanston, Row Peterson, 1956 (2 ed. New York, Harper & Row, 1965). *22, 49, 69*.

PESEK, BORIS P., and THOMAS R. SAVING (1967), *Money, Wealth and Economic Theory*, New York, The Macmillan Co., 1967. *22, 172, 204*.

PETERSON, D. E. (1969), *A Quantitative Framework for Financial Management*, Homewood, Ill., Richard D. Irwin, Inc., 1969. *204*.

PINKHAM, ROGER S. (1960), "Measures of Operating Quality for Inventory Systems," *Navy Supply Systems Research, Study I*, Princeton, N.J., Mathematica, Inc., July 1960 (Multilith). *116*.

POOLE, WILLIAM (1968), "Commercial Bank Reserve Management in a Stochastic Model: Implications For Monetary Policy," *Journal of Finance* 23, 1968 (769-791). *43*.

PORTER, RICHARD (1961), "A Model of Bank Portfolio Selection," *Yale Economic Essays* 1, 1961 (323-357). *131*.

RADNER, ROY (1968), "Competitive Equilibrium Under Uncertainty," *Econometrica* 36, 1968 (31-58). *42*.

ROOS, C. S. (1925), "A Mathematical Theory of Competition," *American Journal of Mathematics* 47, 1925 (163-175). *25*.

SAMUELSON, PAUL (1946), *Foundations of Economic Analysis*, Cambridge, Mass., Harvard University Press, 1946. *25*.

SAVAGE, RICHARD I. (1962), "Surveillance Problems," *Naval Research Logistics Quarterly* 9, 1962 (187-210). *70.*

SCARF, HERBERT (1960), "The Optimality of (s, S) Policies in the Dynamic Inventory Problem" in Arrow, Karlin and Suppes (ed.), *Mathematical Methods in the Social Sciences*, 1959, Stanford, Stanford University Press, 1960. *37, 67, 205.*

TEIGEN, RONALD (1964), "Demand and Supply Functions for Money in the United States: Some Structural Estimates," *Econometrica* 32, 1964 (476-509). *204.*

TELSER, LESTER G., and ROBERT L. GRAVES (1968), "Continuous and Discrete Time Approaches to a Maximization Problem," *Review of Economic Studies* 35, 1968 (307-326). *115.*

THEIL, HENRI (1961), *Economic Forecasts and Policy*, Amsterdam, North-Holland Publishing Co., 1961. *116.*

THORE, STEN (1968), "Programming Bank Reserves Under Uncertainty," *Swedish Journal of Economics* 70, 1968 (123-137). *43.*

TISDELL, CLEMENT A. (1968), *The Theory of Price Uncertainty, Production and Profit*, Princeton, Princeton University Press, 1968. *29.*

TOBIN, JAMES (1947), "Liquidity Preference and Monetary Policy," *Review of Economics and Statistics* 29, 1947 (124-131). *204.*

TOBIN, JAMES (1956), "The Interest Elasticity of the Transactions Demand for Cash," *Review of Economics and Statistics* 38, 1956 (241-247). *33, 46, 145, 196.*

TOBIN, JAMES (1958), "Liquidity Preference as Behavior Toward Risk," *Review of Economic Studies* 25, 1958 (65-86). *22, 187, 189, 192, 205.*

TOBIN, JAMES (1968), "The Consumption Function," *International Encyclopedia of the Social Sciences*, Chicago, Macmillan and The Free Press, 1968. *146.*

TOBIN, JAMES (1969), "Reply to Borch and Feldstein," *Review of Economic Studies* 36, 1969 (13-14). *205.*

USPENSKY, J. V. (1937), *An Introduction to Mathematical Probability*, New York, McGraw-Hill, 1937. *15.*

VAN HORNE, JAMES C. (1968), *Financial Management and Policy*, Englewood Cliffs, N.J., Prentice-Hall, Inc., 1968. *204.*

WALD, ABRAHAM (1944), "On Cumulative Sums of Random Variables," *Annals of Mathematical Statistics* 15, 1944 (283-296). *22, 72.*

WALD, ABRAHAM (1946), "Differentiation Under the Expectation Sign in the Fundamental Identity of Sequential Analysis," *Annals of Mathematical Statistics* 18, 1946 (493-497). *72, 95, 132.*

WALD, ABRAHAM (1947), *Sequential Analysis*, New York, John Wiley & Sons, 1947. *72.*

WEITZMAN, MARTIN (1968), "A Model of the Demand for Money by Firms: Comment," *Quarterly Journal of Economics* 82, 1968 (161-164). *102, 113, 206.*

WHITIN, T. M. (1953, 1957), *The Theory of Inventory Management*, Princeton, Princeton University Press, 1953 (2 ed. 1957). *12, 146.*